Trauma-informed Criminal Justice

"This is a book that will change the way we think about criminal justice. Rather than ask how we might best 'manage' those who appear in our courts and are held in our prisons, it challenges us to think more carefully about what it is that brings a person into the system and how the foundation for rehabilitative success is compassion and healing."

—Professor Andrew Day, *University of Melbourne, Australia*

"This much-needed book weaves a beautifully written narrative on the importance of compassionate criminal justice. Not only does this book cover ground yet to be addressed in other titles, but it also provides imperative practical and theoretical insights for students, practitioners, and academics on how to further trauma-centric practices in the justice system. I recommend this as a must-read for anyone in the field interested in the nexus of trauma and criminal justice."

—Dr. Colleen M. Berryessa, *Rutgers University, USA*

"For too long, the criminal justice system has ignored the impacts of trauma on the lives of those who fill our courtrooms and prison cells. This book provides a clear-eyed analysis of the interactions between trauma and crime before developing a framework for trauma-informed sentencing, especially in the context of First Nations people. Grounded in rigorous research and first-hand experience, it makes a compelling case for compassion. It is essential reading for all who want to work towards a kinder, more effective justice response."

—Lorana Bartels, *Professor of Criminology, Australian National University, Adjunct Professor of Law, University of Canberra and University of Tasmania, Australia*

"Dr. McLachlan offers us a comprehensive, compassionate, culturally attuned re-imagining of a criminal justice system that acknowledges and responds to the pain and unique needs of those who have experienced trauma. A system that considers the traumatic experiences of people who have offended – often representing multiple unconvicted crimes, which result in an accumulation of neglected scars of injustice in that person's life. Criminal justice workers' vicarious trauma is also addressed. A remarkable vision and a significant contribution to the field."

—Lawrence Jones, *Head of Psychology, Rampton Hospital, England*

"Trauma-informed Criminal Justice is a landmark book that maps out the many ways in which trauma affects the justice system. It is a must-read for anyone trying to understand how to improve the situation for people inside the system, including the workforce. Its insights and recommendations give a road map for the future built on evidence and compassion."

—Professor Peter G. Miller, *School of Psychology, Deakin University, Australia*

Katherine J. McLachlan

Trauma-informed Criminal Justice

Towards a More Compassionate Criminal Justice System

palgrave
macmillan

Katherine J. McLachlan
Criminology, College of Business,
Government and Law
Flinders University
Adelaide, SA, Australia

ISBN 978-3-031-59289-8 ISBN 978-3-031-59290-4 (eBook)
https://doi.org/10.1007/978-3-031-59290-4

Cover credit: GOLDsquirrel/Getty Images

This Palgrave Macmillan imprint is published by the registered company Springer Nature Switzerland AG
The registered company address is: Gewerbestrasse 11, 6330 Cham, Switzerland

Paper in this product is recyclable.

I dedicate this book to Charlotte, the indomitable Father Gary, and the late Robert McLachlan Manson.

Preface

I have been fascinated with why people commit crimes since childhood when I read true crime books and studied crime scene photos by torch-light under my quilt. Later, I studied law and psychology with aspirations of becoming a criminal profiler. I started working in the criminal justice system in 2001 as an Intelligence Analyst examining offending patterns in reported sexual assaults. During that time, I worked with an FBI-trained profiler, and she was clear that profiling was not a viable career path in Australia. Over the following decade, I worked in various criminal and social justice public sector roles. In 2014, as a Board Member of the Victim Support Service in Adelaide, I first heard the term "trauma-informed". The service embraced the phrase, even though the social workers could not articulate its meaning clearly. It seemed to me that they thought it just meant doing a good job. Soon after, I was appointed to the Parole Board of SA in 2015 as a victim advocate. It was in this role that I began to understand the significance of trauma as a precursor to offending.

As a Parole Board member, I have interviewed more than 1000 adults. The people I speak with are not homogenous. However, there is a large cohort of people who have been convicted of diverse offences, including drug offences, property offences, driving offences, and violent offences. They often report traumatic childhoods. Women commonly have a history of childhood sexual abuse and abuse within domestic/intimate relationships. Men are often raised in households without father figures; their childhoods are characterised by abuse, neglect, drug use, and domestic abuse perpetrated by a series of "stepfathers". Many of these individuals used drugs as children and disengaged from school. They came to the attention of the child protection and youth justice systems. Some adult male parolees I recognise as graduates of the youth justice system from my work years before, highlighting the failure of multiple government agencies—child protection, education, health, human services, police, and correctional services—to effectively intervene and break the cycle of disadvantage and offending.

I learned that people who continue to offend into adulthood regularly exhibit manifestations of complex trauma: they cannot control their impulses and find it challenging to regulate their emotions, make rational decisions, or deal with the repeated adversity plaguing their lives. Drugs sometimes offer a way of coping with or escaping reality. Many of these individuals return repeatedly to be managed by Corrections due to re-offending or breaching justice conditions (often by continuing to use drugs, absconding, or ceasing to report). The prevalence of unresolved trauma in the lives of people who offend—reflecting their parents' lives and their children's lives—led me to question how we were responding.

This book is for students, academics, practitioners, and "pracademics" like me. I ask you to consider: What if we realise that what has happened to people in the past can impact their functioning and (criminal) behaviour? What if we recognise how trauma might relate to offending and respond in a way that avoids re-traumatisation? What if we focus on rebuilding relationships and connections through compassionate practices?

Throughout the chapters in this book, I invite you to reflect on how trauma-informed criminal justice may promote a more effective justice system.

Adelaide, SA, Australia

Katherine J. McLachlan

Acknowledgements

I acknowledge and pay my respect to the traditional custodians of the lands of the Kaurna people, where this research was undertaken. I was born in a small town on the land of the Eastern Maar peoples, and I also pay my respects to their peoples, country, and ancestors. I join in celebrating the resilience of Aboriginal peoples, their ongoing cultures and connections to Australia's land, skies, and waters.

The foundations of this book began as a Ph.D. thesis supported by an Australian Government Research Training Program (RTP) Scholarship. Thank you to my Ph.D. supervisors: Associate Professor Ben Livings, Emeritus Professor Rick Sarre, Professor Andrew Day, and Dr. Judith De Lang. A particular thank you to Andrew Day for editorial reviews, constant support, cheer, and ideas beyond my Ph.D. years. Working with you on the Magnolia Project is the best fun and a rich opportunity to explore opportunities for compassionate justice.

Thank you to my Ph.D. assessors, Emeritus Professors Loraine Gelsthorpe and Kate Warner. What an honour to have you both read and reflect on my work. Your advice and support were invaluable.

Big hugs to the Village: Tracey Johnson, Dr. Ruth Fazakerley, and Rebecca Medhurst.

Thanks also to my esteemed colleagues at the Parole Board over the years, particularly Frances Nelson KC, Nick Floreani KC, Stephen Ey, Bill Boucaut KC, Dr. Ken O'Brien, and the late Denis Edmonds APM for our chats about the judiciary and the foibles of the sentencing process.

Finally, thanks to Senior Constable First Class Andy Francis, South Australia Police, for demonstrating a trauma-informed police response when my father had a cardiac arrest in January 2024.

Contents

Abbreviations

ABS	Australian Bureau of Statistics
ACEs	Adverse Childhood Experiences
ACJR	Aboriginal Community Justice Reports
ACT	Australian Capital Territory
ADD	Attention Deficit Disorder
ADHD	Attention Deficit Hyperactivity Disorder
AIHW	Australian Institute of Health and Welfare
ANS	Autonomic Nervous System
AOD	Alcohol and Other Drugs
APA	American Psychiatric Association or American Psychological Association
BPD	Borderline Personality Disorder
CBT	Cognitive Behavioural Therapy
CJS	Criminal Justice System
cPTSD	Complex Post-traumatic Stress Disorder
CVWEW	Commissioner for Victims and Witnesses in England and Wales (UK)
DCS	Department for Correctional Services (SA)
DPP	Director of Public Prosecutions
DSM	Diagnostic and Statistical Manual of Mental Disorders

EMDR	Eye Movement Desensitisation and Reprocessing
EOC	Equal Opportunity Commission (SA)
IACP	International Association of Chiefs of Police
ICD-11	International Classification of Diseases 11th Revision
ISTSS	International Society for Traumatic Stress Studies
JCV	Judicial College of Victoria
JJGPPS	Juvenile Justice Geography, Policy, Practice and Statistics (US)
LSS	Legal Services Society (Canada)
LTSO	Long-Term Supervision Order (Canada)
NSW	New South Wales (Australia)
NT	Northern Territory (Australia)
OOHC	Out-of-Home Care
PTSD	Post-Traumatic Stress Disorder
Qld	Queensland (Australia)
RCIADIC	Royal Commission into Aboriginal Deaths in Custody (Australia)
RCT	Randomised Control Trials
RNR	Risk-Need-Responsivity
SA	South Australia
SAC	Sentencing Advisory Council
SAMHSA	Substance Abuse and Mental Health Services Administration (US)
SCEW	Sentencing Council for England and Wales
SEWB	Social and Emotional Wellbeing
Tas	Tasmania (Australia)
TC	Therapeutic Community
TF-CBT	Trauma-Focused Cognitive Behavioural Therapy
TICC	Trauma-informed Correctional Care
TPAV	The Police Association of Victoria
UK	United Kingdom (England, Scotland, Wales, Northern Ireland)
US	United States of America
Vic	Victoria (Australia)
VIS	Victim Impact Statement
VSS	Victim Support Service (SA)
WA	Western Australia
WHO	World Health Organization
WWI	World War One (1914–1918)
WWII	World War Two (1939–1945)

List of Figures

List of Tables

1
Introduction

1.1 Introduction

Trauma-informed care and practice was developed only 20 years ago and is emerging as an important way of working for the police, in corrections and courts, and in broader contexts such as health and education services. Nevertheless, few academics have examined whether trauma-informed practice exists across criminal justice agencies or in sentencing. This book uses a framework developed by the Substance Abuse and Mental Health Services Administration (SAMHSA, 2014) to explore the degree to which criminal justice agencies are trauma-informed. This book examines the relevance of trauma for practitioners, people who are victims of crime and people who have committed offences. This book is the first to examine how victim and defendant trauma is realised, recognised, and responded to by justice agencies and sentencing judges and how re-traumatisation can be resisted.

K. J. McLachlan, *Trauma-informed Criminal Justice*,
https://doi.org/10.1007/978-3-031-59290-4_1

1.2 What Is Compassionate Criminal Justice?

While compassionate justice is sometimes synonymous with faith-based ideals, particularly in the US, the concept is secular. ***Compassion*** centres around a collective and empathic understanding of human suffering. It involves an intention to respond in a way that relieves the suffering of others. The causes and drivers of crime are complex. As stated by Shadd Maruna and Anna King (2008), "[j]ustice is, at its heart, an emotional, symbolic process, not simply a matter of effectiveness and efficiency" (p. 347). Thus, ***compassionate justice*** aims to understand and better respond to the commission and impact of crime through a lens of empathy and humanity (see Rowles & Haji, 2020). Compassion has been used to justify "victim-focused" punitive political rhetoric (Walklate, 2012). Yet, compassionate criminal justice focuses on the broader community, including but not limited to victims of crime. Indeed, Anthony Hopkins et al. (2022) recommend a compassionate justice approach as an antidote to penal populism. The term ***penal populism*** describes when politicians take at face value public expressions of punitiveness (i.e., that sentencing courts are too lenient) and respond by developing increasingly punitive criminal justice policies (SACV, 2019, p. 1). Penal populism occurs in the absence of actual research evidence indicating that the public supports punitive justice policies (Day et al., 2021a, 2021b). Hopkins et al. (2022) focus not on "tough on crime" responses, but on humanising the people who offend "to understand the individual and systemic causes of their criminality…" (p. 2). Thus, a compassionate approach is evidence-informed, focused on addressing the drivers of crime, ultimately to aim to improve community safety.

1.3 Trauma and the Criminal Justice System

The criminal justice system and its agencies aim to "contribute to a safe and secure community and promote a law abiding way of life" (SCRGSP, 2023, p. 1). This book explores the idea that justice outcomes might significantly improve if the criminal justice system was "trauma-informed". Trauma is often defined as an event or experience. However, it perhaps more helpfully can be regarded as "a biopsychosocial *response* to external events that is mediated by personal meaning of those events" (Willmot & Jones, 2022, p. 3). ***Trauma***, in this book, is understood to mean the latter, that is, the impact of adversity (i.e., potentially traumatic events and experiences) on an individual's functioning and wellbeing. A substantial proportion of people who offend have life histories replete with adversity, including exposure to violence, familial mental illness and substance abuse, intergenerational trauma, death, and loss. Certainly, many people in the community experience adversity, yet most have the internal and external resources to manage and resolve its impact. For people entrenched in the criminal justice system, their trajectory into further criminality is often influenced by the ongoing impacts of unresolved trauma. This somewhat begs the question: Why do those in the criminal justice system not have the resources to resolve the impacts?

This book is written from an Australian perspective, but the ideas within it are intended to be applied more broadly. In 2021–2022, the direct operating costs related to incarceration in Australia were $AUD4.44 billion (SCRGSP, 2023, p. 94; approx. $US2.85 billion). Australia has 201 people in prison per 100,000 adult population (as of 30 June 2022, ABS, 2023), which is higher than Aotearoa New Zealand, Scotland, England, and Wales and more than double the Canada and Northern Ireland imprisonment rates (Department of Corrections, 2023; Fair & Walmsley, 2021). Regarding Western jurisdictions, only the US has us beaten at 531 per 100,000 in 2021 (Fair & Walmsley, 2021). The incarceration rate for Aboriginal and Torres Strait Islander peoples in Australia is 2330 people in prison per 100,000 First Nations population. Aboriginal and Torres Strait Islander peoples represent 32% of the prison population (ABS, 2023) but only 3% of the general population (ABS, 2022). Approximately 2.5% of the adult Aboriginal and Torres Strait Islander population is incarcerated at any point in time (Leigh, 2020). As noted by Thalia Anthony (2017), Aboriginal Australians and Torres Strait Islanders are the most incarcerated population in the world. This is not because Indigenous Australians are inherently criminal, but rather criminalisation is associated with the compounded trauma resulting from chronic adversity and disadvantage since colonisation (Heffernan et al., 2014; RCIADIC, 1991), as is examined in Chapters 4 and 10.

While prison may incapacitate people in the short term, most incarcerated individuals will be released into the community, so the justice system must enable effective rehabilitation and reintegration strategies. Nevertheless, the justice system has been criticised for not considering empirical evidence when sentencing to reduce recidivism and promote desistance from crime (Cullen et al., 2011; Martin, 2010). Re-offending rates relative to baseline offending and assessed risk are a proxy measure of the criminal justice system's ability to keep the community safe. In Australia in 2021–2022, almost half the people (42.7%) released from prison returned to prison with a new sentence within two years (SCRGSP, 2023). While recidivism rates are difficult to compare because of significant variations in definitions and reporting practices, it has been reported, in a systematic review, that Australia's rates of reimprisonment and reconviction are relatively high compared to similar Westminster jurisdictions (Yukhnenko et al., 2020). When people are sentenced to a churn of multiple, consecutive periods of incarceration—ostensibly to rehabilitate, incapacitate, and deter—their criminal behaviour and traumatic experiences often become entrenched and life-defining. Punitive sentences can cause or exacerbate trauma for people who offend (SACV, 2016). Thus, current criminal justice system practices often compound the multiple disadvantages and existing adversity and trauma in defendants' lives.

The larger Australian prison population may be attributed (in part) to the widely held assumption endorsed by politicians, the media, and some members of the judiciary that public confidence in the criminal justice system is low and can be bolstered by punitive approaches (Day et al., 2021a, 2021b). Populism has driven punitive sentencing legislation with increasing restrictions on judicial discretion (Freiberg, 2017). Populism has also resulted in the imposition of longer sentences, more punitive legislative frameworks, the mass incarceration of First Nations peoples, and increased difficulty in accessing bail (with an associated increase in unsentenced prisoners; ABS, 2023). Finally, the "tough on crime" rhetoric has also influenced government investment in prisons and tertiary crime prevention rather than primary and secondary crime prevention strategies, which might better achieve community safety (e.g., the Pathways to Prevention project, National Crime Prevention, 1999).

Prison is expensive, it is both criminogenic and traumatic (i.e., it causes crime and results in further trauma), and it is not designed to address the underlying causes of crime (Cullen et al., 2011; Levenson & Willis, 2019). For example, when people remanded in custody are sentenced, their sanction is often backdated, meaning opportunities to achieve rehabilitative gains (and behaviour change) through targeted intervention are lost. Incarceration also erodes protective factors such as stable housing, work and study skills and opportunities, treatment and support programs, and relationships with pro-social family members and associates (Leigh, 2020). Nevertheless, the criminal justice system continues to rely on prisons ostensibly to protect community safety through incapacitation in the short term and an expected (but rarely realised) reduction in future offending. It follows that given their discretionary powers, judges and the criminal justice system would benefit from a broader range of "smarter" sanctions to be used depending on the individuals involved and their offending trajectory and behaviour.

Despite calls for decarceration and the abolition of prisons, we are far from this becoming a reality in Australia or any other country with a Westminster system of law. While an adversarial legal system and prisons remain, the criminal justice system should uphold human and victims' rights and reduce the likelihood of secondary trauma and victimisation. By addressing the underlying drivers and causes of crime, the fundamental purpose of the criminal justice system—to protect community safety by preventing and reducing crime—is best achieved. This is not a soft-on-crime option; this is a smart justice option based on emerging evidence of the impacts of direct and intergenerational trauma.

1.4 Trauma-informed Criminal Justice

Trauma-informed practice requires that service providers realise the potentially traumatic impact of adversity, recognise the relationships between trauma and crime, respond in ways that are safe and trustworthy, and promote choice, collaboration, and empowerment while also resisting further traumatisation (SAMHSA, 2014). The concept of "trauma-informed" emerged in 2001 in the work of Maxine Harris and Roger Fallot (2001). Trauma-informed practice is not designed to treat trauma (the purpose of "trauma-focused" practice). Instead, trauma-informed practice requires that service providers at all organisational levels understand the potentially traumatic effects of adversity on an individual's ability to function and interact with the world and promote service environments conducive to recovery and avoid further traumatisation (Kezelman & Stavropoulos, 2016). The term "trauma-informed" emerged simultaneously with the recognition of the broad and devastating impact of adverse childhood experiences (ACEs) on health and wellbeing (Felitti et al., 1998). Since then, trauma-informed practice has been refined, particularly by mental health and substance abuse professionals. There has been a substantial increase in trauma-informed publications across various disciplines over the last decade.

Trauma-informed practice extends across health and therapeutic services, education, disability, and community services. Trauma-informed practice also exists within the criminal justice system. ***Trauma-informed correctional care*** (TICC) is being applied in mainstream prisons, and trauma-informed lawyering and trauma-informed youth justice is emerging. In addition to trauma-informed practices currently existing within and across the criminal justice system, this book focuses on the overlooked issue of trauma-informed sentencing—particularly how judges currently acknowledge and address defendant trauma in sentencing (Jackson et al., 2021).

1.5 Purpose of the Book

This book is designed to help professionals and students (future professionals) understand the relevance and significance of trauma and trauma-informed practice in the criminal justice system. Whether you are a student or practitioner of social work, law, criminology or psychology, a police officer, or a corrections officer, understanding trauma is vital. Professionals should know how trauma influences criminal behaviour, its relevance to crime prevention strategies and how trauma may also impact their wellbeing and functioning. The idea of trauma-informed criminal justice is both an ideal and a reality. Small gestures can be and are currently being made daily to promote compassionate justice for victims of crime, people who offend and practitioners of the justice system. A compassionate justice system aspires to understand and respond better to the commission and impact of crime through a lens of empathy and humanity. Trauma-informed practice and care is one mechanism to help achieve such an approach.

1.6 Outline of the Book

The book is divided into three parts:

- Recognising relationships between adversity, trauma, and crime,
- Trauma-informed responses in the criminal justice system, and
- Responding to traumatised defendants: Trauma-informed sentencing.

Each chapter in this book is designed to be a standalone resource. Whether you are interested in the relationship between trauma and crime, how you might combat or prevent your own experiences of secondary trauma, or how to professionally behave in a mindful, compassionate, and trauma-informed way, each chapter is designed to help develop your knowledge in specific areas relevant to trauma-informed criminal justice.

The first part of the book examines how adversity, trauma, and crime are related. The word "trauma" can be used in various ways. Chapter 2 explains the difference between adversity and trauma. In this book, "trauma" is regarded as the impact of adversity (i.e., one or more potentially distressing or life-threatening events) on an individual's social and emotional wellbeing. While adversity does not always result in trauma, adverse experiences (including crime victimisation) may result in various symptoms or negative impacts on wellbeing and functioning. Chapter 3 then examines the relationship between trauma and crime, showing that, while trauma cannot be considered a cause of crime, it is a risk factor for criminality. Indeed, past adversities, such as adverse childhood experiences and intergenerational trauma, can also impact the social and emotional wellbeing and criminal behaviour of an adult, as demonstrated in Chapter 4.

The second part of the book focuses on trauma-informed practice in the criminal justice system concerning people who have offended, victims of crime, and the professionals who work within the system. A key weakness in the academic discussion of trauma-informed criminal justice is the absence of tangible strategies that people can use to inform their own practice. This book offers current examples from around the world where criminal justice agencies have worked to operationalise trauma-informed practice. Chapter 5 examines the current defendant-focused practices within the criminal justice system informed by trauma and discusses the future of trauma-informed criminal justice across the police, corrections, and court. Chapter 6 then considers how justice agencies work to identify, understand, and provide trauma-informed care for victims of crime. Chapter 7 explores how professionals—police officers, correctional service workers, lawyers, and the judiciary—are impacted by exposure to the trauma of defendants and victims of crime in terms of secondary trauma. The chapter then examines current responses to secondary trauma for criminal justice professionals.

The third part of the book focuses on responding to defendants through trauma-informed sentencing. Sentencing offers an opportunity for compassionate justice through therapeutic jurisprudence and judicial empathy (Hopkins et al., 2022). Chapter 8 outlines the process of sentencing—the sentencing calculus that judges apply to reach a decision about sanction—and the role of SAMHSA's (2014) 4Rs framework in this process. Chapter 9 demonstrates how trauma-informed sentencing can be identified in practice, drawing a South Australian case study. In that case study, sentencing judges were found to recognise the relevance of adversity in adulthood as impacting an individual's social and emotional wellbeing but minimise or overlook intergenerational and compounded trauma that impacted Aboriginal defendants. Chapter 10 examines the relevance of intergenerational trauma and direct trauma when sentencing First Nations defendants.

These chapters demonstrate how trauma-informed sentencing might better achieve community safety than current strategies through the imposition of evidence-informed sanctions that target the underlying drivers of crime.

1.7 Conclusion

Decades of criminal justice system failure to effectively reduce re-offending is hidden behind the false comfort offered by penal populism, that more prisons will bring about greater levels of safety. In fact, better social welfare and conditions reduce violence and crime (Currie, 2016). Compassion is the key to crime reduction; compassion for people who are victims, people who offend, the many people who are both, and the communities affected. Back when I was reading true crime under the covers, I believed in goodies and baddies; serial killers and criminal profiling; victims and offenders. But I have learned to let these false dichotomies go. Everyday people in mock jury studies, armed with information and facts, do the same (SACV, 2019). People make smart decisions when they understand the social and personal drivers of crime, rather than simply relying on media tropes and lazy political beat ups.

Trauma-informed practice is about understanding the relevance and significance of adversity and resulting trauma, and responding in a way that promotes safety, trust, empowerment, collaboration, and choice as well as giving regard to factors such as culture and gender. It follows that, for example, if trauma-informed practice and care are applied in a way that helps reduce the over-representation of First Nations peoples in the criminal justice system, then the same approaches can be applied to anyone caught up in the churn of chronic offending and re-offending. For too long we have blamed the "others" for crime. This book examines what might happen if we focus on understanding the human suffering that often sits behind criminal acts. Accepting that the criminal justice system aims to "contribute to a safe and secure community and promote a law abiding way of life" (SCRGSP, 2023, p. 1), this book argues that the solution is to move away from focusing on baddies and the myth of a just world (where bad things only happen to bad people) and instead use trauma-informed ways of working (beyond the siloes of the criminal justice system) better to achieve a safer and more secure community for everyone.

References

Anthony, T. (2017, June 6). FactCheck: Are First Australians the Most Imprisoned People on Earth? *The Conversation.*

Australian Bureau of Statistics (ABS). (2023). *Prisoners in Australia.* ABS.

Australian Bureau of Statistics (ABS). (2022). *Australia: Aboriginal and Torres Strait Islander Population Summary.* ABS.

Cullen, F. T., Jonson, C. L., & Nagin, D. S. (2011). Prisons Do Not Reduce Recidivism: The High Cost of Ignoring Science. *The Prison Journal, 91*(3_suppl), 48S–65S. https://doi.org/10.1177/0032885511415224

Currie, E. (2016). *The Roots of danger: violent crime in global perspective.* Oxford University Press.

Day, A., Ross, S., & McLachlan, K. (2021a). *The Effectiveness of Minimum Non-parole Period Schemes for Serious Violent, Sexual and Drug Offenders and Evidence-Based Approaches to Community Protection, Deterrence, and Rehabilitation.* Queensland Sentencing Advisory Council.

Day, A., Ross, S., & McLachlan, K. (2021b). *Technical Report: Scoping Review Methodology and Results of the Report on the Effectiveness of Minimum Non-parole Period Schemes.* Queensland Sentencing Advisory Council.

Department of Corrections. (2023). *Annual Report 1 July 2022–30 June 2023.* New Zealand Government.

Fair, H., & Walmsley, R. (2021). *World Prison Population List* (13th ed.). Institute for Crime and Justice Policy Research (ICPR).

Felitti, V. J., Anda, R. F., Nordenberg, D., Williamson, D. F., Spitz, A. M., Edwards, V., Koss, M. P., & Marks, J. S. (1998). Relationship of Childhood Abuse and Household Dysfunction to Many of the Leading Causes of Death in Adults: The Adverse Childhood Experiences (ACE) Study. *American Journal of Preventative Medicine, 14*(4), 245–258. https://doi.org/10.1016/s0749-3797(98)00017-8

Freiberg, A. (2017). Parole, Populism and Penal Policy. *Alternative Law Journal, 42*(4), 247. https://doi.org/10.1177/1037969XI7733160

Harris, M., & Fallot, R. D. (2001). Envisioning a Trauma-Informed Service System: A Vital Paradigm Shift. *New Directions for Mental Health Services, 2001*(89), 3–22. https://doi.org/10.1002/yd.23320018903

Heffernan, E., Andersen, K., McEntyre, E., & Kinner, S. (2014). Mental Disorder and Cognitive Disability in the Criminal Justice System. In P. Dudgeon, H. Milroy, & R. Walker (Eds.), *Working Together: Aboriginal and Torres Strait Islander Mental Health and Wellbeing Principles and Practice* (pp. 165–178). Commonwealth of Australia.

Hopkins, A., Dodd, S., Nolan, M., & Bartels, L. (2022). At the Heart of Sentencing: Exploring Whether More Compassionate Delivery of Sentencing Remarks Increases Public Concern for People Who Offend. *Psychiatry, Psychology and Law, 30*(4), 459–485. https://doi.org/10.1080/13218719.2022.2040398

Jackson, V., Sullivan, D. H., Mawren, D., Freiberg, A., Kulkarni, J., & Darjee, R. (2021). Trauma-Informed Sentencing of Serious Violent Offenders: An Exploration of Judicial Dispositions with a Gendered Perspective. *Psychiatry, Psychology and Law, 28*(5), 748–773. https://doi.org/10.1080/13218719.2020.1855267

Kezelman, C., & Stavropoulos, P. (2016). *Trauma and the Law: Applying Trauma-Informed Practice to Legal and Judicial Contexts.* Blue Knot Foundation.

Leigh, A. (2020). *The Second Convict Age: Explaining the Return of Mass Imprisonment in Australia* (Vol. IZA DP No. 13025). IZA—Institute of Labor Economics.

Levenson, J. S., & Willis, G. M. (2019). Implementing Trauma-Informed Care in Correctional Treatment and Supervision. *Journal of Aggression, Maltreatment & Trauma, 28*(4), 481–501. https://doi.org/10.1080/10926771.2018.1531959

Martin, W. (2010). Popular Punitivism—The Role of the Courts in the Development of Criminal Justice Policies. *Australian and New Zealand Journal of Criminology, 43*(1), 1–16.

Maruna, S., & King, A. (2008). Selling the Public on Probation: Beyond the Bib. *Probation Journal, 55*(4), 337–451. https://doi.org/10.1177/0264550508096491

National Crime Prevention. (1999). *Pathways to Prevention: Developmental and Early Intervention Approaches to Crime in Australia.* Attorney-General's Department.

Rowles, L., & Haji, I. (Eds.). (2020). *Humane Justice: What Role Do Kindness, Hope and Compassion Play in the Criminal Justice System?* Monument Fellowship.

Royal Commission into Aboriginal Deaths in Custody (RCIADIC). (1991). *National Report* (Vol. 2). Australian Government.

Sentencing Advisory Council of Victoria (SACV). (2016). *Sentencing Guidance in Victoria Report*. Victoria State Government.

Sentencing Advisory Council of Victoria (SACV). (2019). *Public Opinion About Sentencing: A Research Overview*. Victoria State Government.

Steering Committee for the Review of Government Service Provision (SCRGSP). (2023). *Report on Government Services 2023. Part C: Justice*. Productivity Commission.

Substance Abuse and Mental Health Services Administration (SAMHSA). (2014). *SAMHSA's Concept of Trauma and Guidance for a Trauma-Informed Approach*. US Department of Health and Human Services.

Walklate, S. (2012). Courting Compassion: Victims, Policy, and the Question of Justice. *The Howard Journal, 51*(2), 109–121. https://doi.org/10.1111/j.1468-2311.2011.00698.x

Willmot, P., & Jones, L. (2022). Introduction. In P. Willmot & L. Jones (Eds.), *Trauma-Informed Forensic Practice* (pp. 1–11). Routledge. https://doi.org/10.4324/9781003120766-1

Yukhnenko, D., Sridhar, S., & Fazel, S. (2020). A Systematic Review of Criminal Recidivism Rates Worldwide: 3-Year Update. *Wellcome Open Research, 4*(28), 1–26. https://doi.org/10.12688/wellcomeopenres.14970.3

Part I

Part I: Recognising Relationships Between Adversity, Trauma and Crime

2

Adversity and Trauma: Realising the Basics

2.1 Introduction

This chapter provides an overview of adversity and trauma, primarily for people who work in or study the criminal justice system. Trauma is relevant for people who work in the criminal justice system for three reasons. First, evidence shows that trauma is prevalent in the lives of many children and adults who are justice-involved. Second, victims of crime are sometimes (but not always) traumatised due to their experiences of crime and with the criminal justice system. And finally, practitioners themselves may experience trauma from exposure to the devastating, relentless, and often cruel impacts of crime. No consensus exists regarding the definition of trauma, even among experts who practice and teach in the area. Trauma may refer to a distressing event or the impact of that event. In this chapter, trauma is understood to be the latter: the impact of distressing or adverse events on a person's social and emotional well-being. This is because the significance of trauma is the psychological, cognitive, and behavioural impact on an individual, not the nature of the event itself. Oftentimes, judges and others will focus on the nature of the adversity (e.g., chronic childhood sexual abuse) and may use stereotypes and generic assumptions about the likely impact based on the severity of

K. J. McLachlan, *Trauma-informed Criminal Justice*,
https://doi.org/10.1007/978-3-031-59290-4_2

the adversity rather than recognising that the impact of adversity is individualised, influenced by the broader context of internal and external supports.

2.2 Adversity and Trauma

2.2.1 Trauma is the Distressing Impact of Adversity on a Person's Social and Emotional Wellbeing

No universally accepted definition or understanding of trauma exists (Walklate, 2016). Experts use the term "trauma" when referring to events and experiences and the impact of those adverse experiences. The Substance Abuse and Mental Health Services Administration (SAMHSA, 2014) states that:

> Individual trauma results from an event, series of events, or set of circumstances that is experienced by an individual as physically or emotionally harmful or life threatening and that has lasting adverse effects on the individual's functioning and mental, physical, social, emotional, or spiritual well-being. (p. 7)

Thus, trauma is "a biopsychosocial *response* to external events..." rather than the adverse events or experiences themselves (Willmot & Jones, 2022, p. 3).

Adverse events or circumstances include acute "overwhelming and uncontrollable" (van der Kolk, 1987, p. 2) experiences or "traumatic or stressful events... [such as] actual or threatened death, serious injury, or sexual violence" (APA, 2022), as well as chronic traumatic experiences. Chronic traumatic experiences may be either a series of repeated experiences (e.g., a series of relationships characterised by domestic abuse)or ongoing traumatic experiences (e.g., prolonged intrafamilial childhood sexual abuse, exposure to war or combat, bullying, and racism). Adverse events and experiences may occur in childhood (including but not limited to Adverse Childhood Experiences or ACEs) or across the life-course, as shown in Table 2.1. While adversity may include crime victimisation and violence, the concepts of "trauma" and "victimisation" should not be conflated (Walklate, 2016). It is possible to be a crime victim without being traumatised; equally, many people may be traumatised without being victims of crime.

Table 2.1 Examples of adverse events and experiences

Adverse Childhood Experiences (Felitti et al., 1998; Reavis et al., 2013)	Adversity across the life-course (Weathers et al., 2018)
1. Psychological abuse	1. Natural disasters (e.g., flood, hurricane, tornado, earthquake)
2. Physical abuse	2. Fire or explosion
3. Sexual abuse	3. Transportation accident (e.g., car accident, boat accident, train wreck, plane crash)
4. Household substance abuse	4. Serious accident at work, home, or during recreational activity
5. Household mental illness	5. Exposure to toxic substances (e.g., dangerous chemicals, radiation)
6. Family violence/Domestic abuse	6. Physical assault (e.g., being attacked, hit, slapped, kicked, beaten up)
7. Household member incarcerated	7. Assault with a weapon (e.g., being shot, stabbed, threatened with a knife, gun, bomb)
8. Emotional neglect	8. Sexual assault (e.g., rape, attempted rape, made to perform any type of sexual act through force or threat of harm)
9. Physical neglect	9. Other unwanted or uncomfortable sexual experiences
10. Parental separation/divorce	10. Combat or exposure to a warzone (in the military or as a civilian)
	11. Captivity (e.g., being kidnapped, abducted, held hostage, prisoner of war)
	12. Life-threatening illness or injury
	13. Severe human suffering
	14. Sudden violent death (e.g., homicide, suicide)
	15. Sudden accidental death
	16. Serious injury, harm, or death you caused to someone else
	17. Any other very stressful event or experience

Trauma is subjective and individualised, such that not all exposure to adversity results in trauma (APA, 2022; Griffin & Sallen, 2013). Often, the severity of the trauma and the ability of an individual to cope and recover depends on the characteristics of the adversity (e.g., the trauma load: how severe it was, how often it happened), individual characteristics (e.g., the developmental age when the adversity occurred), and the availability of formal and informal supports to aid recovery (Neller et al., 2005; Widom, 2017). Indeed, for some people with sufficient support and protective factors, trauma "may also be a positive and life changing experience, through post-traumatic growth" (Voigt et al., 2017, p. 373).

Trauma may manifest as "a spectrum of conditions" (Herman, 2015, p. 102), including temporary stress responses or a range of unresolved neuropsychological, emotional, and behavioural impacts that together may meet diagnostic criteria of "trauma- and stressor-related disorders" in the DSM-5-TR (APA, 2022). These disorders include post-traumatic stress disorder (PTSD), acute stress disorder, and adjustment disorders (APA, 2022). The World Health Organization (2018) also recognises complex PTSD (cPTSD), as outlined below.

2.2.2 Unresolved Complex Trauma

Unresolved trauma refers to the unaddressed impact of past, chronic adversity on current functioning (Boswell, 2016). Unresolved trauma particularly relates to interrupted neuropsychological, social, and emotional development. ***Complex trauma*** refers to the cumulative or compounded impact of multiple or prolonged traumatic stressors, leading to "underlying" dysfunction across a person's life (Kezelman & Stavropoulos, 2019). Specifically, complex trauma may be caused by:

> [e]xposure to severe stressors that (1) are repetitive or prolonged, (2) involve harm or abandonment by caregivers or other ostensibly responsible adults, and (3) occur at developmentally vulnerable times in a victim's life, such as early childhood or adolescence (when critical periods of brain development are rapidly occurring or being consolidated. (Ford & Courtois, 2014, p. 13)

Cathy Kezelman et al. (2015) go so far as to argue that all developmental trauma (i.e., the negative impact of chronic adversity in childhood) is complex because it changes the developing brain "from a 'learning' brain to a 'survival' brain" (p. 14). Complex trauma is influenced by the characteristics of both the adversity and the individual experiencing it (Wall & Quadara, 2014).

2.3 How Does Trauma Manifest?

Adversity can result in trauma, which impacts a person's functioning and wellbeing in several ways. Unresolved complex trauma may impair functioning across various human domains, including physiological (neurological), psychological and emotional, cognitive, physical, behavioural, and social (Wall & Quadara, 2014), as illustrated in Fig. 2.1. The specific impacts of developmental trauma are further examined in Chapter 4. Often, complex trauma can manifest as changes in "personality structure" (Kezelman & Stavropoulos, 2019, p. 35). This is because chronic adversity can have a long-term impact on the body, brain, and nervous system. From a therapeutic perspective, psychological and emotional trauma symptoms may be "'expectable and adaptive' reactions to traumatic childhood experiences, i.e., the outgrowth of normal protective responses to abnormal conditions" (Kezelman & Stavropoulos, 2019, p. 38, quoting Courtois et al., 2009, p. 93).

Trauma-based behaviour may serve important adaptive functions to survive and cope with adversity. While such behaviours (e.g., hypervigilance, aggression, impulsivity, and non-compliance) make sense in the context in which they emerge, they may be perceived as counterproductive if they continue after the risk of harm has ceased. However, the law takes a deficit approach, such that collectively, psychological, neurological, and emotional trauma may be evidence of "cognitive impairment", further discussed in Chapters 3 and 8. Psychological and emotional trauma are examined in more detail below.

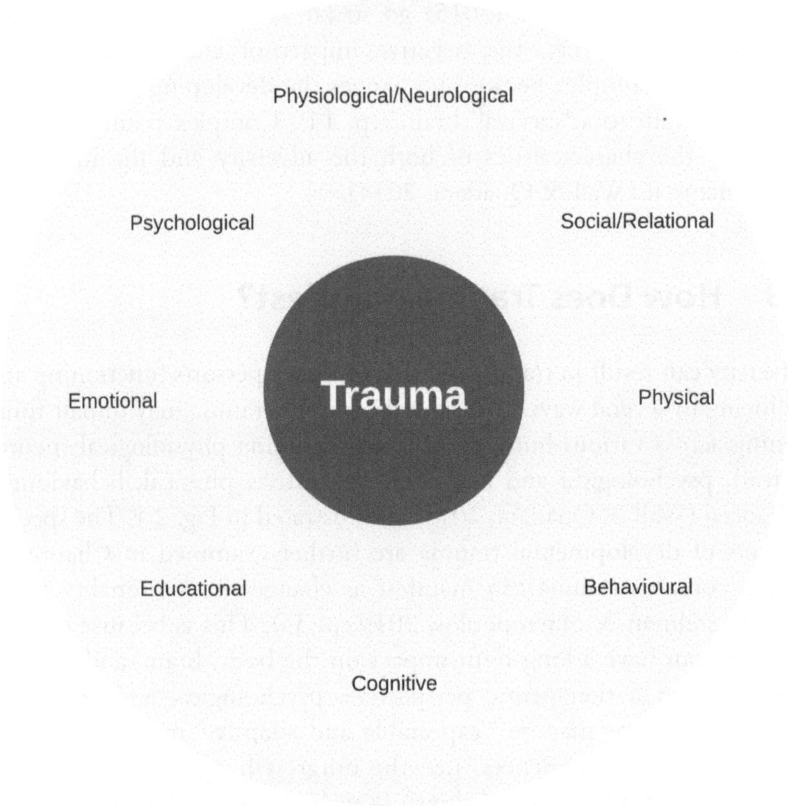

Fig. 2.1 The possible manifestations of trauma, across human domains

2.3.1 Psychological and Emotional Trauma

The impact of adversity on mental health may be referred to as "psychological trauma", i.e., "an emotional state of discomfort and stress resulting from memories of an extraordinary catastrophic experience which shattered the survivor's sense of invulnerability to harm" (Figley, 1985, p. xviii). The association between exposure to adversity and psychological trauma is widely accepted (Cloitre et al., 2009; D'Andrea et al., 2012; Sweeney et al., 2016). According to Dutch-American psychiatrist Bessel van der Kolk (1987), psychological trauma occurs:

> when one loses the sense of having a safe place to retreat to within or outside oneself to deal with frightening emotions or experiences. This results in a state of helplessness, a feeling that one's actions have no bearing on the outcome of one's life. (p. 31)

Psychological, emotional, and social trauma caused by chronic adversity can impair an individual's way of perceiving and responding to the world (van der Kolk, 2005), leading to dysfunctional coping and protective mechanisms (Kezelman & Stavropoulos, 2019) as well as difficulty regulating emotions. As highlighted by the American Psychiatric Association's *Diagnostic and Statistical Manual of Mental Disorders* (DSM-5-TR: APA, 2022), the way trauma manifests can vary between individuals.

2.3.1.1 Poor Emotional Regulation

Poor emotional regulation may present as a "poor tolerance for psychological and physiological arousal" (van der Kolk, 1987, p. 3), a limited ability to regulate anger, and a tendency to respond to triggers or provocation in either a withdrawn or aggressive manner (van der Kolk, 1987, p. 37; Malvaso et al., 2017). As noted by Marylene Cloitre et al. (2009):

> [d]isturbances in self-regulation account for both overactivation and deactivation/avoidance in emotions and interpersonal behaviors as seen in dysphoria and anger as well as dissociation; and in interpersonal behaviors that are aggressive or dependent, as well as those that are distant and avoidant. (p. 400)

Impaired self-regulation includes high levels of impulsivity, "a personality trait related to reacting rapidly or in unplanned ways to behavioral or emotional stimuli without proper regard for negative impacts" (Shin et al., 2018, p. 118). High impulsivity has again been correlated with a history of emotional abuse and neglect but may exist without a medical diagnosis (Shin et al., 2018). Hyperarousal, or excessive agitation, is associated with high anxiety levels (Kezelman & Stavropoulos, 2019).

Dissociation is a disconnection between a person's thoughts, memories, feelings, actions, or sense of who they are (APA, 2022) and is associated with aggression and violence (Altintas & Bilici, 2018).

2.3.1.2 PTSD, cPTSD, and Mental Health Diagnoses

Psychological trauma may result in diagnoses relating to psychosis, such as schizophrenia and drug-induced psychosis, PTSD, diagnoses associated with dissociation, anxiety, and depression, personality disorders (including but not limited to borderline personality disorder, BPD), and bipolar disorder. However, the use of these labels must be treated with caution. There is emerging discontent among mental health practitioners about the usefulness of psychiatric diagnoses (e.g., Johnstone et al., 2018).

The DSM-5-TR (APA, 2022) states PTSD requires a psychiatric diagnosis based on specific symptoms: "(1) re-experiencing of painful memories, (2) effortful avoidance of trauma cues, (3) emotional numbing, and (4) hyperarousal. The disorder arises from exposure to one or more potentially life-threatening events" (summarised by Bottalico & Bruni, 2012, p. 112). The adoption of the diagnostic label of PTSD in the DSM-III in 1980 was in direct response to Vietnam War veterans in the US who had experienced delayed and chronic manifestations of trauma. From early in World War One (WWI), it had been acknowledged that soldiers might experience "shell-shock", first attributing:

> … their symptoms to the concussive effects of exploding shells… though it soon became clear that the syndrome could be found in soldiers who had not been exposed to any physical trauma. Gradually military psychiatrists were forced to acknowledge that the symptoms of shell shock were due to psychological trauma. The emotional stress of prolonged exposure to violent death was sufficient to produce a neurotic syndrome resembling hysteria in men. (Herman, 2015, p. 24)

Strategies in WWI (and WWII) to treat soldiers with symptoms of psychological trauma involved "forward treatment": keeping traumatised patients near the front line, conveying expectations that the patient would recover and fight on (Crocq & Crocq, 2000; Herman, 2015). After the war, ongoing psychological trauma experienced by returned soldiers was disregarded and fundamentally treated as an embarrassing issue not for discussion (Herman, 2015).

By the time of the Vietnam War, the sheer volume of Vietnam veterans who required psychological support (almost a quarter of all US soldiers sent to Vietnam from 1964 to 1973), meant that there was a significant push for the recognition of the psychological impact of exposure to war and combat (Crocq & Crocq, 2000). As noted by van der Kolk:

> [t]he PTSD diagnosis was a result of intense advocacy and was created against huge opposition… The people who advocated for the PTSD diagnosis came from outside of academia: Vietnam veterans and two psychoanalysts, Robert J Lifton and Chaim Shatan, who wanted to create a diagnosis that was not stigmatizing. (van der Kolk with Najavits, 2013, p. 516)

Since its inclusion in the DSM in 1980, the diagnostic criteria for PTSD have changed with each new edition, and there is now a push to de-medicalise post-traumatic stress (Smith & Whooley, 2015). There is debate about changing the "D" of PTSD from disorder to response (PTSR) or injury (PTSI) or dropping it all together (PTS), given that the symptoms of PTSD are not at all disordered but reasonable and natural reactions to a traumatic event (Smith & Whooley, 2015).

Many studies—and criminal justice practitioners such as judges—use PTSD as a definite indicator of the presence of trauma. However, researchers and practitioners have found that relying on a PTSD diagnosis as a measure of traumatisation is limited because:

> the diagnostic category of PTSD was developed in response to the symptoms seen in survivors of one-off, or relatively contained events, such as a natural disaster. Many researchers in the fields of psychiatry, traumatology, and social work do not see PTSD as adequately capturing the effects of chronic and/or multiple types of victimisation. (Wall & Quadara, 2014, p. 2)

Thus, PTSD, by definition, is a medicalised marker of the presence and impact of trauma, but it is not the only reliable indicator.

In 1992, Judith Herman (2014, 2015), a psychiatrist at Harvard Medical School who is an expert in trauma, introduced complex PTSD (cPTSD) to explain the psychological trauma exhibited by people who had experienced prolonged adversity, particularly sexual violence. She identified three symptoms of cPTSD: somatisation, dissociation, and affect dysregulation. Such symptoms "were found particularly in survivors of childhood abuse, less commonly in those abused in adolescence or adulthood, and rarely in people who had endured a single acute trauma that was not of human design" (Herman, 2014, p. xiii).

The PTSD Working Group for the DSM-IV initially supported the inclusion of cPTSD in the DSM-IV. However, this was overruled at higher levels (Herman, 2014; van der Kolk with Najavits, 2013). While cPTSD is not a recognised medical condition in the DSM, the World Health Organization (WHO) recognised cPTSD in the International Classification of Diseases (ICD-11) in 2018. WHO (2018) describes cPTSD as:

> … a disorder that may develop following exposure to an event or series of events of an extremely threatening or horrific nature, most commonly prolonged or repetitive events from which escape is difficult or impossible (e.g., torture, slavery, genocide campaigns, prolonged domestic violence, repeated childhood sexual or physical abuse). All diagnostic requirements for PTSD are met. In addition, Complex PTSD is characterized by severe and persistent 1) problems in affect regulation; 2) beliefs about oneself as diminished, defeated or worthless, accompanied by feelings of shame, guilt or failure related to the traumatic event; and 3) difficulties in sustaining relationships and in feeling close to others. These symptoms cause significant impairment in personal, family, social, educational, occupational or other important areas of functioning.

The Clinical Division of the British Psychological Society has acknowledged that ideas such as "complex trauma" and cPTSD are more helpful than DSM diagnoses for people experiencing problems with their mental health, emotional regulation, social relationships, and cognition due to unresolved complex trauma (Johnstone et al., 2018).

The diagnosis of cPTSD was excluded from the DSM because "it does not fit neatly under the category of anxiety disorders. It might fit equally well under dissociative disorders, or somatization disorders, or even personality disorders" (Herman, 2014, p. xiii). The impact of chronic adversity has been associated with a range of DSM-5 psychological and personality disorder diagnoses (Ford & Courtois, 2014). None of them truly capture the range of impacts that exposure to chronic trauma may have on functioning and wellbeing. Indeed, the DSM's PTSD diagnosis can be made through hundreds of thousands of different symptom combinations (Galatzer-Levy & Bryant, 2013). Field tests of the DSM-5 found that of the 23 DSM disorder classifications, only five "achieved scientifically acceptable (kappa) levels of agreement" (van der Kolk with Najavits, 2013, p. 516). Cohen's kappa coefficient is used to measure inter-rater reliability; in this case, it refers to the degree to which different clinicians reach the same diagnostic conclusion when evaluating individuals' self-reports of symptoms and distress. Across DSM editions, diagnostic criteria have changed, leading to decreased kappa coefficients for some disorders, such as schizophrenia (Greenberg, 2013). Overall, the DSM has been criticised by practitioners, including psychiatrists who helped develop it, for lacking a robust empirical evidence base (Greenberg, 2013). If the experts do not fully agree on how or what is trauma evidence, this is a challenge for trauma-informed criminal justice.

Despite the lack of consensus regarding trauma-related diagnoses, the diagnosis of cPTSD is upheld by many psychiatrists (e.g., Judith Herman, Sandra Bloom, John Briere, Bruce Perry, Bessel van der Kolk), psychologists (e.g., Maxine Harris), social workers (e.g., Stephanie Covington), and counsellors with frontline experience. They have identified the importance of responding to the personal impact of ongoing, interpersonal trauma—particularly the impact of domestic abuse and chronic child abuse and neglect. This trauma-informed work has led to a broader understanding of trauma than the clinical model, where:

> trauma is viewed not as a single discrete event but rather as a defining and organizing experience that forms the core of an individual's identity… The impact of trauma is thus felt throughout an individual's life in areas of functioning that may seem quite far removed from the abuse, as well

> as in areas that are more obviously connected to the trauma. (Harris & Fallot, 2001, p. 312)

This definition goes beyond the DSM-5-TR (APA, 2022) criteria for PTSD, recognising that individuals may experience lingering trauma-related distress or dysfunction in unique and individualised ways. The cPTSD model underpins the understanding of trauma upon which trauma-informed work—and this book—is based.

> *Trauma usually has much more of an interpersonal aspect than what the PTSD diagnosis recognizes. Ignoring this leaves out the vast majority of traumatized individuals. (van der Kolk with Najavits, 2013, p. 518)*

2.4 Trauma Experienced by People who Offend

The prevalence of adversity and trauma is higher in the lives of adults and children who are known to offend than in the general population (Edalati et al., 2017; Malvaso et al., 2021). Justice-involved women tend to experience greater levels of adversity and complex trauma than justice-involved men (Kubiak et al., 2017). A recent study of 221 incarcerated men in London identified that 16.7% met the diagnosis for cPTSD (Facer-Irwin et al., 2021). A meta-analysis of 56 studies conducted across 20 countries involving 21,099 people in prison found that men and women in prison were five to eight times, respectively, more likely to be diagnosed with PTSD at some point in their lives than non-incarcerated people (Baranyi et al., 2018). The elevated prevalence rates of PTSD show that people who have been incarcerated are significantly more likely than the general population to meet the threshold of PTSD diagnostic criteria (i.e., to have experienced at least one adverse event that has had a significant impact on their functioning). Contact with the justice system itself is often traumatic and may result in further re-traumatisation. Chapter 3 examines the links between trauma and offending behaviour in more detail.

2.5 Trauma Experienced by People who are Victims of Crime

Herman (2015) has said that:

> Traumatic events are extraordinary, not because they occur rarely but rather because they overwhelm the ordinary adaptations to life. Unlike commonplace misfortunes, traumatic events generally involve threats to life or bodily integrity, or a close personal encounter with violence and death. They confront human beings with the extremities of helplessness and terror and evoke the responses of catastrophe. (p. 35)

Crimes such as sexual assault, physical assault, and home invasion are all examples of adverse events. These crimes are often highly traumatic—particularly when there is a relationship of trust, love, or reliance between the victim and the person committing the offence, such as between a parent and a child or intimate partners. An insensitive, judgemental, or ignorant criminal justice system response can exacerbate the impacts of crimes, resulting in re-traumatisation for some people who are victims. Chapter 6 explores criminal justice responses to victims of crime.

> *People's perceptions do more damage than your own perception because you take it on. I already had a hard enough time dealing with me and hating me without having to deal with other people's perceptions of me. ("Jane" a victim of sexual violence, discussing her experience with police; McLachlan, 2007, p. 157)*

However, an adverse event such as a crime may not always lead to psychological trauma. This is because everyone responds to traumatic events differently, and not all adversity is identified by the individual as traumatic. Paul Rock (2006) argued that the widespread assumption that all victims of crime are broken, traumatised people is unhelpful. While there is no doubt that many victims of crime are traumatised by either or both their experiences and the criminal justice response, Rock (2006) argues that it does victims of crime a disservice to presume that a standard and "normal" response to crime is that a victim will be traumatised. Victim impact statements (VIS) demonstrate the individualised trauma that results from crime victimisation.

2.6 Secondary Trauma Experienced by Criminal Justice Practitioners

The traumatic impact of crime can indirectly impact professionals in the criminal justice system. Vicarious trauma is a pervasive, long-lasting change to someone's social and emotional wellbeing, caused by exposure to the trauma of others and disrupting people's beliefs regarding themselves, other people, and the social world (Rauvola et al., 2019, p. 303). The manifestations of secondary or indirect trauma, such as vicarious trauma, can be the same for criminal justice practitioners, such as judges, lawyers, and police officers, as they are for people who have been directly traumatised, and include psychological distress, avoidance behaviours, hypervigilance, irritability, and poor emotional regulation (Duran & Woodhams, 2022). While some research has focused on the impact of specific types of stressors on criminal justice professionals, such as child sex offences (Polak et al., 2019) or being exposed to audio-visual evidence of violent crimes (Birze et al., 2023), vicarious trauma is more likely to occur in response to chronic and repeated exposure to a broad range of offending behaviours or outcomes. The issue of vicarious trauma and secondary traumatisation is examined further in Chapter 7.

2.7 Trauma Recovery

2.7.1 Treating PTSD

Most people's trauma symptoms abate naturally over time, often due to internal and informal social supports that aid recovery (Neller et al., 2005; Widom, 2017). Trauma-focused (or trauma-specific) therapeutic practices traditionally focus on PTSD, recurrent memories of the adverse experience, and hyperarousal symptoms. Evidence-informed approaches include long-term, trauma-focused cognitive behavioural therapy (TF-CBT), contextual behaviour trauma therapy, and reprocessing therapies such as Eye Movement Desensitisation and Reprocessing (EMDR). There is also moderate evidence to suggest pharmacotherapy can help address physiological damage to the brain when coupled with psychotherapy (Thomaes et al., 2014). Interventions such as EMDR are more successful with young people than with adults, reinforcing the benefit of early intervention (Buckingham, 2016). Trauma can be counteracted by protective factors: a supportive, pro-social partner, family, or social network; employment and education; personal resilience; and external supports, including therapeutic counselling (McCartan, 2020). These factors are also protective against criminality, but protective factors are often not available to justice-involved people.

2.7.2 Treating cPTSD

PTSD has been described as a post-traumatic *threat* disorder compared with cPTSD, which is better regarded as a post-traumatic *betrayal* disorder (Kezelman & Stavropoulos, 2019). Thus, best practices in treating cPTSD differ from treatment for PTSD (Kezelman & Stavropoulos, 2019; van der Kolk with Najavits, 2013). As summarised by van der Kolk:

> … what is missing [from evidence-based PTSD treatment] is the whole issue of attachment, betrayal, and abandonment, which interferes with normal developmental pathways. Our treatments almost entirely ignore

> what happens when trauma meets the attachment system. (van der Kolk with Najavits, 2013, p. 518f)

Resolving cPTSD requires recognition of "the loss of emotional, social, cognitive and psychological competencies that either failed to develop properly or that deteriorated due to prolonged exposure to complex trauma" (Cloitre et al., 2012, p. 5). Strategies to achieve this are emerging, although:

> … there has been a lack of focus on developing treatments that addressed the inability to concentrate and modulate affective arousal. In recent years, we have seen the beginning of attention to mindfulness techniques and neurofeedback methods to deal with those problems. But treatment research on how to deal with loss of attention, concentration, and engagement is still in its infancy. (van der Kolk with Najavits, 2013, p. 518f)

While multiple new and emerging treatment approaches exist for cPTSD, the best evidence currently endorses a phased approach based on Herman's Trauma Theory (Herman, 2015; Kezelman & Stavropoulos, 2019). The International Society for Traumatic Stress Studies (ISTSS) commissioned a survey of 50 expert clinicians and found that most (84%) recommended a phased approach in treating cPTSD. This approach was supported by seven randomised control trials (RCTs) and two other studies on treating cPTSD in adults (see also Kezelman & Stavropoulos, 2019). Herman's phased approach allows the individual to work through the stages of recovery: by first, establishing a sense of safety; second, by reconstructing and integrating the trauma; and third, by reconnecting with the community. The first phase requires establishing a sense of safety, including physical safety. While the preferred approach to achieving safety is individual therapy, it can be achieved in small, therapist-led groups (Cloitre et al., 2012). Physical safety and individual therapy are both unlikely to be achievable in prison.

Once a person feels physically safe, Phase 2 in treating cPTSD is reconstructing and integrating trauma memories. Phase three involves "consolidating the gains" through (re)connecting with the community "to strengthen safe and supportive social networks and to build and enhance intimate and family relationships. Plans for education, employment, recreation and social activities or meaningful hobbies should be considered and organized" (Cloitre et al., 2012, p. 10). Again, Phase 3 is best achieved in the community. This three-phase approach may take between four months and two years to have lasting effects (Cloitre et al., 2012).

2.7.3 Move from Diagnoses to a Focus on Social and Emotional Wellbeing

Many trauma practitioners have moved away from a diagnostic model and instead focus on treating trauma symptoms, such as emotion regulation difficulties, impaired interpersonal skills, dissociation, maladaptive beliefs, and hypervigilance (Kezelman & Stavropoulos, 2019). The British Psychological Society Clinical Division developed the Power Threat Meaning Framework (PTM Framework). The PTM Framework draws from theory and research and involves four interrelated aspects:

- power and how it is used negatively,
- that threatens an individual's safety and wellbeing,
- the meaning that individual gives to the ways power and threat influence their lives,
- resulting in threat responses that individuals draw upon to protect themselves or others (Johnstone et al., 2018).

This approach shifts from "treating" the protective coping mechanisms (i.e., symptoms) to a more holistic approach that identifies and addresses the underlying trauma.

The shift from a diagnostic model to a broader understanding of mental health is particularly relevant for the over-represented First Nations populations caught up in the criminal justice system. First Nations peoples take a holistic view of mental health (Dudgeon et al., 2014). As such, ***social and emotional wellbeing*** (SEWB) may be regarded as incorporating cultural and historical factors, including connection to land, ancestry, and spirituality, and the impact of intergenerational trauma (discussed in Chapter 4), such as family breakdown, social disadvantage, and cultural dislocation (Newton et al., 2015). Current IQ tests, standardised tools, and diagnostic labels are often not developed with SEWB or cultural understandings of mental health in mind, resulting in further marginalisation of First Nations peoples through misdiagnosis and cultural bias (Gillies, 2013; Newton et al., 2015).

2.7.4 The Importance of Trauma Recovery for Criminal Justice Practitioners

Chapter 3 examines the relationship between trauma and crime (and criminality). As such, in addition to understanding trauma recovery services in the community (i.e., offered by mainstream health services), criminal justice practitioners should understand trauma recovery in the context of criminogenic risk and correctional care to manage and treat trauma. Clearly, evidence-informed practice to resolve trauma—relying on establishing a sense of safety, long-term intervention, and re-connection with the community—is not easily achieved in prison. Trauma-informed and trauma-focused care requires ongoing safety and stability, which is often absent in custody. Depending on sentence plans, security ratings, breaches, and prison capacity, people in prison may be moved between facilities and away from services and family. There are elements of trauma-informed practice in group work programs available for some people in prison addressing substance abuse issues or violent offending (see DCS, 2019). However, there are limited opportunities to safely work with individuals in prison one-on-one to develop self-regulation or psychosocial skills. General individual mental health counselling and therapy are not offered by correctional service agencies or available in custody, leaving community-based services to provide specialised services. Treatment models require a long-term commitment to enable skill acquisition regarding emotional regulation and distress tolerance. Long-term therapy is not always possible while a person remains under the supervision of Corrections (whether in custody or the community), and people who offend rarely have the personal resources to access specialised trauma counselling. Indeed, low or no-cost trauma-informed counselling services are limited for anyone, including perpetrators and victims of crime.

2.8 Conclusion

Trauma is the impact of distressing or adverse events on a person's social and emotional wellbeing. Criminal justice practitioners should realise the importance of trauma and understand how to recognise and reduce trauma and re-traumatisation. Trauma is prevalent in the lives of people who offend, influencing criminogenic (i.e., crime-causing) attitudes and behaviour. Additionally, victims of crime may be traumatised due to their experiences of crime and with the criminal justice system. Finally, practitioners themselves may experience trauma from exposure to the experiences of justice-involved people. Trauma is relevant for professionals in the criminal justice system in ensuring their ability to do their jobs well and maintain their social and emotional wellbeing. Trauma can be counteracted by internal and external protective factors, including (but not limited to) therapeutic counselling. While trauma-focused (or trauma-specific) therapeutic practices may help promote recovery, efficacious models can be difficult to access in the community due to cost and waiting times and are rarely or not available in custody.

Key Points

- Trauma is relevant for people who work in the criminal justice system for three reasons: first, evidence shows that trauma is prevalent in the lives of both children and adults who are justice-involved. Second, victims of crime are sometimes (but not always) traumatised due to their experiences of crime and with the criminal justice system. Finally, practitioners themselves may experience trauma from exposure to the devastating, relentless, and often cruel impacts of crime.
- Trauma can be counteracted by protective factors such as support from family or social networks, employment and education, personal resilience, as well as external supports, including therapeutic counselling. However,

while trauma-focused (or trauma-specific) therapeutic support may help promote recovery, effective models can be difficult to access in the community and are rarely accessible in custody.

References

Altintas, M., & Bilici, M. (2018). Evaluation of Childhood Trauma with Respect to Criminal Behavior, Dissociative Experiences, Adverse Family Experiences and Psychiatric Backgrounds Among Prison Inmates. *Comprehensive Psychiatry, 82*, 100–107. https://doi.org/10.1016/j.comppsych.2017.12.006

American Psychiatric Association (APA). (2022). *Diagnostic and Statistical Manual of Mental Disorders* (5th ed., Text Revised [DSM-5-TR®]). American Psychiatric Publishing. https://doi.org/10.1176/appi.books.9780890425787

Baranyi, G., Cassidy, M., Fazel, S., Priebe, S., & Mundt, A. P. (2018). Prevalence of Posttraumatic Stress Disorder in Prisoners. *Epidemiologic Reviews, 40*(1), 134–145. https://doi.org/10.1093/epirev/mxx015

Birze, A., Regehr, K., & Regehr, C. (2023). Workplace Trauma in a Digital Age: The Impact of Video Evidence of Violent Crime on Criminal Justice Professionals. *Journal of Interpersonal Violence, 38*(1–2), 1654–1689. https://doi.org/10.1177/08862605221090571

Boswell, G. (2016). Trauma Experiences in the Backgrounds of Violent Young Offenders. *Pakistan Journal of Criminology, 8*(2), 12–24.

Bottalico, B., & Bruni, T. (2012). Post Traumatic Stress Disorder, Neuroscience, and the Law. *International Journal of Law and Psychiatry, 35*(2), 112–120. https://doi.org/10.1016/j.ijlp.2011.12.001

Buckingham, S. (2016). Trauma Informed Juvenile Justice. *The American Criminal Law Review, 53*(3), 641–692.

Cloitre, M., Courtois, C., Ford, J., Green, B., Alexander, P., Briere, J., Herman, J. L., Lanius, R., Pearlman, L. A., Stolbach, B., Spinazzola, J., van der Kolk, B., & van der Hart, O. (2012). *The ISTSS Expert Consensus Treatment Guidelines for Complex PTSD in Adults*. ISTSS.

Cloitre, M., Stolbach, B. C., Herman, J. L., Kolk, B. V. D., Pynoos, R., Wang, J., & Petkova, E. (2009). A Developmental Approach to Complex PTSD: Childhood and Adult Cumulative Trauma as Predictors of Symptom Complexity. *Journal of Traumatic Stress, 22*(5), 399–408. https://doi.org/10.1002/jts.20444

Courtois, C. A., Ford, J. D., & Cloitre, M. (2009). Best Practices in Psychotherapy for Adults. In C. A. Courtois & J. D. Ford (Eds.), *Treating Complex Traumatic Stress Disorders: An Evidence-Based Guide* (pp. 82–103). Guilford Publications.

Crocq, M.-A., & Crocq, L. (2000). From Shell Shock and War Neurosis to Posttraumatic Stress Disorder: A History of Psychotraumatology. *Dialogues in Clinical Neuroscience, 2*(1), 47–55.

D'Andrea, W., Ford, J., Stolbach, B., Spinazzola, J., & Van Der Kolk, B. A. (2012). Understanding Interpersonal Trauma in Children: Why We Need a Developmentally Appropriate Trauma Diagnosis. *American Journal of Orthopsychiatry, 82*(2), 187–200. https://doi.org/10.1111/j.1939-0025.2012.01154.x

Department for Correctional Services (DCS). (2019). *Rehabilitation Programs Branch: Model of Service.* Government of South Australia.

Dudgeon, P., Wright, M., Paradies, Y., Garvey, D., & Walker, I. (2014). Aboriginal Social, Cultural and Historical Contexts. In P. Dudgeon, H. Milroy, & R. Walker (Eds.), *Working Together: Aboriginal and Torres Strait Islander Mental Health and Wellbeing Principles and Practice* (pp. 3–24). Commonwealth of Australia.

Duran, F., & Woodhams, J. (2022). Impact of Traumatic Material on Professionals in Analytical and Secondary Investigative Roles Working in Criminal Justice Settings: A Qualitative Approach. *Journal of Police and Criminal Psychology, 37*, 904–917. https://doi.org/10.1007/s11896-022-09532-8

Edalati, H., Nicholls, T. L., Crocker, A. G., Roy, L., Somers, J. M., & Patterson, M. L. (2017). Adverse Childhood Experiences and the Risk of Criminal Justice Involvement and Victimization Among Homeless Adults with Mental Illness. *Psychiatric Services, 68*(12), 1288–1295. https://doi.org/10.1176/appi.ps.201600330

Facer-Irwin, E., Karatzias, T., Bird, A., Blackwood, N., & MacManus, D. (2021). PTSD and Complex PTSD in Sentenced Male Prisoners in the UK: Prevalence, Trauma Antecedents, and Psychiatric Comorbidities. *Psychological Medicine, 52*(13): 2794–2804.https://doi.org/10.1017/S0033291720004936

Felitti, V. J., Anda, R. F., Nordenberg, D., Williamson, D. F., Spitz, A. M., Edwards, V., Koss, M. P., & Marks, J. S. (1998). Relationship of Childhood Abuse and Household Dysfunction to Many of the Leading Causes of Death in Adults: The Adverse Childhood Experiences (ACE) Study. *American Journal of Preventative Medicine, 14*(4), 245–258. https://doi.org/10.1016/s0749-3797(98)00017-8

Figley, C. R. (Ed.). (1985). *Trauma and Its Wake: The Study and Treatment of Post-Traumatic Stress Disorder.* Brunner/Mazel.

Ford, J. D., & Courtois, C. A. (2014). Defining and Understanding Complex Trauma and Complex Traumatic Stress Disorders. In C. A. Courtois & J. D. Ford (Eds.), *Treating Complex Traumatic Stress Disorders: Scientific Foundations and Therapeutic Models* (pp. 13–30). Guilford.

Galatzer-Levy, I. R., & Bryant, R. A. (2013). 636,120 Ways to Have Posttraumatic Stress Disorder. *Perspectives on Psychological Science, 8*(6), 651–662. https://doi.org/10.1177/1745691613504115

Gillies, C. (2013). Establishing the United Nations' Declaration on the Rights of Indigenous Peoples as the Minimum Standard for All Forensic Practice with Australian Indigenous Peoples. *Australian Psychologist, 48*(1), 14–27. https://doi.org/10.1111/ap.12003

Greenberg, G. (2013) *The Book of Woe: The DSM and the Unmaking of Psychiatry*. Scribe.

Griffin, G., & Sallen, S. (2013). Considering Child Trauma Issues in Juvenile Court Sentencing. *Children's Legal Rights Journal, 34*(1), 1–22.

Harris, M., & Fallot, R. D. (2001). Envisioning a Trauma-Informed Service System: A Vital Paradigm Shift. *New Directions for Mental Health Services, 2001*(89), 3–22. https://doi.org/10.1002/yd.23320018903

Herman, J. L. (2014). Foreword. In C. A. Courtois & J. D. Ford (Eds.), *Treating Complex Traumatic Stress Disorders: Scientific Foundations and Therapeutic Models* (pp. xiii–xvii). Guilford.

Herman, J. L. (2015). *Trauma and Recovery: The Aftermath of Violence—From Domestic Abuse to Political Terror*. Basic Books.

Johnstone, L., Boyle, M., with Cromby, J., Dillon, J., Harper, D., Kinderman, P., Longden, E., Pilgrim, D., & Read, J. (2018). *The Power Threat Meaning Framework: Towards the Identification of Patterns in Emotional Distress, Unusual Experiences and Troubled or Troubling Behaviour, as an Alternative to Functional Psychiatric Diagnosis.* British Psychological Society.

Kezelman, C., Hossack, N., Stavropoulos, P., & Burley, P. (2015). *The Cost of Unresolved Childhood Trauma and Abuse in Adults in Australia.* Adults Surviving Child Abuse and Pegasus Economics.

Kezelman, C., & Stavropoulos, P. (2019). *Practice Guidelines for Clinical Treatment of Complex Trauma.* Blue Knot Foundation.

Kubiak, S. P., Covington, S. S., & Hillier, C. (2017). Trauma-Informed Corrections. In D. Springer & A. Roberts (Eds.), *Social Work in Juvenile and Criminal Justice Systems* (4th ed., pp. 92–104.). Charles C. Thomas.

Malvaso, C., Day, A., Casey, S., & Corrado, R. (2017). Young Offenders, Maltreatment, and Trauma: A Pilot Study. *Psychiatry, Psychology and Law, 24*(3), 458–469. https://doi.org/10.1080/13218719.2016.1247682

Malvaso, C., Day, A., Delfabbro, P., Cale, J., Hackett, L., & Ross, S. (2021). *Adverse Childhood Experiences and Trauma among Young People in the Youth Justice System.* Australian Institute of Criminology.

McCartan, K. F. (2020). *Trauma-Informed Practice.* Her Majesty's Inspectorate of Probation.

McLachlan, K. (2007). *Grounds for Hope and Disappointment: Victims'/Survivors' Perceptions of South Australia Police Responses to Rape.* LLM, Flinders University.

Neller, D., Denney, R., Pietz, C., & Thomlinson, R. (2005). Testing the Trauma Model of Violence. *Journal of Family Violence, 20*(3), 151–159. https://doi.org/10.1007/s10896-005-3651-z

Newton, D., Day, A., Gillies, C., & Fernandez, E. (2015). A Review of Evidence-Based Evaluation of Measures for Assessing Social and Emotional Well-Being in Indigenous Australians. *Australian Psychologist, 50*, 40–50. https://doi.org/10.1111/ap.12064

Polak, S., Bailey, R., & Bailey, E. (2019). Secondary Traumatic Stress in the Courtroom: Suggestions for Preventing Vicarious Trauma. *Juvenile & Family Court Journal, 70*(2), 69–75. https://doi.org/10.1111/jfcj.12137

Rauvola, R. S., Vega, D. M., & Lavigne, K. N. (2019). Compassion Fatigue, Secondary Traumatic Stress, and Vicarious Traumatization: A Qualitative Review and Research Agenda. *Occupational Health Science, 3*, 297–336. https://doi.org/10.1007/s41542-019-00045-1

Reavis, J. A., Looman, J., Franco, K. A., & Rojas, B. (2013). Adverse Childhood Experiences and Adult Criminality: How Long Must We Live Before We Possess Our Own Lives? *The Permanente Journal, 17*(2), 44–48. https://doi.org/10.7812/TPP/12-072

Rock, P. (2006). Aspects of the Social Construction of Crime Victims in Australia. *Victims & Offenders, 1*(3), 289–321. https://doi.org/10.1080/15564880600767397

Shin, S. H., McDonald, S. E., & Conley, D. (2018). Profiles of Adverse Childhood Experiences and Impulsivity. *Child Abuse & Neglect, 85*, 118–126. https://doi.org/10.1016/j.chiabu.2018.07.028

Smith, R. T., & Whooley, O. (2015). Dropping the Disorder in PTSD. *Contexts, 14*(4), 38–43. https://doi.org/10.1177/1536504215609300

Substance Abuse and Mental Health Services Administration (SAMHSA). (2014). *SAMHSA's Concept of Trauma and Guidance for a Trauma-Informed Approach*. US Department of Health and Human Services.

Sweeney, A., Clement, S., Filson, B., & Kennedy, A. (2016). Trauma-Informed Mental Healthcare in the UK: What is it and How Can We Further its Development? *The Mental Health Review, 21*(3), 174–192. https://doi.org/10.1108/MHRJ-01-2015-0006

Thomaes, K., Dorrepaal, E., Draijer, N., Jansma, E. P., Veltman, D. J., & van Balkom, A. J. (2014). Can Pharmacological and Psychological Treatment Change Brain Structure and Function in PTSD? A Systematic Review. *Journal of Psychiatric Research, 50*, 1–15. https://doi.org/10.1016/j.jpsychires.2013.11.002

van der Kolk, B. A. (Ed.). (1987). *Psychological Trauma*. American Psychiatric Press.

van der Kolk, B. A. (2005). Developmental Trauma Disorder: Towards a Rational Diagnosis for Children with Complex Trauma Histories. *Psychiatric Annals, 35*(5), 401–408.

van der Kolk, B., with Najavits, L. M. (2013). Interview: What is PTSD Really? Surprises, Twists of History, and the Politics of Diagnosis and Treatment. *Journal of Clinical Psychology: In Session, 69*(5), 516–522. https://doi.org/10.1002/jclp.21992

Voigt, T., Balandin, S., & Day, A. (2017). What is the Impact of Acts of Bravery? *Journal of Trauma and Treatment, 6*(2), 373. https://doi.org/10.4172/2167-1222.1000373

Walklate, S. (2016). The Metamorphosis of the Victim of Crime: From Crime to Culture and the Implications for Justice. *International Journal for Crime, 5*(4), 4–16. https://doi.org/10.5204/ijcjsd.v5i4.280

Wall, L., & Quadara, A. (2014). Acknowledging Complexity in the Impacts of Sexual Victimisation Trauma. *ACSSA Issues, 16*, 1–24.

Weathers, F., Blake, D., Schnurr, P., Kaloupek, D., Marx, B., & Keane, T. (2018). *The Life Events Checklist for DSM-5 (LEC-5)—Standard. [Measurement Instrument]*. National Center for PTSD.

Widom, C. S. (2017). Long-Term Impact of Childhood Abuse and Neglect on Crime and Violence. *Clinical Psychology: Science and Practice, 24*(2), 186–202. https://doi.org/10.1111/cpsp.12194

Willmot, P., & Jones, L. (2022) Introduction. In P. Willmot & L. Jones (Eds.), *Trauma-Informed Forensic Practice* (pp. 1–11). Routledge. https://doi.org/10.4324/9781003120766-1

World Health Organization (WHO). (2018). *International Classification of Diseases (ICD)—11*. WHO.

3

Recognising the Relationships Between Trauma and Offending

3.1 Introduction

If you work in the criminal justice system long enough, you come to realise that many people who have offended have experienced much higher levels of adversity and trauma than the average citizen. As the previous chapter outlined, "trauma" is the distressing impact of adverse events and experiences on an individual's social and emotional wellbeing. The significance of trauma is the emotional, cognitive, and behavioural impact of an adverse event, not the nature of the adversity itself. This chapter explores the associations between trauma and crime for people who offend, including children, women, and Aboriginal people. While trauma is prevalent in the lives of both children and adults who are justice-involved, there is a lack of evidence showing a causal relationship between trauma and criminality. Nevertheless, many criminogenic risk factors for crime are associated with trauma. Adversity and trauma remain a crucial focus for criminal justice agencies when developing policies and practices to reduce offending behaviour.

K. J. McLachlan, *Trauma-informed Criminal Justice*,
https://doi.org/10.1007/978-3-031-59290-4_3

3.2 Trauma is Associated with Crime

Criminal "[b]ehaviour has three main components—thinking (cognitions), feeling (emotions, affect) and actions" (SCEW, 2020, p. Annex A). While criminal thoughts and feelings are not themselves crimes, antisocial attitudes, values, and beliefs are risk factors for criminal behaviour (Andrews et al., 2010). Trauma (i.e., the distressing impact of adverse events and experiences on an individual's wellbeing) may manifest as impaired or negative thoughts (i.e., neuropsychological trauma), feelings (emotional trauma), and actions (physical or social trauma), as discussed in detail below.

3.2.1 Psychological Trauma, Psychiatric Diagnoses, and Crime

The ways that psychological trauma manifests are often considered symptoms of various psychiatric diagnoses, including diagnoses relating to psychosis, diagnoses associated with dissociation, anxiety and depression, and personality disorders (as discussed in Chapter 2). Developmental trauma (i.e., the negative impact of chronic adversity in childhood) increases the prevalence of both affective and anxiety disorders more so than adulthood-onset trauma (although adversity in adulthood may compound developmental trauma; Chu et al., 2013). US research involving 491 women who had offended found that a history of traumatic adversity (in either childhood or adulthood) was not directly associated with offending. Instead, it was when trauma manifested as poor mental health outcomes, including substance misuse disorders, that there was an increased likelihood of offending behaviour (Lynch et al., 2013).

The Australian Institute of Health and Welfare (AIHW, 2023) reported that more than half of people entering prison in Australia had been told they had a mental health issue at some stage in their lives. Despite this, about three in five self-reported that their mental health was good, very good, or excellent on admission to prison, with lower rates of positive reporting for women. Time in prison improved the self-reported mental health of men and women (AIHW, 2023). Despite this, research using the Kessler 10 (K10) found that[1]:

> Prison entrants (43%) were more than 3 times as likely to score high or very high levels of psychological distress as the general population (15%) in 2020–21. Prison discharges (26%) were also more likely to score high or very high levels of psychological distress than the general population (15%) in 2020–21. (AIHW, 2023, p. 48, reference removed)

People entering prison are more than four times as likely to report illicit drug use in the 12 months prior to being surveyed (73%) as people in the general community (17%; AIHW, 2020). In terms of substance abuse, 2021 data from 2223 police detainees across Australia found that 77% of detainees were positive for at least one drug at the time of arrest, most often methamphetamines (50%) and cannabis (45%). Self-reported alcohol use around the time of arrest was also high (27%; Voce & Sullivan, 2022).

There is a clear association between a diagnosis of post-traumatic stress disorder (PTSD) or complex PTSD (cPTSD) and crime. A meta-analysis of 56 studies conducted across 20 countries involving 21,099 people in prison found that men and women in prison were (respectively) five to eight times more likely to be diagnosed with PTSD at some point in their lives than non-incarcerated people (Baranyi et al., 2018). The elevated prevalence rates of PTSD show that people who have been incarcerated are significantly more likely than the general population to meet the threshold of PTSD diagnostic criteria. A diagnosis of PTSD may be predictive of impulsive behaviour, aggression, and affect dysregulation (Ardino, 2012), and is prevalent in prisoner populations, particularly women prisoners (Butler et al., 2005). Some people may have complex trauma or cPTSD, where their trauma stems from prolonged adversity and a betrayal of trust (e.g., child sexual abuse or domestic abuse; see Gagnon et al., 2017). Nevertheless, the DSM-III-R

[1] "A widely used and well-validated survey tool designed to measure participants' levels of psychological distress through questions about depression and anxiety symptoms over the preceding four weeks" (AIHW, 2023, p. 47).

included a cautionary note that diagnoses made using the DSM "may not be wholly relevant to legal judgments, for example, that take into account such issues as individual responsibility… or competency…" (APA, 1987, p. xxvi).

Violent offending co-occurs with multiple mental health diagnoses, including PTSD, Panic Disorder, and Alcohol Use Disorder. The underlying factors for violence may be similar to those underlying various diagnoses. Indeed, in their research with 349 incarcerated men in the US, Alexa Barrett et al. (2021) found that 25% of men who had committed violent offences met the criteria for all three disorders. Suppose the diagnostic symptoms of PTSD and Panic Disorder are specifically considered. In that case, it becomes clearer how unresolved trauma (i.e., the unaddressed impact of past, chronic adversity on current functioning) may impact a person's interpretation and response to social situations. Julia Ahrens and Lillian Rexford (2014) summarise this approach, stating that it creates a "self-perpetuating cycle of violence":

> The expectancy of threat leads to increased acting out and/or numbing. They suggested that the state of hyperalertness often engendered by experiencing trauma predisposes individuals to heightened sensitivity to threat, which is often misperceived in even innocuous stimuli. The resultant acting out, avoidance, or withdrawal can reinforce beliefs that the world is a dangerous place, which becomes a self-fulfilling prophecy of aggression, withdrawal, or vacillation between the two. (p. 203)

Claude Chemtob et al. (1988) agreed. They argued that people develop strategies to keep themselves safe when exposed to chronic adversity, such as hypervigilance, aggression, or withdrawal. These strategies may continue as maladaptive behaviour in their daily lives, potentially leading to unprovoked aggression and violence.

3.2.2 Neurophysiological Trauma and Crime

Adverse experiences may also result in neurological trauma, changing the physical structure of a person's brain (Peckham, 2023). Adversity may impact the neurosequential development of the brain (Perry,

2009). Mirjam Rinne-Albers et al. (2017) explain that the prefrontal cortex: "an area central to higher cognitive functioning and involved in emotion regulation, matures relatively late and continues to develop into adulthood, this structure is thought to be especially vulnerable for the effects of [adverse childhood experiences]" (p. 1164). Additionally, adversity may change the brain's structure via neuroplastic mechanisms. ***Neuroplasticity***:

> refers to the capacity of neural systems to adapt and change in response to experience and injury... [it] is greatest during development but neuroplasticity is a property of living neural systems, a dynamic process that continues throughout life into aging. (Peckham, 2023, p. 21)

Neurophysiological trauma may lead to impulsive, unpredictable, or violent behaviour due to changes in the volume and functioning in areas of the brain associated with emotional regulation and problem-solving (Bollinger et al., 2017; Rinne-Albers et al., 2017). Many people who offend have experienced chronic adversity and have "marked abnormal development" (McDermott, 2004, p. 276) with a "poor tolerance for psychological and physiological arousal" (van der Kolk, 1987, p. 3), a limited ability to regulate their anger and the tendency to respond to triggers or provocation in either a withdrawn or aggressive manner (van der Kolk, 1987). Neuropsychological trauma can be reversed with targeted interventions and through connection and positive relationships with others (Peckham, 2023).

3.2.3 Emotional Trauma, Attachment, and Crime

Unresolved or untreated trauma or "traumatic grief" may be associated with both incarceration and re-offending (Leach et al., 2008).Raelene Leach et al. (2008) defined ***traumatic grief*** as "a betrayal of attachment" (p. 104), occurring "when a person has suffered a significant loss of attachment, and the results of that loss have left the grieving process unresolved. Traumatic grief has its roots in attachment behaviour, separation distress and traumatic distress. It is a mixture of trauma and loss…" (p. 107). Leach et al. (2008) proposed that untreated developmental trauma, regardless of its cause, is associated with substance abuse and criminal activity, as well as maladaptive coping mechanisms such as hyperarousal, associated with the potential for increased aggression (see also Honorato et al., 2016). Criminality and contact with the criminal justice system may also compound and exacerbate unresolved trauma.

Bessel van der Kolk (1989) explored the idea of a "compulsion to trauma", finding that traumatised people may seek to unconsciously replicate their traumatic experience, putting themselves at risk of re-traumatisation. Lawrence Jones (2018) referred to an:

> 'acquired callousness' in people who have been abused who go on to offend. Dissociation and cutting off emotionally as a coping response can also have the effect of desensitising the individual to the effects of violence or offending on others… Trauma can contribute to offending through people reacting pre-emptively to what they misconstrue as a threat to themselves or a background of exposure to violence, desensitisation to distress and associated dissociation can allow instrumental violence to flourish. (p. 97)

Although "violent offending is the exception and not the rule" (Piquero et al., 2012, p. 176), people with unresolved complex trauma—particularly those who have been the victims of or who have witnessed violence—may make up a disproportionately large percentage of that violent offender population, and the chronic offending population (Hahn Fox et al., 2015; Neller et al., 2006; Piquero et al., 2012). In their US study of almost 4000 incarcerated men, Nancy Wolff and Jing Shi (2012) found that childhood physical abuse was predictive of poor emotional regulation and high levels of aggression. In addition to being associated with criminal behaviour, trauma and past victimisation in childhood may also increase the risk of future victimisation as an adult (Ogloff et al., 2012; Wall & Quadara, 2014).

3.2.4 Social and Behavioural Trauma and Crime

Traumatised people may also lack the ability to read and respond appropriately to social cues and be unable to form functional relationships and healthy social networks. Social trauma (often due to insecure attachment) is associated with violent offending (Schimmenti et al., 2014) and sexual offending (Grady et al., 2017). Richard Johnson and colleagues have explored how adults identify interpersonal social behaviours and found that standing in a boxer's stance, invading someone's personal space, and putting hands in pockets or clenched hands are often associated with perceived impending violence (Johnson, 2015; Johnson & Aaron, 2013). Social trauma (especially as the product of adversity in childhood) may lead to misinterpretation of facial expressions and misread body language. People with social trauma may misread a casual glance towards themselves (or, for example, a woman across a bar by another man) as aggression or suggestion, leading to violent and aggressive responses as a means of self-protection (Pfaltz et al., 2019).

3.3 Trauma is a Risk Factor for Crime

The association between trauma and crime is such that trauma may be considered a risk factor for crime (Baglivio et al., 2015; Caspi et al., 2002; Grady et al., 2022; Widom, 1989; Willmot, 2022). ***Risk factors*** are characteristics of a person, or their life associated with criminality. Intervention programs in the UK, Australia, Canada, and other common law jurisdictions are typically based on the Risk-Need-Responsivity (RNR) model of Don Andrews and James Bonta (Andrews et al., 2010; Heseltine et al., 2011).

> The Risk principle suggests that higher risk offenders stand to benefit more from rehabilitation programs than low risk offenders; the Needs principle suggests that programs should target individual 'criminogenic' needs, or those dynamic risk factors that are directly related to offending behaviour, and the Responsivity principle refers to those internal and external factors that may impede an individual's response to interventions,

> such as weak motivation or program content and delivery. (Howells et al., 2004, p. 71)

The Needs principle within the RNR model emphasises the "central eight" criminogenic risk factors, namely:

- substance abuse,
- relationship problems,
- poor engagement with education or employment,
- poor engagement with leisure and recreational activities,
- antisocial behaviour (including criminal history),
- antisocial personality,
- antisocial attitudes, values, and beliefs, and
- antisocial friends and family (Andrews et al., 2010).

The latter four ***criminogenic needs*** are known as the "big four", which are described as "the major predictor variables and indeed the major causal variables in the analysis of criminal behavior of individuals" (Andrews et al., 2010, p. 55). Intervention programs offered by corrections are designed to target the "central eight" criminogenic needs that increase the likelihood of criminal behaviour (Andrews et al., 2010; Heseltine et al., 2011).

Criminogenic needs are static or dynamic. Dynamic needs may be amenable to change and include factors such as:

- an individual's (un)employment status,
- antisocial personality,
- antisocial attitudes, values, and beliefs,
- antisocial friends and family,
- substance abuse,
- relationship problems, and
- mental health (Andrews et al., 2010).

Static needs cannot be managed or mitigated by intervention (e.g., gender, current age, age at first offence, past criminal convictions). Despite their unchangeable nature, static risk factors strongly predict future criminal behaviour. Exposure to adversity in childhood has been described as a static risk factor (Bates-Maves & O'Sullivan, 2017).

However, developmental trauma from childhood adversity is dynamic. Developmental trauma can change over time and its symptoms or manifestations may resolve.

Accepting that trauma is the impact of adversity (and not the event or experience itself), if we use the language of the RNR model, trauma may be regarded as a factor that directly influences dynamic criminogenic needs. Trauma influences responsivity: specifically, a person's capacity and ability to focus and engage, which may be referred to under the RNR model as issues of "poor engagement". Using the RNR model, Katarina Fritzon et al. (2021) recently undertook a narrative literature review exploring the association between trauma and offending behaviour. They found that trauma contributes to the "central eight" needs. Similarly, Michael Baglivio et al. (2021) noted that:

> ...the majority, if not all, of the "Central Eight" risk factors espoused by the RNR framework have been empirically linked to traumatic exposure, where many of the RNR risk factors are symptoms of trauma, whereas RNR considers them causes of delinquency/offending. (p. 256, emphasis in original)

Lorraine Cuadra and colleagues examined 338 adult males with histories of child abuse and neglect. They found clear links between exposure to adversity (i.e., child abuse), criminal thinking (due to trauma's impacts on social and emotional wellbeing), and criminal behaviour (Cuadra et al., 2014, p. 1407). These cognitive distortions allowed the individuals to rationalise their behaviour, avoid evidence-informed problem-solving or follow through with intended actions (Cuadra et al., 2014).

Many criminogenic needs are associated with the neuropsychological, emotional, or social traumata outlined above. These are sometimes captured by the umbrella legal term ***cognitive impairments***. The legal concept of cognitive impairment includes developmental disabilities, acquired disabilities, and mental illness (e.g., *Sentencing Act 2017* (SA), ss 5, 11(1)(f)). Arguably, cognitive impairments include the psychological and physiological impacts of adversity articulated in this chapter (e.g., neurological disability or diagnoses such as PTSD), which affect how people think, feel, and act. When trauma remains unresolved and/

or is exacerbated by additional adversity or substance abuse, it is the unresolved and untreated symptoms of trauma (rather than the adversity itself) that increase the likelihood of criminal behaviour (Halsey, 2017; Leach et al., 2008).

Some factors, such as culture, are protective in forging a strong sense of identity and connectedness with family and community, as discussed in Chapter 10. However, culture may be associated with experiences such as intergenerational trauma, racism and bullying, poverty, and homelessness, which may be associated with criminogenic needs. Chapter 4 examines intergenerational trauma in greater detail.

3.3.1 Trauma and Drug-Related Offences

The central eight criminogenic needs include substance abuse. While not all substance abuse is driven by trauma, research has found definite links between trauma and the abuse of alcohol and other drugs (Asberg & Renk, 2012; Khoury et al., 2010; Najavits et al., 2017). People who report substance dependency—as opposed to substance abuse—report high levels of trauma (Edwards et al., 2006). Further, people are often diagnosed with co-occurring substance abuse disorders and traumatic stress disorders, such as PTSD (Najavits et al., 2017). Carla Edwards et al. (2006) emphasise that "the intricate nature of internal traumatic stress symptoms that may more fully explain the relationship between symptoms of stress and higher levels of substance use is not completely understood" (p. 2095). A genetic predisposition may influence a person's propensity to be significantly impacted by adversity and abuse of substances. After exposure to adversity, particularly ACEs, the abuse of substances has also been explained as ***avoidant coping*** (Asberg & Renk, 2012, p. 800). Avoidant coping might be understood as an "[attempt] to self-medicate or to dampen mood symptoms associated with a dysregulated biological stress response" (Khoury et al., 2010, p. 1078); to "numb depression, hypomania or distress" (Pemberton et al., 2019, p. 17).

There are different pathway theories proposed to help understand the association between trauma and drugs (i.e., drug use, drug abuse, and drug-related offending). As stated above, people may use drugs to ***self-medicate*** to help manage painful emotions (Najavits et al., 2017). Richard Hammersley (2011) proposed that adversity may result in short-term intense drug use for some people before natural desistance from drugs. There may be "disruptions in several neurotransmitter levels, including dopamine, norepinephrine, and serotonin" associated with both substance misuse and trauma (Najavits et al., 2017, p. 197). For people with chronic drug use histories, exposure to future adversity and re-traumatisation is more likely to result in a resumption of drug use than for others without a history of substance use or abuse. Drug use can also compound trauma by putting people with trauma histories in high-risk situations, leading to further adversity and re-traumatisation (Hammersley, 2011).

Drug and alcohol abuse is frequent in the lives of people who offend, particularly women (Asberg & Renk, 2012; Grella et al., 2005). The Australian Institute of Health and Welfare (AIHW, 2023) reported that in 2022, almost three-quarters (73%) of all prisoners had used illicit drugs in the previous year, most commonly cannabis (53%) followed by methamphetamines/amphetamines (46%). Illicit drug use in the general population is much lower; in 2019, only 1.3% of people aged 14 and over reported using amphetamines in the last 12 months and 11.6% reported cannabis use (AIHW, 2020). Drug use, including alcohol abuse and poly-drug use, is also associated with people who have developmental trauma (Asberg & Renk, 2012; Khoury et al., 2010). In their Australian Institute of Criminology report, Jeremy Pritchard and Jason Payne (2005) drew from Paul Goldstein's tripartite model (1985), which hypothesised that the link between drug use and crime could be explained in three ways:

- drug use leads to crime;
- crime leads to drug use; and
- drug use and crime are not causally related, but are the result of a third factor.

The first explanation can be divided into three hypotheses. These are that the use of drugs leads to crime because of: the psychopharmacological effects of the drugs; the costs of the drugs encouraging users to acquire money via crime; or the violence associated with the drug trade. The second explanatory model suggests that engaging in criminal activity draws offenders into criminal subcultures where drugs (and alcohol) are readily available. Offenders are influenced by the norms of the subculture, one of which is drug and alcohol use. The final model views both drug use and criminality as behaviours that are symptomatic of a third common cause. These might include childhood experiences of abuse, family problems or academic failure. (p. 16, citations removed)

Based on these explanations, trauma may be directly linked with crime, or the relationship between trauma and crime may be mediated through factors such as drug use. Many theories aim to explain the link between trauma and criminal behaviour (in this case, illicit drug use). Co-morbidity research (i.e., regarding people with mental health and substance abuse issues) recognises the link between substance abuse, mental health issues, and crime, such that "substance abuse dramatically increases the rates at which the mentally ill come into contact with the criminal justice system" (Edgely, 2009, p. 243). However, substance abuse may be associated with crime in the absence of a mental disorder (Day & Howells, 2008). Substance abuse may itself be the foundation for a criminal conviction or may be a precursor to further offending. Some people with a history of adversity who have drug offence convictions may commit other offences, such as drug dealing and property offences (to fund drug use), and other offences committed under the disinhibiting influence of drugs.

Substance use is a significant risk factor for women who offend, more so than for men. For women who offend, substance use co-occurs with life-course exposure to adversity and associated psychological symptoms of unresolved trauma (Pemberton et al., 2019; Stathopoulos & Quadara, 2014). The causes and pathways into offending for women differ from those of men. Simon Pemberton et al. (2019) reviewed 360 international studies related to women who offend. They found that women commit fewer and less serious, less violent crimes than men and that women's offending behaviour tended to begin earlier in life and was associated with complex trauma and victimisation. Indeed, their review found that women who offend "disproportionately have experiences of childhood sexual abuse and later violence from partners and criminogenic peers, who consequently self-medicate as a result of these life experiences and who also find themselves at society's margins in terms of accommodation and employment" (Pemberton et al., 2019, p. 13).

3.4 Does Trauma Cause Crime?

The relationship between trauma and crime is complex. This chapter has examined the general association between trauma and crime and demonstrated that while trauma may be a risk factor for crime, it does not cause crime.

3.4.1 Will Addressing Trauma also Address and Reduce Crime?

Most people desist from crime as they age (Moffitt, 1993). ***Desistance*** from crime is "the long-term abstinence from criminal behaviour among those for whom offending had become a pattern of behaviour" (McNeill et al., 2012, p. 3). Lesley McAra and Susan McVie (2022), in the Edinburgh Study of Youth Transitions and Crime, found that desistance from offending for children and young adults is delayed or prevented due to impulsivity, substance abuse, and frequent crime victimisation. This is likely to also be true for adults who offend. Poor self-regulation (i.e., impulsivity) and substance abuse can be manifestations of trauma (as discussed earlier in the chapter). Maria Sapouna et al. (2015) speculated, in their literature review of "what works", that "Desisters do not necessarily face fewer social problems than recidivists but there is evidence to suggest they are more psychologically resilient showing higher levels of self-efficacy and better coping skills" (p. 39). Therefore, by addressing some of the psychological and emotional manifestations of trauma, it may be possible to reduce re-offending by promoting a level of functioning that is conducive to desistance from crime.

Correctional service agencies tend to develop RNR-based intervention programs that focus on the "central eight" criminogenic needs to reduce recidivism (Andrews et al., 2010). ***Recidivism*** occurs when someone who has previously offended re-offends. Trauma may be relevant in the "process of recidivism" (Zamble & Quinsey, 1997, p. 6), which relates to the acute factors which influence re-offending. Trauma may manifest as impaired social and emotional wellbeing, reducing a person's capacity to deal with fresh adversity, such as a relationship breakdown or death of a loved one. Adverse life experiences often occur within 24–48 hours of a relapse into substance abuse, re-offending, or a breach of justice conditions (e.g., a "cut and run" when someone cuts off their electronic monitoring device and absconds; Zamble & Quinsey, 1997).

Trauma is generally not regarded by RNR practitioners as a criminogenic need. Currently, there is just not enough research to say definitively if trauma-focused interventions that aim to reduce psychological trauma also reduce dynamic criminogenic risks and recidivism (Baglivio et al., 2021). Thus, it is not possible to say yet whether addressing trauma will reduce recidivism. However, current group intervention programs offered by in custody, based on the RNR model and cognitive behavioural therapy (CBT), *at best* reduce the risk of recidivism by 20–30% (Beaudry et al., 2021). In fact, the first meta-analysis of 29 randomised controlled trials (from the US, Canada, UK, Sweden, Norway, Germany, and Japan) examining the effectiveness of psychological interventions delivered in prisons to reduce recidivism found that there was "no strong evidence of reduced reoffending after participation in CBT-based programmes in prison" (Beaudry et al., 2021, p. 768). Gabrielle Beaudry et al. (2021) proposed a greater need for tailored and individualised interventions with psychosocial supports at and after release. Clearly, there is room for new ways of working. It makes sense that if trauma-focused interventions can help a person deal with new forms of adversity, curb their impulsive and reactive behaviours, take a moment to read social cues accurately, respond proportionately, and think about the best course of action, then trauma-focused work may help to influence the process of recidivism and reduce re-offending.

To enhance RNR models, some jurisdictions have embedded a strengths-based desistance approach. Tony Ward's ***Good Lives Model*** (GLM) may be used to extend the RNR model (Ward & Maruna, 2007). The GLM highlights that:

> ... people acquire a sense of who they are and what really matters from what they do. What this means for correctional practitioners is that it is not enough simply to equip individuals with skills to control or reduce their risk factors; it is essential that they are also given the opportunity to acquire a more adaptive personal identity, one that gives them a sense of meaning and fulfilment. (Ward & Maruna, 2007, p. 117)

The importance of social ties and a pro-social self-identity is supported by desistance research (McNeill et al., 2012; Sampson & Laub, 2003) and Compassion-Focused Therapy (CFT; Gilbert, 2017).

Desistance theory accepts that individuals can change when sufficient supports are in place. As highlighted by Astrid Birgden (2015):

> Supporting desistance requires human capital (internal capacities to change) and social capital (external opportunities to exercise those capacities to change), redeems or restores the person who makes positive contributions to local communities, and is an active process in which agency or autonomy (the ability to make choices and govern one's life) is realized; interventions therefore focus on strengths, resilience, and protective factors. (p. 19f)

Paul Gilbert (2017) champions the effectiveness of CFT, particularly for people who have a history of trauma associated with shame and self-criticism. Many people who have trauma and offending histories cannot be compassionate towards themselves or others. The purpose of CFT is "to create an inner, compassion-focused, motivational state that will impact on (re)organising emotion, cognition and behavioural patterns" (Gilbert, 2017, p. 60). It aims to teach individuals compassion for themselves and others, recognise how their behaviour may impact others, shift the focus from shame to responsibility, and promote pro-social behaviour and new ways to cope with stressors and triggers (D'Souza & Lawrence, 2021).

There is a broader acceptance that trauma influences a person's responsivity, with trauma-informed services potentially increasing a person's ability to effectively engage in intervention programs (Miller & Najavits, 2012; Sapouna et al., 2015; Vitopoulos et al., 2019). One of the founding fathers of the RNR model, James Bonta (2021), has endorsed the integration of trauma-informed approaches into the responsivity principles as an opportunity to "enrich the RNR model". US researchers Julie Bates-Maves and Deirdre O'Sullivan (2017) proposed a model that embeds trauma-informed principles into the RNR model. They argue that, including:

> trauma-assessments as part of the RNR process, enhances the needs-matching and responsivity outcomes. Given the over-representation of trauma exposure in the corrections population, and the wide-ranging symptoms and impacts on individuals, system-wide screening is recommended for all as part of a comprehensive RNR assessment. (Bates-Maves & O'Sullivan, 2017, p. 98)

Their model would implement trauma-informed correctional care (TICC, refer to Chapter 5) across the entire correctional services workforce, as well as trauma-focused treatment as part of the intervention provided for people with trauma symptoms associated with the central eight needs (i.e., substance abuse, relationship problems, limited education or employment and leisure and recreational activities, antisocial behaviour, and antisocial attitudes, values, and beliefs; Andrews et al., 2010).

3.5 Conclusion

This chapter has examined the links between trauma and crime. Trauma-crime pathways are neither linear, simple, nor easily applied. Trauma should be regarded as a dynamic criminogenic need associated with other "central" needs, such as antisocial and criminal behaviour and attitudes, family and relationship problems, problems with social achievement (education/employment), a lack of pro-social activities, and substance abuse. Trauma symptoms can be managed or treated, but for many people who offend, the compounding effect of chronic or repeated adversity makes psychological, emotional, and social trauma more challenging to resolve. If correctional intervention programs were expanded beyond just RNR models to incorporate trauma-focused strategies, CFT, and desistance evidence, such programs might be even more effective.

Key Points

- Trauma is associated with crime.
- Trauma is a risk factor for crime.
- Trauma does not cause crime.
- Trauma is closely associated with criminogenic needs. Addressing the manifestations of trauma (e.g., psychological, behavioural, and cognitive impairments) may help reduce recidivism. More work is needed in this area.

References

Ahrens, J., & Rexford, L. (2014). Cognitive Processing Therapy for Incarcerated Adolescents with PTSD. In R. Greenwald (Ed.), *Trauma and Juvenile Delinquency: Theory, Research, and Interventions* (pp. 201–216). Taylor and Francis. https://doi.org/10.4324/9781315808819

American Psychiatric Association (APA). (1987). *Diagnostic and Statistical Manual of Mental Disorders* (3rd ed., Revised [DSM-III-R]). American Psychiatric Publishing.

Andrews, D. A., Bonta, J., & Holsinger, A. M. (2010). *The Psychology of Criminal Conduct*. Taylor & Francis Group.https://doi.org/10.4324/9781315677187

Ardino, V. (2012). Offending Behaviour: The Role of Trauma and PTSD. *European Journal of Psychotraumatology, 3*(10), 1–4.

Asberg, K., & Renk, K. (2012). Substance Use Coping as a Mediator of the Relationship Between Trauma Symptoms and Substance Use Consequences Among Incarcerated Females with Childhood Sexual Abuse Histories. *Substance Use & Misuse, 47*(7), 799–808. https://doi.org/10.3109/10826084.2012.669446

Australian Institute of Health and Welfare (AIHW). (2020). *National Drug Strategy Household Survey 2019.*

Australian Institute of Health and Welfare (AIHW). (2023). *The Health of People in Australia's Prisons 2022.*

Baglivio, M. T., Wolff, K. T., Piquero, A. R., & Epps, N. (2015). The Relationship Between Adverse Childhood Experiences (ACE) and Juvenile Offending Trajectories in a Juvenile Offender Sample. *Journal of Criminal Justice, 43*(3), 229–241. https://doi.org/10.1016/j.jcrimjus.2015.04.012

Baglivio, M. T., Zettler, H., Craig, J. M., & Wolff, K. T. (2021). Evaluating RNR-Based Targeted Treatment and Intervention Dosage in the Context of Traumatic Exposure. *Youth Violence and Juvenile Justice, 19*(3), 251–276. https://doi.org/10.1177/1541204020988575

Baranyi, G., Cassidy, M., Fazel, S., Priebe, S., & Mundt, A. P. (2018). Prevalence of Posttraumatic Stress Disorder in Prisoners. *Epidemiologic Reviews, 40*(1), 134–145. https://doi.org/10.1093/epirev/mxx015

Barrett, A. J., Taylor, S. L., Kopak, A. M., & Hoffmann, N. G. (2021). PTSD, Panic Disorder and Alcohol Use Disorder as a Triple Threat for Violence Among Male Jail Detainees. *Journal of Criminal Psychology, 11*(1), 21–29.

Bates-Maves, J. K., & O'Sullivan, D. (2017). Trauma-Informed Risk Assessment in Correctional Settings. *International Journal of Criminology and Sociology, 6*, 93–102.

Beaudry, G., Yu, R., Perry, A. E., & Fazel, S. (2021). Effectiveness of Psychological Interventions in Prison to Reduce Recidivism: A Systematic Review and Meta-Analysis of Randomised Controlled Trials. *Lancet Psychiatry, 8*, 759–773.

Birgden, A. (2015). Maximizing Desistance: Adding Therapeutic Jurisprudence and Human Rights to the Mix. *Criminal Justice and Behavior, 42*(1), 19. https://doi.org/10.1177/0093854814550024

Bollinger, J., Scott-Smith, S., & Mendes, P. (2017). How Complex Developmental Trauma, Residential Out-of-Home Care and Contact with the Justice System Intersect. *Children Australia, 42*(2), 108–112. https://doi.org/10.1017/cha.2017.9

Bonta, A. (2021, November 25). Childhood Trauma, Crime, and RNR. *LinkedIn*. https://www.linkedin.com/pulse/childhood-trauma-crime-rnr-james-bonta/

Butler, T., Allnutt, S., Cain, D., Owens, D., & Muller, C. (2005). Mental Disorder in the New South Wales Prisoner Population. *Australian and New Zealand Journal of Psychiatry, 39*(5), 407–413. https://doi.org/10.1111/j.1440-1614.2005.01589.x

Caspi, A., Mcclay, J., Moffitt, T. E., Mill, J., Martin, J., Craig, I. W., Taylor, A., & Poulton, R. (2002). Role of Genotype in the Cycle of Violence in Maltreated Children. *Science, 297*(5582), 851–854. https://doi.org/10.1126/science.1072290

Chemtob, C., Roitblat, H. L., Hamada, R. S., Carlson, J. G., & Twentyman, C. T. (1988). A Cognitive Action Theory of Post-traumatic Stress Disorder. *Journal of Anxiety Disorders, 2*(3), 253–275. https://doi.org/10.1016/0887-6185(88)90006-0

Chu, D. A., Williams, L. M., Harris, A. W. F., Bryant, R. A., & Gatt, J. M. (2013). Early Life Trauma Predicts Self-reported Levels of Depressive and Anxiety Symptoms in Nonclinical Community Adults: Relative Contributions of Early Life Stressor Types and Adult Trauma Exposure. *Journal of Psychiatric Research, 47*(1), 23–32. https://doi.org/10.1016/j.jpsychires.2012.08.006

Cuadra, L. E., Jaffe, A. E., Thomas, R., & DiLillo, D. (2014). Child Maltreatment and Adult Criminal Behavior: Does Criminal Thinking Explain the Association? *Child Abuse & Neglect, 38*(8), 1399–1408. https://doi.org/10.1016/j.chiabu.2014.02.005

D'Souza, L., & Lawrence, D. (2021). Is There Adequate Evidence to Support the Use of Compassion Focused Therapy Group Interventions with Forensic Mental Health Service Users? A Rapid Evidence Assessment. *Forensic Update, 1*(136). https://doi.org/10.53841/bpsfu.2021.1.136.39

Day, A., & Howells, K. (2008). Problems in Responding to Co-occurring Mental Health and Drug-Related Problems: A Criminal Justice Perspective. In S. Allsop (Ed.), *Drug Use and Mental Health: Effective Responses to Co-occurring Drug and Mental Health Problems* (pp. 78–89). IP Communications.

Edgely, M. (2009). Common Law Sentencing of Mentally Impaired Offenders in Australian Courts: A Call for Coherence and Consistency. *Psychiatry, Psychology and Law, 16*(2), 240–261. https://doi.org/10.1080/13218710802242037

Edwards, C., Dunham, D., Ries, A., & Barnett, J. (2006). Symptoms of Traumatic Stress and Substance Use in a Non-clinical Sample of Young Adults. *Addictive Behaviors, 31*(11), 2094–2104. https://doi.org/10.1016/j.addbeh.2006.02.009

Fritzon, K., Miller, S., Bargh, D., Hollows, K., Osborne, A., & Howlett, A. (2021). Understanding the Relationships Between Trauma and Criminogenic Risk Using the Risk-Need Responsivity Model. *Journal of Aggression, Maltreatment & Trauma, 30*(3), 294–323. https://doi.org/10.1080/10926771.2020.1806972

Gagnon, K. L., Lee, M. S., & DePrince, A. P. (2017). Victim–Perpetrator Dynamics Through the Lens of Betrayal Trauma Theory. *Journal of Trauma & Dissociation, 18*(3), 373–382. https://doi.org/10.1080/15299732.2017.1295421

Gilbert, P. (2017). Exploring Compassion Focused Therapy in Forensic Settings: An Evolutionary and Social-Contextual Approach. In J. Davies & C. Nagi (Eds.), *Individual Psychological Therapies in Forensic Settings: Research and Practice* (pp. 59–84). Routledge/Taylor & Francis Group.

Goldstein, P. J. (1985). The Drugs/Violence Nexus: A Tripartite Conceptual Framework. *Journal of Drug Issues, 39*(Fall), 143–174.

Grady, M. D., Levenson, J. S., & Bolder, T. (2017). Linking Adverse Childhood Effects and Attachment: A Theory of Etiology for Sexual Offending. *Trauma, Violence & Abuse, 18*, 433–444. https://doi.org/10.1177/1524838015627147

Grady, M. D., Levenson, J. S., Glover, J., Kavanagh, S., & Carter, K. (2022). "Hurt People Hurt Other People": The Link Between Past Trauma and Sexual Offending. *Sexual Offending: Theory, Research, and Prevention, 17*(e7361), 1–28. https://doi.org/10.5964/sotrap.7361

Grella, C. E., Stein, J. A., & Greenwell, L. (2005). Associations Among Childhood Trauma, Adolescent Problem Behaviors, and Adverse Adult Outcomes in Substance-Abusing Women Offenders. *Psychology of Addictive Behaviors, 19*(1), 43–53. https://doi.org/10.1037/0893-164X.19.1.43

Hahn Fox, B., Perez, N., Cass, E., Baglivio, M. T., & Epps, N. (2015). Trauma Changes Everything: Examining the Relationship Between Adverse Childhood Experiences and Serious, Violent and Chronic Juvenile Offenders. *Child Abuse & Neglect, 46*, 163–173. https://doi.org/10.1016/j.chiabu.2015.01.011

Halsey, M. (2017). Child Victims as Adult Offenders: Foregrounding the Criminogenic Effects of (Unresolved) Trauma and Loss. *British Journal of Criminology, 58*(1), 17–36. https://doi.org/10.1093/bjc/azw097

Hammersley, R. (2011). Pathways Through Drugs and Crime: Desistance, Trauma and Resilience. *Journal of Criminal Justice, 39*(3), 268–272. https://doi.org/10.1016/j.jcrimjus.2011.02.006

Heseltine, K., Sarre, R., & Day, A. (2011). Prison-Based Correctional Rehabilitation: An Overview of Intensive Interventions for Moderate to High-Risk Offenders. *Trends & Issues in Crime and Criminal Justice, 412*, 1–6.

Honorato, B., Caltabiano, N., & Clough, A. R. (2016). From Trauma to Incarceration: Exploring the Trajectory in a Qualitative Study in Male Prison Inmates from North Queensland Australia. *Health and Justice, 4*(3), 1–10. https://doi.org/10.1186/s40352-016-0034-x

Howells, K., Heseltine, K., Sarre, R., Davey, L., & Day, A. (2004). *Correctional Offender Rehabilitation Programs: The National Picture in Australia.* Criminology Research Council.

Johnson, R. R. (2015). Perceptions of Interpersonal Social Cues Predictive of Violence Among Police Officers Who Have Been Assaulted. *Journal of Police and Criminal Psychology, 30*, 87–93. https://doi.org/10.1007/s11896-014-9145-2

Johnson, R. R., & Aaron, J. L. (2013). Adults' Beliefs Regarding Nonverbal Cues Predictive of Violence. *Criminal Justice and Behavior, 40*(8), 881–894. https://doi.org/10.1177/0093854813475347

Jones, L. (2018). Trauma-Informed Care and 'Good Lives' in Confinement: Acknowledging and Offsetting Adverse Impacts of Chronic Trauma and Loss of Liberty. In G. Akerman, A. Needs, & C. Bainbridge (Eds.), *Transforming Environments and Rehabilitation: A Guide for Practitioners in Forensic Settings and Criminal Justice* (pp. 92–114). Routledge.

Khoury, L., Tang, Y. L., Bradley, B., Cubells, J. F., & Ressler, K. J. (2010). Substance Use, Childhood Traumatic Experience, and Posttraumatic Stress Disorder in an Urban Civilian Population *Depression and Anxiety, 27*, 1077–1086. https://doi.org/10.1002/da.20751

Leach, R. M., Burgess, T., & Holmwood, C. (2008). Could Recidivism in Prisoners be Linked to Traumatic Grief? A Review of the Evidence. *International Journal of Prisoner Health, 4*(2), 104–119. https://doi.org/10.1080/17449200802038249

Lynch, S. M., DeHart, D. D., Belknap, J., & Green, B. L. (2013). Women's Pathways to Jail: Examining Mental Health, Trauma, and Substance Use. *BJA Policy Brief*, 1–4.

McAra, L., & McVie, S. (2022). *Causes and Impacts of Offending and Criminal Justice Pathways: Follow-up of the Edinburgh Study Cohort at Age 35* (Edinburgh Study of Youth Transitions and Crime Report). University of Edinburgh.

McDermott, B. M. (2004). Child and Youth Emotional Trauma: An Explanatory Model of Adverse Outcomes. *Psychiatry, Psychology and Law, 11*(2), 269–279. https://doi.org/10.1375/pplt.2004.11.2.269

McNeill, F., Farrall, S., Lightowler, C., & Maruna, S. (2012). How and Why People Stop Offending: Discovering Desistance. *IRISS Insights, 15*, 1–12.

Miller, N. A., & Najavits, L. M. (2012). Creating Trauma-Informed Correctional Care: A Balance of Goals and Environment. *European Journal of Psychotraumatology, 3*, 1–8. https://doi.org/10.3402/ejpt.v3i0.17246

Moffitt, T. E. (1993). Adolescence-Limited and Life-Course-Persistent Antisocial Behavior: A Developmental Taxonomy. *Psychological Review, 100*(4), 674–701.

Najavits, L. M., Hyman, S. M., Ruglass, L. M., Hien, D. A., & Read, J. P. (2017). Substance Use Disorder and Trauma. In S. N. Gold (Ed.), *APA Handbook of Trauma Psychology: Foundations in Knowledge* (pp. 195–213). American Psychological Association. https://doi.org/10.1037/0000019-012

Neller, D. J., Denney, R. L., Pietz, C. A., & Thomlinson, R. P. (2006). The Relationship Between Trauma and Violence in a Jail Inmate Sample. *Journal of Interpersonal Violence, 21*(9), 1234–1241. https://doi.org/10.1177/0886260506290663

Ogloff, J. R., Cutajar, M. C., Mann, E., & Mullen, P. (2012). Child Sexual Abuse and Subsequent Offending and Victimisation: A 45 Year Follow-Up Study. *Trends & Issues in Crime and Criminal Justice, 440*, 1–6.

Peckham, H. (2023). Introducing the Neuroplastic Narrative: A Non-pathologizing Biological Foundation for Trauma-Informed and Adverse Childhood Experience Aware Approaches. *Frontiers in Psychiatry, 14*(1103718), 1–21. https://doi.org/10.3389/fpsyt.2023.1103718

Pemberton, S., Balderston, S., & Long, J. (2019). *Trauma, Harm and Offending Behaviour: What Works to Address Social Injury and Criminogenic Need with Criminal Justice Involved Women?* University of Birmingham.

Perry, B. D. (2009). Examining Child Maltreatment through a Neurodevelopmental Lens: Clinical Applications of the Neurosequential Model of Therapeutics. *Journal of Loss and Trauma, 14*(4), 240–255. https://doi.org/10.1080/15325020903004350

Pfaltz, M. C., Passardi, S., Auschra, B., Fares-Otero, N. E., Schnyder, U., & Peyk, P. (2019). Are You Angry at Me? Negative Interpretations of Neutral Facial Expressions are Linked to Child Maltreatment But Not to Post-traumatic Stress Disorder. *European Journal of Psychotraumatology, 10*(1), 1682929. https://doi.org/10.1080/20008198.2019.1682929

Piquero, A. R., Jennings, W. G., & Barnes, J. C. (2012). Violence in Criminal Careers: A Review of the Literature from a Developmental Life-Course Perspective. *Aggression and Violent Behavior, 17*(3), 171–179. https://doi.org/10.1016/j.avb.2012.02.008

Pritchard, J., & Payne, J. (2005). *Alcohol, Drugs and Crime: A Study of Juveniles in Detention.* Australian Institute of Criminology.

Rinne-Albers, M. A., Pannekoek, J. N., van Hoof, M.-J., van Lang, N. D., Lamers-Winkelman, F., Rombouts, S. A., van der Wee, N. J., & Vermeiren, R. R. (2017). Anterior Cingulate Cortex Grey Matter Volume

Abnormalities in Adolescents with PTSD After Childhood Sexual Abuse. *European Neuropsychopharmacology, 27*(11), 1163–1171. https://doi.org/10.1016/j.euroneuro.2017.08.432

Sampson, R. J., & Laub, J. H. (2003). Life-Course Desisters—Trajectories of Crime among Delinquent Boys followed to Age 70*. *Criminology, 41*(3), 555–592. https://doi.org/10.1111/j.1745-9125.2003.tb00997.x

Sapouna, M., Bisset, C., Conlong, A.-M., & Matthews, B. (2015). *What Works to Reduce Reoffending: A Summary of the Evidence*. Scottish Government.

Schimmenti, A., Passanisi, A., Pace, U., Manzella, S., Di Carlo, G., & Caretti, V. (2014). The Relationship Between Attachment and Psychopathy: A Study with a Sample of Violent Offenders. *Current Psychology, 33*(3), 256–270. https://doi.org/10.1007/s12144-014-9211-z

Sentencing Council for England and Wales (SCEW). (2020). *Sentencing Offenders with Mental Disorders, Developmental Disorders, or Neurological Impairments*. Ministry of Justice.

Stathopoulos, M., & Quadara, A. (2014). *Women as Offenders, Women as Victims. The Role of Corrections in Supporting Women with Histories of Sexual Abuse*. Corrective Services NSW.

van der Kolk, B. A. (1987). The Psychological Consequences of Overwhelming Life Experiences. In B. A. van der Kolk (Ed.), *Psychological Trauma* (pp. 1–30). American Psychiatric Press.

van der Kolk, B. A. (1989). The Compulsion to Repeat the Trauma: Re-enactment, Revictimization, and Masochism. *Psychiatric Clinics of North America, 12*(2), 389–411.

Vitopoulos, N. A., Peterson-Badali, M., Brown, S., & Skilling, T. A. (2019). The Relationship Between Trauma, Recidivism Risk, and Reoffending in Male and Female Juvenile Offenders. *Journal of Child & Adolescent Trauma, 12*, 351–364. https://doi.org/10.1007/s40653-018-0238-4

Voce, A., & Sullivan, T. (2022). *Drug use Monitoring in Australia: Drug Use Among Police Detainees, 2021* (AIC Statistical Report 40). Australian Institute of Criminology.

Wall, L., & Quadara, A. (2014). Acknowledging Complexity in the Impacts of Sexual Victimisation Trauma. *ACSSA Issues, 16*, 1–24.

Ward, T., & Maruna, S. (2007). *Rehabilitation: Beyond the Risk Paradigm*. Routledge.

Widom, C. (1989). The Cycle of Violence. *Science, 244*(4901), 160–165.

Willmot, P. (2022) Childhood Maltreatment and Its Links to Offending. In P. Willmot & L. Jones (Eds.), *Trauma-Informed Forensic Practice* (pp. 15–31). Routledge. https://doi.org/10.4324/9781003120766-3

Wolff, N., & Shi, J. (2012). Childhood and Adult Trauma Experiences of Incarcerated Persons and Their Relationship to Adult Behavioral Health Problems and Treatment. *International Journal of Environmental Research and Public Health, 9*(5), 1908–1926. https://doi.org/10.3390/ijerph9051908

Zamble, E., & Quinsey, V. L. (1997). *The Criminal Recidivism Process.* Cambridge University Press.

Legislation

Sentencing Act 2017 (SA).

4 Recognising the Significance of the Past: Developmental and Intergenerational Trauma

4.1 Introduction

Adults who offend often have complex trauma associated with adverse childhood experiences (ACEs), particularly chronic childhood physical abuse, neglect, and family disruption (Craig et al., 2017; Sampson & Laub, 2003). For some First Nations children, this may extend to forceable removal from their families and communities by the State (Menzies, 2019). While people who offend may also experience adversity in adulthood, the impact of these experiences tends to compound the pre-existing symptoms of developmental trauma. Justice-involved adults, particularly First Nations peoples, also often have a history of intergenerational trauma, the legacy of centuries of oppression, adversity, racism, and harm to their parents, grandparents, communities, and ancestors. While past trauma may be discounted as something that occurred in childhood (i.e., developmental trauma) or because its effects are indirect (i.e., intergenerational trauma), this chapter argues that such adversity has a significant bearing on the social and emotional wellbeing of many individuals caught up in the criminal justice system.

K. J. McLachlan, *Trauma-informed Criminal Justice*,
https://doi.org/10.1007/978-3-031-59290-4_4

4.2 Developmental Trauma

Developmental trauma refers to the negative impacts of acute or chronic adversity in childhood on an individual's social and emotional wellbeing. Specific examples or triggers of developmental trauma include ***adverse childhood experiences (ACEs).*** ACEs emerged from a US study of chronic health conditions (Felitti et al., 1998). Vincent Felitti et al. (1998) identified that ACEs were positively related to chronic disease in later life. Initially, they identified seven ACEs: psychological abuse, physical abuse, sexual abuse, household substance abuse, household mental illness, exposure to domestic abuse, and having a household member imprisoned (Felitti et al., 1998). In their later work, Felitti et al. modified the ACE scale to 10 items, adding emotional neglect, physical neglect, and parental separation/divorce (Reavis et al., 2013). Most people are exposed to at least one ACE (Joshi et al., 2021) and suffer no long-term effects. However, Felitti et al. (1998) found that the harmful effects of ACEs were compounded such that the more ACEs experienced by an individual, the poorer their physical and mental health outcomes and the greater their likelihood of substance abuse.

Felitti et al. (1998) were not focused on the association between ACEs and crime. However, childhood adversity and developmental trauma are associated with future criminality, such that the link between childhood adversity and criminal behaviour is "extremely complex" (Willmot, 2022, p. 15). As noted by Catia Malvaso et al. (2023), the prevalence of ACEs "in justice-involved populations encourages us to think more deeply about how exposure to ACEs interacts with other criminogenic risk factors that underlie offending pathways" (p. 103). Developmental and life-course criminology—particularly the work of David Farrington et al.—has examined explanatory ***risk factors*** for offending (i.e., factors that predict a high probability of someone committing crime) and found that in addition to ACEs (such as child abuse and neglect and family dysfunction), other types of childhood adversity may be relevant to future criminality, including other family factors (e.g., inattentive or ineffective parenting) and social factors (e.g., low socioeconomic status, poverty, inadequate or unstable housing, and living in a high-crime neighbourhood; Farrington, 2015; Farrington et al., 2017).

Exposure to adversity does not always result in trauma, and trauma is not always associated with criminality. However, when childhood adversity is associated with developmental trauma, some symptoms or manifestations are common in people with trauma who offend. Farrington (2015), for example, has found that individuals with criminal careers that span childhood into adulthood often behave impulsively, with limited self-control. Arguably, this behaviour may be an indicator of developmental (neurophysiological) trauma.

4.2.1 Neurophysiological Trauma

While adversity can occur at any time in a person's life, as previously acknowledged, trauma during childhood can have the most significant and detrimental effects. As noted by Sarah Font and Reeve Kennedy (2022):

> studies demonstrate that [childhood] maltreatment gets under the skin, altering biological processes and interfering with development in areas of the brain related to the stress response system, emotion processing and emotion regulation, learning and memory, and cognitive functioning. (p. 375)

A human brain develops in a specific order (Kambam et al., 2009; Stiles & Jernigan, 2010), and, depending on when a child experiences adversity, brain development may be interrupted or disrupted.

There are strong indicators that developmental trauma can result in structural abnormalities in the limbic system (i.e., prefrontal cortex, hippocampus, and amygdala), which impacts an individual's ability to regulate stress, reason, and control their impulses and emotions (Paquola et al., 2016; Willmot, 2022). Studies have found that people diagnosed with post-traumatic stress disorder (PTSD) have decreased activity in the medial prefrontal cortex and increased activity in the amygdala and hippocampus (Bottalico & Bruni, 2012). Changes associated with PTSD have also been found in the grey matter volume of the dorsal anterior cingulate cortex (involved in cognitive processing; Rinne-Albers et al., 2017), prefrontal cortex (involved in higher cognitive functioning and emotional regulation), and the hippocampus (Boukezzi et al., 2017). Stephen Porges' Polyvagal Theory proposes that early adversity may change how the autonomic nervous system (ANS) functions (Porges, 2022). This may affect how a person interacts with stimuli within the world around them, resulting in social and behavioural trauma. Adversity may lead to an increase in impulsive, unpredictable, or violent behaviour due to changes in the volume and functioning of areas of the brain associated with emotional regulation and problem-solving (Rinne-Albers et al., 2017).

Developmental trauma may affect children's brain development. As summarised by American psychiatrist Bruce Perry (2009):

> Maltreatment disrupts this hardy process; trauma, neglect, and related experiences of maltreatment such as prenatal exposure to drugs or alcohol and impaired early bonding all influence the developing brain. These adverse experiences interfere with normal patterns of experience-guided neurodevelopment by creating extreme and abnormal patterns of neural and neurohormonal activity. (p. 241)

Indeed, both enrichment and deprivation experiences can impact the development of brain structure and function in children (Stiles & Jernigan, 2010). However, most justice-involved people experience chronic levels of adversity and deprivation.

Children with neurophysiological trauma may recover through a positive change in their care environment or therapeutic services (Font & Kennedy, 2022; Malvaso et al., 2018). Developmental trauma may be resolved in childhood by addressing safety issues, dealing with traumatic re-enactments, and promoting mastery, i.e., "the feeling of being in charge, calm, and able to engage in focused efforts to accomplish goals" (van der Kolk, 2005, p. 8). However, if developmental trauma symptoms remain, they may become entrenched or exacerbated by additional adversity later in life. Adversity can result in cognitive trauma (as per Fig. 2.1), altering a child's beliefs and cognitive schemas (Evans & Graves, 2018). People who have experienced multiple or ongoing adversity throughout their lives may rely on fear-based schemas to make sense of themselves and the world around them (Ahrens & Rexford, 2014). Ongoing or additional adversity may also lead to the retention of coping mechanisms, which may have been protective in the short term but are maladaptive in adulthood, such as hypersensitivity to triggers and perceived threats.

4.2.2 Attachment and Emotional Regulation

Childhood adversity associated with parental abandonment or maltreatment may negatively impact children's attachment (Willmot, 2022). John Bowlby, an English psychologist and psychiatrist, established the original concept that a child's ***attachment*** to someone means she or "he is strongly disposed to seek proximity to and contact with a specific figure and to do so in certain situations, notably when he (sic) is frightened, tired or ill" (Bowlby, 1969/1997, p. 371) to establish a secure base, as a survival mechanism. Children with secure attachment to caregivers feel protected and can trust and communicate their emotions and thoughts about the world (van der Kolk, 2005). Unstable attachment may affect an individual's ability to regulate their emotions. Children who cannot trust their caregivers to keep them safe, particularly in cases where the caregivers are the source of traumatic experiences (noting most child maltreatment is perpetrated by parents and caregivers; van der Kolk, 2005), cannot interpret and manage distress and often suffer neurophysiological and psychological damage as a result (Cloitre et al., 2009; van der Kolk, 1987). This is sometimes referred to as ***"betrayal trauma"***, when abuse is perpetrated by the person who a child trusts and relies upon (Kaehler et al., 2013; Willmot, 2022, p. 17). Children with unstable attachments cannot interpret or predict dangerous situations or regulate their emotional responses appropriately. They often feel helpless to influence their lives and respond to situations with excessive anger, anxiety, or neediness (van der Kolk, 2005). Family violence, family breakdown, and parental absence affect a child's attachment.

The impacts of unstable attachment may also be regarded as unresolved traumatic grief, as discussed in Chapter 3, which occurs "when a person has suffered a significant loss of attachment and the results of that loss have left the grieving process unresolved" (Leach et al., 2008, p. 107). In adulthood, unstable attachment is characterised by the inability to form and maintain successful relationships with others (Anda et al., 2006) as well as an increased risk of criminality (Craig et al., 2017; Farrington et al., 2016; Griffin & Sallen, 2013; Malvaso et al., 2017a; Sampson & Laub, 2003).

4.3 Developmental Trauma and Criminality

Longitudinal studies have demonstrated that multiple experiences of childhood adversity and associated developmental trauma (e.g., impaired neurophysiological development and functioning, poor emotional regulation, antisocial attitudes and behaviours, and unstable attachment) are prevalent in the lives of people who offend and a predictor of both youth and adult offending (Craig et al., 2017; Farrington et al., 2016; Griffin & Sallen, 2013; Malvaso et al., 2017a; Sampson & Laub, 2003). People who offend are more likely than people without offending histories to have been exposed to chronic adversity (i.e., multiple, concurrent ACEs) rather than a single traumatic event (Baglivio et al., 2015; Malvaso et al., 2022; Segrave & Carlton, 2010).

Recent Australian research (Mathews et al., 2023) examined the prevalence of ***child maltreatment*** (i.e., physical abuse, sexual abuse, emotional abuse, neglect, and exposure to domestic abuse) among 8503 adult Australians. Mathews et al. (2023) examined the association between the experience of child maltreatment and criminal justice system involvement. This study did not include adversity related to household dysfunction, focusing only on childhood maltreatment, a specific type of ACEs. They found that:

- 610 out of all 813 persons who reported being arrested had experienced maltreatment (75.0%), compared with 203 who had not (24.9%). Participants who experienced three or more types of maltreatment ("chronic multi-type maltreatment") were more likely to be arrested than other participants. Overall, the odds of ever being arrested were more than twice as high for participants who experienced maltreatment compared to those who did not, and a person was

2.5 times more likely to be arrested if they had experienced chronic multi-type maltreatment.

- Men who reported maltreatment were 2 to 2.5 times more likely to have been convicted of a crime than men without maltreatment and significantly more likely to be imprisoned (4.6%) relative to their non-maltreated counterparts (2.1%; Mathews et al., 2023).

Importantly, the researchers noted that most maltreated individuals (85%) did not report a history of criminal justice involvement:

> simultaneously suggest[ing] the resilience of many maltreated individuals, as shown by the absence of criminal justice system involvement, and the significant challenge criminal justice systems face in responding to individuals who have experienced child maltreatment. (Mathews et al., 2023, p. 13)

Further, the associations between childhood maltreatment and criminality were consistently noted for men but not women (Mathews et al., 2023). This may be partly attributed to the much smaller numbers of women who offend, the nature of the childhood adversity experienced by girls not captured in the study, and/or the compounding impact of adulthood adversity for women, including chronic or repeated domestic and sexual abuse (Baldry, 2010; Fuentes, 2013; Gelb, 2019).

The nature of the childhood adversity a person has experienced can influence the nature and seriousness of their offending behaviour. In Canada, Hanie Edalati et al. (2017) examined 2255 subjects. They found that criminal justice involvement in the previous six months (i.e., detention or arrest by police or court appearance) was significantly correlated with seven of the 10 categories of ACEs, excluding emotional neglect, sexual abuse, and household mental illness. Edalati et al. (2017) concluded:

> ... the greatest effect on criminal justice involvement was seen among participants who reported parental separation and divorce and an incarcerated household member... It has been suggested that family disruption is associated with weak parental attachment; emotional problems; and exposure to discrimination, violence, and abuse, which consequently

> increase the risk of delinquency among the children of these parents. (p. 1292)

It is important to note here that childhood adversity does not cause criminality. Therefore, there remains a need to understand better how trauma might mediate the relationship between adversity and crime, recognising that no single pathway will apply.

A Queensland study of a cohort of 41,700 children also found that physical abuse and neglect were stronger predictors of future offending than sexual or emotional abuse (Stewart et al., 2002). Finally, Bryanna Hahn Fox et al. (2015) focused on a sample in Florida of 22,575 youth who had offended. They concurred that physical and emotional abuse, family violence, and an incarcerated family member were most correlated with serious, violent, and chronic youth offending. Emotional neglect, sexual abuse, and household mental illness were the least common ACEs associated with offending. While experiences of (and exposure to) physical abuse may result in future violent behaviour, as shown above, a linear relationship does not exist between being a victim of child sexual abuse and perpetrating sexual violence (Ogloff et al., 2012).

4.4 From Child Protection to Prison: The Welfare to Justice Continuum

Some children who offend have also had contact with the child protection system (SAC, 2020; Walsh, 2019). Malvaso et al. (2018) systematically reviewed the literature examining the association between maltreatment and offending. From their analysis of 62 prospective and longitudinal studies (58 from the US, three from Australia, and one from Sweden), they concluded:

> [y]oung people can be subjected to different types of abuse, at different times throughout their childhood or adolescent years, and at different levels of severity and frequency. Similarly, young people may experience various levels of intervening services, from placement in out-of-home care down to the type, stability, and length of placement services… there is

> evidence that these factors can influence the nature of the association between maltreatment and offending. (p. 30)

In the longitudinal study of 74,673 children and young people in SA's child protection or youth justice systems, Malvaso et al. (2017b) found that a small but significant proportion of young people had been the subject of both a notification to child protection authorities and convicted for a crime as a young person. Malvaso et al. (2017b) found that 71.1% ($n = 1455$) of young people with convictions ($n = 2045$) were involved with the child protection system, with 747 of these children (36.5% of young people with convictions) placed in out-of-home care (OOHC).

Ironically, children are removed from the care of their birth families and placed in OOHC because their home environments are considered too dangerous due to issues such as parental criminality and household conflict (Malvaso et al., 2019), and yet a significant body of research from Australia (Baidawi et al., 2014; Marien, 2012; Stewart et al., 2002), the US (Dierkhising et al., 2013), and the UK (Boswell, 2016) has emphasised the association between family separation, OOHC, and future criminality (Colvin et al., 2018). In the study cited above, children in OOHC were 22.4 times more likely to be convicted of an offence than children not placed in OOHC (Malvaso et al., 2017b). In further research focusing on 1,819 young people in SA secure care, Malvaso et al. found that young people with convictions for violence had experienced persistent maltreatment (i.e., abuse, neglect), particularly exposure to conflict in the home (Malvaso et al., 2018). The maltreated children placed in OOHC were 70% more likely to be convicted of a violent crime. This significance of OOHC as a risk for criminality may be relevant in several ways.

- First, it may indicate the range, chronicity, and severity of childhood adversity already experienced by the child.
- Second, OOHC may undermine and destroy family and community ties, affecting a young person's sense of self, attachment, and belonging (McLean et al., 2016).

- Third, people who work as foster carers and professional carers may themselves present a risk of harm to the safety of children in their care, leading to re-traumatisation.
- Fourth, OOHC arrangements may expose children to abusive behaviour, resulting in children learning to use aggression and violence to keep themselves safe and to resolve conflict (Willmot, 2022).
- Finally, a young person in OOHC acting out is more likely to be reported to the police and have their behaviour criminalised by a professional carer than a parent (Malvaso et al., 2017c).

In her research with 200 young people who had committed serious offences and had "graduated" to adult prison in England and Wales, Gwyneth Boswell found 91% had experienced childhood adversity in the form of child abuse or traumatic loss, the latter "in the shape of bereavement and separation from family which the young people had not been helped to understand or come to terms with" (Boswell, 2016, p. 16). Susan Baidawi et al. (2014) interviewed 77 professionals in Victoria who worked with "order clients". They found:

> The respondents largely viewed offending behaviour in OHC [out of home care] populations as a 'trauma-related outcome'... the symptoms of trauma (including difficulties managing emotions and moderating behaviour) led young people in out of home care to experience rejection and exclusion from OHC placements (e.g., placement breakdowns) and school environments (e.g., suspension and expulsion). Three key factors which mediate the association between experiences of trauma and later offending behaviour were identified: substance use, educational disengagement/exclusion and association with antisocial peers. (p. 32)

Emma Colvin et al. (2018) interviewed 46 workers in NSW between 2014 and 2016 about children missing from OOHC. Many professionals (i.e., care workers, police, lawyers, youth justice, and child protection workers) equated running away with criminality. Indeed, young people were sometimes arrested on a warrant for absconding from care (*Children and Young Persons (Care and Protection) Act 1998* (NSW), s 109B). The researchers noted "[p]articipants often referred to missing children as 'absconders' and spoke of 'apprehending' and 'arresting'...

[these] inherently troublesome and delinquent [children]" (Colvin et al., 2018, p. 238f). The young people's vulnerability and their reasons for "running away" were rarely acknowledged, with only three police officers recognising that sometimes children ran away from "unsuitable or unsafe" placements (Colvin et al., 2018, p. 241). Broader research indicates that the few young people in residential care are highly vulnerable to further victimisation and abuse. Running away from out-of-home placements indicates "clear and serious" risks that must be identified and addressed to avoid entrenching these young people in the justice system.

There is significantly more research exploring the link between developmental trauma and crime (particularly offending during childhood) than between adult criminality and adversity across the life-course (Wolff & Shi, 2012). Evidence shows developmental trauma is a predictor of further trauma (or re-traumatisation) in adulthood. In addition, in the absence of developmental trauma, criminal behaviour may be associated with adult-onset trauma (Wolff & Shi, 2012) and intergenerational trauma. As previously stated, while the cause of trauma is less relevant than its severity, people exposed to multiple forms of childhood adversity or intergenerational trauma are highly likely to experience complex trauma and increased contact with the youth justice and adult justice agencies.

4.5 Intergenerational Trauma

Intergenerational or transgenerational trauma refers to the trauma experienced by children and descendants of those directly exposed to adversity (Atkinson et al., 2014; Kezelman et al., 2015). Intergenerational trauma may stem from a discrete traumatic event or chronic adversity. Intergenerational trauma may affect a single generation (i.e., be passed from a parent to their child) or traverse multiple generations, such as the complex and entrenched collective trauma that affects Aboriginal people. A range of theoretical approaches can be used to explain intergenerational trauma, including social modelling and "learned problem parenting" (Minh et al., 2013, p. 5477), weakened social bonds, genetics, and epigenetic links (Jiang et al., 2019), and biopsychosocial approaches (Kim et al., 2014).

4.5.1 Intergenerational Trauma Associated with a Parent in Prison

Having a parent in prison is a risk factor for children's future criminal behaviour (Flynn et al., 2016; Halsey & de Vel-Palumbo, 2020; Murray et al., 2012). One in four adults in Australian prisons report that they had a parent in prison during childhood, with more than one-third of Aboriginal and Torres Strait Islander prisoners reporting growing up with an incarcerated parent (AIHW, 2023). The imprisonment of parents can lead to significant emotional distress for children and impact children's life outcomes, including disengagement from school and increased aggressive behaviour (Green et al., 2005). Joseph Murray et al. (2012) undertook a meta-analysis of samples from 40 studies that involved 7374 children with imprisoned parents and 37,325 comparison children (without incarcerated parents) from the US, UK, the Netherlands, Denmark, Sweden, Australia, and Aotearoa New Zealand. Some studies did not differentiate between imprisoned fathers and mothers, with only six focusing solely on imprisoned mothers. Murray et al. found that the risk of future antisocial behaviour was the same for children with imprisoned fathers or mothers. The researchers concluded that separation per se did not increase the risk of criminality; parental imprisonment specifically predicted children's antisocial behaviour because of the specific stigma, strain, and shame associated with prison.

Many more fathers than mothers are incarcerated, and the absence of fathers may be highly impactful on children (Halsey & de Vel-Palumbo, 2020). However, in practical terms, Wendy Kukulies-Smith (2018) concluded that:

> where the mother is the primary caregiver of dependent children the children are likely to be displaced from the family home by her incarceration. Whereas when the father of dependent children is incarcerated, the children are likely to remain in the family home and be cared for by their mother. (p. 16)

Catherine Flynn also found that the incarceration of mothers was particularly distressing for young people. In her Victorian research, she interviewed 20 young people (between 10 and 18 years) who had mothers in prison, of whom eight were required to live with their fathers. These young people were often ambivalent or unhappy with the arrangement because they missed their mothers (their primary carers), and their fathers did not encourage or enable them to see their mothers (Flynn, 2012).

Further, children may feel the loss of their mothers more acutely (in terms of care arrangements), given that many fathers were already absent from their children's lives (Giordano & Copp, 2015). In SA, 60 to 65% of incarcerated women self-identified as mothers, with up to 40% primary carers and up to 20% sole carers of children under 18 years (DCS, 2017). Australian researchers have emphasised that "[c]hildren of incarcerated mothers are more likely to be in out-of-home care (often permanently), and children in out-of-home care are more likely to have contact with the criminal justice system" (AIHW, 2023, p. 58). Given that mothers are often the primary caregivers, the incarceration of mothers may result in developmental trauma by disrupting attachment between mothers and their children rather than through modelling (Murray et al., 2012). Often, the trauma experienced by children separated from their mothers reflects their mothers' own experiences; most incarcerated women have histories of trauma (Green et al., 2005).

Canadian research with mothers who had experienced life-course trauma (i.e., in childhood and adulthood) found:

> The "chain of risk" can be applied to intergenerational patterns of criminality. Risk of criminality for a woman or her children can be enhanced through an accumulation of exposures across generations. Among the women in this study, criminality in many forms—child abuse and neglect, substance use, and intimate partner abuse—spanned the generations. (Minh et al., 2013, p. 5476)

Maternal incarceration impacts attachment and ***attunement***, the ability to reflect the emotions and affect of others, such as a primary caregiver or child (Parkerville Children and Youth Care, 2018, p. 5).

If maternal incarceration or absence occurs across multiple generations, impacting attachment and attunement, this may result in childhood neglect, with mothers unaware of the attachment and attunement needs of their babies and children.

Most women and girls who are criminalised have experienced gender-based adversity in terms of sexual violence and domestic abuse (Gelb, 2019). The domestic abuse histories of mothers in prison are often intergenerational and compound additional experiences of life-course adversity (Minh et al., 2013). Minh et al. (2013) found that while mothers in prison sought to provide safe and secure childhoods for their children, they often had trauma symptoms (e.g., difficulties with emotional regulation, self-worth, and coping strategies) as well as a lack of positive parenting models, which impacted the safety and wellbeing of their children (Minh et al., 2013). Peggy Giordano and Jennifer Copp (2015) found that children of incarcerated parents faced "packages of risk" beyond parental incarceration, including multiple childhood adversities such as parental drug and alcohol abuse, domestic abuse, violence, poverty, and social exclusion. Thus, the issue may not be the imprisonment of parents per se but rather intergenerational trauma and "underlying difficulties and problems that predate incarceration" (Giordano & Copp, 2015, p. 159).

4.5.2 Intergenerational Trauma in the Lives of First Nations Peoples

Present-day adversity experienced by First Nations peoples may be a combination of the legacy of intergenerational traumas and direct adverse experiences. First Nations peoples are over-represented in the criminal justice system as both victims and people who have offended. As noted in Chapter 1, Aboriginal and Torres Strait Islander peoples represent only three percent of the Australian population (ABS, 2022), but they are 32% of the prison population (ABS, 2023). As noted by Thalia Anthony (2017), Aboriginal Australians and Torres Strait Islanders are the most incarcerated population in the world. Similarly, First Nations people are over-represented in the justice systems in Canada and Aotearoa New

Zealand. In Canada, First Nations people represent approximately five percent of the population but around a third of the incarcerated population (Barkaskas et al., 2019, p. 11). In some Canadian provinces/territories, the proportion of prisoners who are Aboriginal people is as high as 75% (Dickson & Smith, 2021). In Aotearoa New Zealand, Māori people represent about 17% of the general population and more than half the prison population (DOC, 2021; Stats NZ, 2023). The over-representation of First Nations peoples in the justice system is associated with the experiences of compounded adversity and disadvantage since colonisation (RCIADIC, 1991; refer to Chapter 10).

4.5.3 The Trauma of Colonisation

Intergenerational trauma is particularly notable for First Nations peoples who have layered experiences of cumulative trauma. The term "intergenerational trauma" may be used interchangeably with "historical trauma" or "collective trauma" or may be explicitly used to refer to trauma within families (Menzies, 2019). ***Historical trauma*** has been defined as resulting "from systematically inflicted and sustained trauma on a subjugated population" (Menzies, 2019, p. 1). Historical trauma caused by colonisation resulted in a loss of cultural knowledge when Elders and senior knowledge holders were killed. In addition, the sexual assault of women and children by White settlers demonstrated that such behaviour was acceptable in the new colonial world (Brock & Gard, 2017). Trauma from colonisation continues to impact Aboriginal peoples after years of being denied access to their languages, laws (and lore), traditions, cultures, lands and sacred places, and ways of life (Bombay et al., 2009; Dodson, 1997; Menzies, 2019). It has been suggested that colonisation and other intergenerational traumas have destroyed cultural links, Aboriginal identity, and a sense of belonging (ALRC, 2017), leading to "social disintegration (i.e., identity confusion between dominant and original culture) and social disadvantage" for many Aboriginal and First Nations peoples (Hill et al., 2010, p. 40).

Colonisation in both Canada and Australia "undermined the social, cultural and economic foundations of Aboriginal peoples" (Parkes et al.,

2012, p. 309). Debra Parkes et al. (2012) highlighted several factors applicable to Canadian First Nations people, which also reflect the Australian Aboriginal peoples' experiences post-colonisation (Brock & Gard, 2017), namely:

- the relocation of Aboriginal people from their country to poor-quality lands,
- criminalisation of traditional Aboriginal practices and use of language,
- restrictions on Aboriginal people's human rights, including freedom of association, movement, speech and assembly, and autonomy,
- forcing Aboriginal men to stay in poverty on reserves or, if they moved away for work or other opportunities, to give up their language and culture as well as any access to welfare services for their families, and
- the removal and assimilation of their children.

Intergenerational trauma for some Aboriginal people may result in "a self-destructive cycle of loss of identity and purpose that fuels anger and trauma behaviours, such as acts of violence and alcohol and drug misuse" (Atkinson, 2008, p. 7). In their work with Canadian First Nations people, Amy Bombay et al. (2009) explained:

> In assessing the intergenerational effects of adverse events on well-being, it needs to be considered that the impact of trauma experiences of one generation are difficult to dissociate from the effects of adverse events encountered in subsequent generations. Specifically, poor well-being may reflect the direct actions of current events, the direct or indirect effects attributable to traumatic experiences in previous generations, or the synergy between the two. (p. 13)

US researchers Laura Quiros et al. (2020) articulated how racially based intergenerational trauma is entrenched, caused by "structural, social, economic, and political" disadvantages experienced by non-White people (Quiros et al., 2020, p. 160), through economic marginalisation and the poverty that ensued for First Nations populations. The DSM-5-TR (APA, 2022) acknowledges that the higher rates of PTSD in First Nations Americans and African Americans than in White Americans are potentially influenced by "exposure to past adversity and racism and discrimination, and in availability or quality of treatment, social support, socioeconomic status, and other social resources that facilitate recovery and are confounded with ethnic and racialized background" (APA, 2022).

Canadian research has proposed that the impact of colonisation on First Nations people includes poor educational achievement, higher unemployment and poverty, poor physical and mental health outcomes, including substance abuse and suicidality, and high levels of criminal justice system engagement (Barkaskas et al., 2019, p. 11). The Canadian Royal Commission on Aboriginal Peoples (RCAP) examined three theories most cited as explanations for the over-incarceration of Aboriginal people in prison: culture clash, socio-economic, and colonialism (Parkes et al., 2012). The RCAP (1996, cited in Parkes et al., 2012) and the Canadian Supreme Court (LSS, 2022) concluded that systematic discrimination, as well as the ongoing impacts of colonisation, have influenced the over-incarceration of First Nations people. Similar systematic discrimination in the Australian criminal justice system has led to over-policing of First Nations communities (ALRC, 2017), high rates of arrest, low access to bail, an inability to access community-based sentences due to a lack of stable or suitable housing, judicial bias, and racism (RCIADIC, 1991), and limited access to quality legal representation (Anthony, 2013).

A more insidious example of re-traumatisation is in the form of microaggressions: small, repeated experiences that may cumulatively lead to trauma responses (Sue, 2017). According to Derald Sue (2017):

> Microaggressions are about experiential reality and about listening to the voices of those most oppressed, ignored, and silenced. Those voices tell stories of the many hurts, humiliations, lost opportunities, need for change, and the often unintentional microaggressions endured as they struggle against an unwelcoming, invalidating and even hostile campus climate and society. (p. 171)

Microaggressions are often associated with the "otherness" of race, culture, and social exclusion. When microaggressions are overlooked or dismissed as insignificant, re-traumatisation may exacerbate their impact (Sue, 2017).

4.5.4 The Re-traumatisation of Government Policies and Statements

Intergenerational and collective trauma can also be exacerbated for First Nations peoples through re-traumatisation. Re-traumatisation is often caused by government laws, policies, and actions, such as past assimilation laws that prevented Aboriginal adults from accessing their language and heritage. The *Australia Policy of Assimilation in 1961* (Assimilation Policy; Hasluck, 1961) stated:

> The policy of assimilation means in the view of all Australian governments that all aborigines and part-aborigines are expected eventually to attain the same manner of living as other Australians and to live as members of a single Australian community enjoying the same rights and privileges, accepting the same responsibilities, observing the same customs and influenced by the same beliefs, hopes and loyalties as other Australians. Thus, any special measures taken for aborigines and part-aborigines are regarded as temporary measures not based on colour but intended to meet their need for special care and assistance to protect them from any ill effects of sudden change and to assist them to make the transition from one stage to another in such a way as will be favourable to their future social, economic and political advancement. (p. 1)

While it did not explicitly acknowledge the removal of Aboriginal children from their families,the Assimilation Policy meant generations of Aboriginal children from the late nineteenth century until the 1960s were removed from their families and communities and placed with non-Aboriginal families or in children's homes (Menzies, 2020). This entrenched destruction of Aboriginal community and family life has led to further generations of Aboriginal children beyond 1969 being removed from their birth parents by child protection services. The intentional destruction of culture and family surrounding the "Stolen

Generations" is also reflected in the collective, historical trauma experienced by First Nations peoples in other countries, such as Canada (refer to Bombay et al., 2009).

Intergenerational trauma is prevalent in families impacted by the "Stolen Generations", where Aboriginal and Torres Strait Islander children were forcibly removed from their families and communities throughout the twentieth century (Menzies, 2019). It has been estimated that one in five living Indigenous Australians born before 1972 are survivors of the Stolen Generations (AIHW, 2021). More than one in three Aboriginal and Torres Strait Islander adults today (36%) and almost half of the SA Indigenous population (47.8%) are descendants of survivors of the Stolen Generations (AIHW, 2021). Living members of the Stolen Generations are reportedly worse off compared with other Indigenous Australians of the same age on a range of health and socioeconomic outcomes, including contact with the criminal justice system (AIHW, 2021; The Healing Foundation, 2021). This is not surprising. These people experienced the intentional destruction of culture and family (Dodson, 1997; The Healing Foundation, 2021). They were told that Aboriginality was something to be ashamed of rather than an enduring strength to celebrate (The Healing Foundation, 2021). Survivors of the Stolen Generations, because of their childhood experiences, were not always exposed to effective and loving families and parenting experiences, and as a result, may find it difficult to establish positive emotional connections with others (The Healing Foundation, 2021). This potentially has a profound impact on their children and descendants.

The children of the Stolen Generations often experience compounded trauma, as explained by Helen Milroy (2015), Australia's first Indigenous doctor and professor in psychiatry.

> The trans-generational effects of trauma occur via a variety of mechanisms including the impact on the attachment relationship with caregivers; the impact on parenting and family functioning; the association with parental physical and mental illness; disconnection and alienation from extended family, culture and society. These effects are exacerbated by exposure to

> continuing high levels of stress and trauma including multiple bereavements and other losses, the process of vicarious traumatisation where children witness the on-going effect of the original trauma, which a parent or other family member has experienced. Even where children are protected from the traumatic stories of their ancestors, the effects of past traumas still impact on children in the form of ill health, family dysfunction, community violence, psychological morbidity and early mortality. (p. xxi)

Whether regarded as intergenerational, historical, or collective trauma, Aboriginal people have experienced trauma, both in the past and present. Recent media and political statements indicate that there continues to be a lack of understanding of the importance of acknowledging the devastating impact of British settlement on Australian Aboriginal and Torres Strait Islander peoples, their identities, and their cultures (Butler, 2024; Hytner, 2021). This ignorance continues to compound the impact of intergenerational and historical trauma.

4.6 Conclusion

This chapter has aimed to highlight the importance of two overlooked forms of past trauma: developmental trauma and intergenerational trauma. Both are based on past adversity, whether years, decades, or centuries ago. Past adversity significantly influences the trajectory of people at risk of—or who engage in—criminal behaviour. This chapter discusses the relevance of unresolved (and compounded) past traumas in current and future criminal behaviour. The impact of recent, direct traumatic experiences may be compounded by developmental and intergenerational trauma. In recognising the significance of the past, often overlooked by practitioners, including judges, I am aware of the limitations of ACEs as a measure of childhood adversity. I am also conscious that I am writing from a non-Indigenous perspective. I have intentionally referred to sources created by First Nations authors, thinkers, and researchers. A source of distress for me and other workers in the criminal justice system is the recognition that we work within a system that is fundamentally flawed and inherently racist. The following chapter outlines how agencies and individuals are working to combat this and respond in a trauma-informed way.

Key Points

- Past adversity that occurred in childhood or previous familial generations can impact individuals' social and emotional wellbeing today.
- Developmental trauma refers to the negative impacts of chronic adversity in childhood on an individual's social and emotional wellbeing. Developmental trauma may present as neurophysiological trauma, changes to attachment, and poor emotional regulation impacting a person's wellbeing and behaviour.
- Longitudinal studies have demonstrated that multiple ACEs and the resulting developmental trauma (e.g., impaired neurophysiological development and functioning, poor emotional regulation, antisocial attitudes and behaviours, and unstable attachment) are prevalent in the lives of people who offend and a predictor of both youth and adult offending.
- Involvement in the child protection system is a risk factor for youth justice involvement, which is often a pathway into the adult justice system.
- Intergenerational or transgenerational trauma refers to the trauma experienced by children and descendants of those directly exposed to adversity.
- Parental incarceration is a risk factor for children's future criminal behaviour.
- First Nations people have experienced centuries of intergenerational trauma as well as direct personal experiences of adversity. Trauma from colonisation continues to impact Aboriginal peoples after years of being denied access to their languages, laws (and lore), traditions, cultures, lands and sacred places, and ways of life. This compounded trauma helps to understand better that it is trauma and not culture that is predictive of the over-representation of First Nations people in the criminal justice system.

References

Ahrens, J., & Rexford, L. (2014). Cognitive Processing Therapy for Incarcerated Adolescents with PTSD. In R. Greenwald (Ed.), *Trauma and Juvenile*

Delinquency: Theory, Research, and Interventions (pp. 201–216). Taylor and Francis. https://doi.org/10.4324/9781315808819

American Psychiatric Association. (APA). (2022). Trauma- and Stressor-Related Disorders. In *Diagnostic and Statistical Manual of Mental Disorders, Fifth Edition—Text Revised (DSM-5-TR®).* American Psychiatric Publishing. https://doi.org/10.1176/appi.books.9780890425787.x07_Trauma_and_Stressor_Related_Disorders

Anda, R., Felitti, V., Bremner, J., Walker, J., Whitfield, C., Perry, B., Dube, S., & Giles, W. (2006). The Enduring Effects of Abuse and Related Adverse Experiences in Childhood. *European Archives of Psychiatry and Clinical Neuroscience, 256*(3), 174–186. https://doi.org/10.1007/s00406-005-0624-4

Anthony, T. (2013). *Indigenous people, crime and punishment*. Routledge.

Anthony, T. (2017, June 6). FactCheck: are first Australians the most imprisoned people on Earth? *The Conversation.*

Atkinson, C. L. (2008). *The Violence Continuum: Australian Aboriginal Male Violence and Generational Post-Traumatic Stress* [PhD, Charles Darwin University].

Atkinson, J., Nelson, J., Brooks, R., Atkinson, C., & Ryan, K. (2014). Addressing Individual and Community Transgenerational Trauma. In P. Dudgeon, H. Milroy, & R. Walker (Eds.), *Working Together: Aboriginal and Torres Strait Islander Mental Health and Wellbeing Principles and Practice* (2nd ed., pp. 289–305). Commonwealth of Australia.

Australian Bureau of Statistics (ABS). (2022). *Australia: Aboriginal and Torres Strait Islander Population Summary.* ABS.

Australian Bureau of Statistics (ABS). (2023) *Prisoners in Australia.* ABS.

Australian Institute of Health and Welfare (AIHW). (2021). *Aboriginal and Torres Strait Islander Stolen Generations Aged 50 and Over: Updated Analyses for 2018–2019 (Cat. no. IHW 257).* AIHW.

Australian Institute of Health and Welfare (AIHW). (2023). *The Health of People in Australian Prisons 2022.* AIHW.

Australian Law Reform Commission (ALRC). (2017). *Pathways to Justice—An Inquiry into the Incarceration Rate of Aboriginal and Torres Strait Islander Peoples: Final Report* (Vol. ALRC Report 133). Commonwealth of Australia.

Baglivio, M. T., Wolff, K. T., Piquero, A. R., & Epps, N. (2015). The Relationship Between Adverse Childhood Experiences (ACE) and Juvenile Offending Trajectories in a Juvenile Offender Sample. *Journal of Criminal Justice, 43*(3), 229–241. https://doi.org/10.1016/j.jcrimjus.2015.04.012

Baidawi, S., Mendes, P., & Snow, P. (2014). 'Setting Them Up to Fail': System Responses to Dual Order Child Protection and Youth Justice Clients. *Alternative Law Journal, 39*(1), 31–35.
Baldry, E. (2010). Women in Transition: From Prison to... *Current Issues in Criminal Justice, 22*(2), 253–267.
Barkaskas, P., Chin, V., Dandurand, Y., & Tooshkenig, D. (2019). *Production and Delivery of Gladue Pre-sentence Reports: A Review of Selected Canadian Programs*. International Centre for Criminal Law Reform and Criminal Justice Policy.
Bombay, A., Matheson, K., & Anisman, H. (2009). Intergenerational Trauma: Convergence of Multiple Processes Among First Nations Peoples in Canada. *Journal of Aboriginal Health, 5*(3), 6–47.
Boswell, G. (2016). Trauma Experiences in the Backgrounds of Violent Young Offenders. *Pakistan Journal of Criminology, 8*(2), 12–24.
Bottalico, B., & Bruni, T. (2012). Post Traumatic Stress Disorder, Neuroscience, and the Law. *International Journal of Law and Psychiatry, 35*(2), 112–120. https://doi.org/10.1016/j.ijlp.2011.12.001
Boukezzi, S., El Khoury-Malhame, M., Auzias, G., Reynaud, E., Rousseau, P.-F., Richard, E., Zendjidjian, X., Roques, J., Castelli, N., Correard, N., Guyon, V., Gellato, C., Samuelian, J.-C., Cancel, A., Comte, M., Latinus, M., Guedj, E., & Khalfa, S. (2017). Grey Matter Density Changes of Structures Involved in Posttraumatic Stress Disorder (PTSD) After Recovery Following Eye Movement Desensitization and Reprocessing (EMDR) Therapy. *Psychiatry Research: Neuroimaging, 266*, 146–152. https://doi.org/10.1016/j.pscychresns.2017.06.009
Bowlby, J. (1969/1997). *Attachment and Loss Volume 1: Attachment*. Pimlico.
Brock, P., & Gard, T. (Eds.). (2017). *Colonialism and its Aftermath: A History of Aboriginal South Australia*. Wakefield Press.
Butler, J. (2024, January 11). Peter Dutton Calls for Boycott of Woolworths After Australia Day Merchandise Dropped. *The Guardian*.
Cloitre, M., Stolbach, B. C., Herman, J. L., Kolk, B. V. D., Pynoos, R., Wang, J., & Petkova, E. (2009). A Developmental Approach to Complex PTSD: Childhood and Adult Cumulative Trauma as Predictors of Symptom Complexity. *Journal of Traumatic Stress, 22*(5), 399–408. https://doi.org/10.1002/jts.20444
Colvin, E., McFarlane, K., Gerard, A., & McGrath, A. (2018). We Don't do Measure and Quotes': How Agency Responses Criminalise and Endanger the Safety of Children Missing in Care in New South Wales, Australia.

Howard Journal of Crime and Justice, 57(2), 231–249. https://doi.org/10.1111/hojo.12253
Craig, J. M., Piquero, A. R., Farrington, D. P., & Ttofi, M. M. (2017). A Little Early Risk Goes a Long Bad Way: Adverse Childhood Experiences and Life-Course Offending in the Cambridge Study. *Journal of Criminal Justice, 53*, 34–45. https://doi.org/10.1016/j.jcrimjus.2017.09.005
Department for Correctional Services (DCS). (2017). *Stronger Together: Safe Children & Strong Families*. Government of South Australia.
Department of Corrections (DOC). (2021). *Corrections Volumes 2019–2020*. New Zealand Government.
Dickson, J., & Smith, K. (2021). Exploring the Canadian Judiciary's Experiences with and Perceptions of Gladue. *Canadian Journal of Criminology and Criminal Justice, 63*(3–4), 23–46. https://doi.org/10.3138/cjccj.2021-0031
Dierkhising, C. B., Ko, S. J., Woods-Jaeger, B., Briggs, E. C., Lee, R., & Pynoos, R. S. (2013). Trauma Histories Among Justice-Involved Youth: Findings from the National Child Traumatic Stress Network. *European Journal of Psychotraumatology, 4*(1), 1–12. https://doi.org/10.3402/ejpt.v4i0.20274
Dodson, M. (1997). Citizenship in Australia: An Indigenous Perspective. *Alternative Law Journal, 22*(2), 57–59.
Edalati, H., Nicholls, T. L., Crocker, A. G., Roy, L., Somers, J. M., & Patterson, M. L. (2017). Adverse Childhood Experiences and the Risk of Criminal Justice Involvement and Victimization Among Homeless Adults with Mental Illness. *Psychiatric Services, 68*(12), 1288–1295. https://doi.org/10.1176/appi.ps.201600330
Evans, C., & Graves, K. (2018). Trauma Among Children and Legal Implications. *Cogent Social Sciences, 4*, 1–9. https://doi.org/10.1080/23311886.2018.1546791
Farrington, D. P. (2015). Prospective Longitudinal Research on the Development of Offending. *Australian and New Zealand Journal of Criminology, 48*(3), 314–335. https://doi.org/10.1177/0004865815590461
Farrington, D. P., Gaffney, H., & Ttofi, M. M. (2017). Systematic Reviews of Explanatory Risk Factors for Violence, Offending, and Delinquency. *Aggression and Violent Behavior, 33*, 24–36. https://doi.org/10.1016/j.avb.2016.11.004
Farrington, D. P., Ttofi, M. M., & Piquero, A. R. (2016). Risk, Promotive, and Protective Factors in Youth Offending: Results from the Cambridge Study in Delinquent Development. *Journal of Criminal Justice, 45*(C), 63–70. https://doi.org/10.1016/j.jcrimjus.2016.02.014

Felitti, V. J., Anda, R. F., Nordenberg, D., Williamson, D. F., Spitz, A. M., Edwards, V., Koss, M. P., & Marks, J. S. (1998). Relationship of Childhood Abuse and Household Dysfunction to Many of the Leading Causes of Death in Adults: The Adverse Childhood Experiences (ACE) Study. *American Journal of Preventative Medicine, 14*(4), 245–258. https://doi.org/10.1016/s0749-3797(98)00017-8

Flynn, C. (2012). Caring for the Children of Imprisoned Mothers: Exploring the Role of Fathers. *Child Abuse Review, 21*(4), 285–298. https://doi.org/10.1002/car.1206

Flynn, C., Naylor, B., & Arias, P. F. (2016). Responding to the Needs of Children of Parents Arrested in Victoria, Australia. The Role of the Adult Criminal Justice System. *Australian & New Zealand Journal of Criminology, 49*(3), 351–369. https://doi.org/10.1177/0004865815585390

Font, S. A., & Kennedy, R. (2022). The Centrality of Child Maltreatment to Criminology. *Annual Review of Criminology, 5*(1), 371–396. https://doi.org/10.1146/annurev-criminol-030920-120220

Fuentes, C. M. (2013). Nobody's Child: The Role of Trauma and Interpersonal Violence in Women's Pathways to Incarceration and Resultant Service Needs. *Medical Anthropology Quarterly, 28*(1), 85–104. https://doi.org/10.1111/maq.12058

Gelb, K. (2019). *Young Women and Girls in Youth Justice: A Review of Literature and Evaluations.* Victorian Department of Justice and Community Safety.

Giordano, P. C., & Copp, J. E. (2015). Packages" of Risk: Implications for Determining the Effect of Maternal Incarceration on Child Wellbeing. *Criminology and Public Policy, 14*(1), 157–168. https://doi.org/10.1111/1745-9133.12118

Green, B. L., Miranda, J., Daroowalla, A., & Siddique, J. (2005). Trauma Exposure, Mental Health Functioning, and Program Needs of Women in Jail. *Crime & Delinquency, 51*(1), 133–151. https://doi.org/10.1177/0011128704267477

Griffin, G., & Sallen, S. (2013). Considering Child Trauma Issues in Juvenile Court Sentencing. *Children's Legal Rights Journal, 34*(1), 1–22.

Hahn Fox, B., Perez, N., Cass, E., Baglivio, M. T., & Epps, N. (2015). Trauma Changes Everything: Examining the Relationship Between Adverse Childhood Experiences and Serious, Violent and Chronic Juvenile Offenders. *Child Abuse & Neglect, 46*, 163–173. https://doi.org/10.1016/j.chiabu.2015.01.011

Halsey, M., & de Vel-Palumbo, M. (2020). *Generations Through Prison: Experiences of Intergenerational Incarceration.* Routledge.

Hasluck, P. (1961). *The Policy of Assimilation: Decisions of Commonwealth and State Ministers at the Native Welfare Conference, Canberra, January 26th and 27th, 1961.* A.J. Arthur, Commonwealth Government Printer.
The Healing Foundation. (2021). *Make Healing Happen: It's Time to Act*. The Healing Foundation.
Hill, J. S., Lau, M. Y., & Sue, D. W. (2010). Integrating Trauma Psychology and Cultural Psychology: Indigenous Perspectives on Theory, Research, and Practice. *Traumatology, 16*(4), 39–47. https://doi.org/10.1177/1534765610388303
Hytner, M. (2021, January 21) Scott Morrison Criticised for Saying 26 January "Wasn't a Flash Day for Those on First Fleet Vessels Either". *The Guardian.*
Jiang, S., Postovit, L., Cattaneo, A., Binder, E. B., & Aitchison, K. J. (2019). Epigenetic Modifications in Stress Response Genes Associated with Childhood Trauma. *Frontiers in Psychiatry, 10*(808), 1–19. https://doi.org/10.3389/fpsyt.2019.00808
Joshi, D., Raina, P., Tonmyr, L., MacMillan, H. L., & Gonzalez, A. (2021). Prevalence of Adverse Childhood Experiences Among Individuals Aged 45 to 85 Years: A Cross-Sectional Analysis of the Canadian Longitudinal Study on Aging. *CMAJ Open, 9*(1), E158–E166.
Kaehler, L. A., Babock, R., DePrince, A. P., & Freyd, J. J. (2013). Betrayal Trauma. In J. D. Ford & C. A. Courtois (Eds.), *Treating Complex Traumatic Stress Disorders in Children and Adolescents: Scientific Foundations and Therapeutic Models* (pp. 62–78). Guilford.
Kambam, P., Thompson, C., Erickson, S. K., & Felthous, A. R. (2009). The Development of Decision-Making Capacities in Children and Adolescents: Psychological and Neurological Perspectives and Their Implications for Juvenile Defendants. *Behavioral Sciences and the Law, 27*(2), 173–190. https://doi.org/10.1002/bsl.859
Kezelman, C., Hossack, N., Stavropoulos, P., & Burley, P. (2015). *The Cost of Unresolved Childhood Trauma and Abuse in Adults in Australia.* Adults Surviving Child Abuse and Pegasus Economics.
Kim, S., Fonagy, P., Allen, J., & Strathearn, L. (2014). Mothers' Unresolved Trauma Blunts Amygdala Response to Infant Distress. *Social Neuroscience, 9*(4), 352–363. https://doi.org/10.1080/17470919.2014.896287
Kukulies-Smith, W. A. (2018). *Punishing Parents: A Study of Family Hardship in Australian Sentencing* [PhD Thesis, Australian National University]. Canberra.
Leach, R. M., Burgess, T., & Holmwood, C. (2008). Could Recidivism in Prisoners Be Linked to Traumatic Grief? A Review of the Evidence. *International*

Journal of Prisoner Health, 4(2), 104–119. https://doi.org/10.1080/17449200802038249

Legal Services Society (LSS). (2022). *Gladue Report Guide: How to Prepare and Write a Gladue Report* (2nd ed.), Legal Aid BC.

Malvaso, C. G., Cale, J., Whitten, T., Day, A., Singh, S., Hackett, L., Delfabbro, P. H., & Ross, S. (2022). Associations Between Adverse Childhood Experiences and Trauma Among Young People Who Offend: A Systematic Literature Review. *Trauma, Violence, & Abuse, 23*(5), 1677–1694. https://doi.org/10.1177/15248380211013132

Malvaso, C., Day, A., Casey, S., & Corrado, R. (2017a). Young Offenders, Maltreatment, and Trauma: A Pilot Study. *Psychiatry, Psychology and Law, 24*(3), 458–469. https://doi.org/10.1080/13218719.2016.1247682

Malvaso, C. G., Delfabbro, P. H., & Day, A. (2017b). The Child Protection and Juvenile Justice Nexus in Australia: A Longitudinal Examination of the Relationship Between Maltreatment and Offending. *Child Abuse & Neglect, 64*, 32–46. https://doi.org/10.1016/j.chiabu.2016.11.028

Malvaso, C. G., Delfabbro, P. H., & Day, A. (2017c). Child Maltreatment and Criminal Convictions in Youth: The Role of Gender, Ethnicity and Placement Experiences in an Australian Population. *Children and Youth Services Review, 73*, 57–65. https://doi.org/10.1016/j.childyouth.2016.12.001

Malvaso, C. G., Delfabbro, P., & Day, A. (2018). The Maltreatment-Offending Association: A Systematic Review of the Methodological Features of Prospective and Longitudinal Studies. *Trauma, Violence & Abuse, 19*(1), 20–34. https://doi.org/10.1177/1524838015620820

Malvaso, C. G., Delfabbro, P. H., Day, A., & Nobes, G. (2019). Young People Under Youth Justice Supervision with Varying Child Protection Histories: An Analysis of Group Differences. *International Journal of Offender Therapy and Comparative Criminology, 63*(2), 159–178. https://doi.org/10.1177/0306624X18791735

Malvaso, C., Harris, D., McGee, T. R., & Craig, J. (2023). The Implications of Adverse Childhood Experiences (ACEs) Research in the Treatment and Prevention of Offending Behaviour Hype or Hope? In C. Malvaso, T. R. McGee & R. Homel (Eds.), *Frontiers in Developmental and Life-Course Criminology: Methodological Innovation and Social Benefit* (pp. 102–114). Routledge. https://doi.org/10.4324/9781003294740-10

Marien, M. (2012). Cross-Over Kids': Childhood and Adolescent Abuse and Neglect and Juvenile Offending. *Judicial Review, 11*(1), 97–126.

Mathews, B., Papalia, N., Napier, S., Malacova, E., Lawrence, D., Higgins, D. J., Thomas, H., Erskine, H., Meinck, F., Haslam, D., Scott, J., Finkelhor,

D., & Pacella, R. (2023). Child Maltreatment and Criminal Justice System Involvement in Australia: Findings from a National Survey. *Trends & Issues in Crime and Criminal Justice, 681*, 1–21. https://doi.org/10.52922/ti77215

McLean, S. (2016). *The Effect of Trauma on the Brain Development of Children: Evidence-Based Principles for Supporting the Recovery of Children in Care*. Australian Institute of Family Studies.

Menzies, K. (2019). Forcible Separation and Assimilation as Trauma: The Historical and Socio-Political Experiences of Australian Aboriginal People. *Social Work and Society, 17*(1), 1–10.

Menzies, K. (2020). A New Paradigm: Bringing a Historical and Sociopolitical Trauma Lens to the Training for Welfare Practitioners Working with Aboriginal Families. *Children and Society*. https://doi.org/10.1111/chso.12375

Milroy, H. (2015). Preface. In S. R. Zubrick, D. M. Lawrence, S. R. Silburn et al. (Eds.), *The Western Australian Aboriginal Child Health Survey: The Social and Emotional Wellbeing of Aboriginal Children and Young People* (Vol. 2, pp. xi–xxi). Curtin University of Technology and Telethon Institute for Child Health Research.

Minh, A., Matheson, F., Daoud, N., Hamilton-Wright, S., Pedersen, C., Borenstein, H., & O'Campo, P. (2013). Linking Childhood and Adult Criminality: Using a Life Course Framework to Examine Childhood Abuse and Neglect, Substance Use and Adult Partner Violence. *International Journal of Environmental Research and Public Health, 10*(11), 5470–5489. https://doi.org/10.3390/ijerph10115470

Murray, J., Farrington, D. P., & Sekol, I. (2012). Children's Antisocial Behavior, Mental Health, Drug Use, and Educational Performance After Parental Incarceration: A Systematic Review and Meta-Analysis. *Psychological Bulletin, 138*(2), 175–210. https://doi.org/10.1037/a0026407

Ogloff, J. R., Cutajar, M. C., Mann, E., & Mullen, P. (2012). Child Sexual Abuse and Subsequent Offending and Victimisation: A 45 Year Follow-Up Study. *Trends & Issues in Crime and Criminal Justice, 440*, 1–6.

Paquola, C., Bennett, M. R., & Lagopoulos, J. (2016). Understanding Heterogeneity in Grey Matter Research of Adults with Childhood Maltreatment—A Meta-Analysis and Review. *Neuroscience & Biobehavioral Reviews, 69*, 299–312. https://doi.org/10.1016/j.neubiorev.2016.08.011

Parkerville Children and Youth Care. (2018). *Taking a Trauma Informed Approach: A Practice Framework*. Parkerville.

Parkes, D., Milward, D., Keesic, S., & Seymour, J. (2012). *Gladue Handbook a Resource for Justice System Participants in Manitoba*. University of Manitoba.

Perry, B. D. (2009). Examining Child Maltreatment Through a Neurodevelopmental Lens: Clinical Applications of the Neurosequential Model of Therapeutics. *Journal of Loss and Trauma, 14*(4), 240–255. https://doi.org/10.1080/15325020903004350

Porges, S. W. (2022). Polyvagal Theory: A Science of Safety. *Frontiers in Integrative Neuroscience, 16*(871227), 1–15. https://doi.org/10.3389/fnint.2022.871227

Quiros, L., Varghese, R., & Vanidestine, T. (2020). Disrupting the Single Story: Challenging Dominant Trauma Narratives Through a Critical Race Lens. *Traumatology, 26*(2), 160–168.

Reavis, J. A., Looman, J., Franco, K. A., & Rojas, B. (2013). Adverse Childhood Experiences and Adult Criminality: How Long Must We Live Before We Possess Our Own Lives? *The Permanente Journal, 17*(2), 44–48. https://doi.org/10.7812/TPP/12-072

Rinne-Albers, M. A., Pannekoek, J. N., van Hoof, M.-J., van Lang, N. D., Lamers-Winkelman, F., Rombouts, S. A., van der Wee, N. J., & Vermeiren, R. R. (2017). Anterior Cingulate Cortex Grey Matter Volume Abnormalities in Adolescents with PTSD After Childhood Sexual Abuse. *European Neuropsychopharmacology, 27*(11), 1163–1171. https://doi.org/10.1016/j.euroneuro.2017.08.432

Royal Commission into Aboriginal Deaths in Custody (RCIADIC). (1991). *National Report—Volume Two.* Australian Government.

Sampson, R. J., & Laub, J. H. (2003). Life-Course Desisters—Trajectories of Crime Among Delinquent Boys Followed to Age 70*. *Criminology, 41*(3), 555–592. https://doi.org/10.1111/j.1745-9125.2003.tb00997.x

Segrave, M., & Carlton, B. (2010). Women, Trauma, Criminalisation and Imprisonment... *Current Issues in Criminal Justice, 22*(2), 287–305.

Sentencing Advisory Council (SAC). (2020). *'Crossover Kids': Vulnerable Children in the Youth Justice System Report 3: Sentencing Children Who Have Experienced Trauma.* Victorian Government.

Stats NZ. (2023, November 16). *Māori Population Estimates: At 30 June 2023.* New Zealand Government.

Stewart, A., Dennison, S., & Waterson, E. (2002). Pathways from Child Maltreatment to Juvenile Offending. *Trends & Issues in Crime and Criminal Justice, 241*, 1–6.

Stiles, J., & Jernigan, T. L. (2010). The Basics of Brain Development. *Neuropsychology Review, 20*, 327–348. https://doi.org/10.1007/s11065-010-9148-4

Sue, D. W. (2017). Microaggressions and "Evidence": Empirical or Experiential Reality? *Perspectives on Psychological Science, 12*(1), 170–172. https://doi.org/10.1177/1745691616664437

van der Kolk, B. A. (1987). The Psychological Consequences of Overwhelming Life Experiences. In B. A. van der Kolk (Ed.), *Psychological Trauma* (pp. 1–30). American Psychiatric Press.

van der Kolk, B. A. (2005). Developmental Trauma Disorder: Towards a Rational Diagnosis for Children with Complex Trauma Histories. *Psychiatric Annals, 35*(5), 401–408.

Walsh, T. (2019). From Child Protection to Youth Justice: Legal Responses to the Plight of 'Crossover Kids.' *University of Western Australia Law Review, 46*(1), 90.

Willmot, P. (2022) Childhood Maltreatment and Its Links to Offending. In P. Willmot & L. Jones (Eds.), *Trauma-Informed Forensic Practice* (pp. 15–31). Routledge. https://doi.org/10.4324/9781003120766-3

Wolff, N., & Shi, J. (2012). Childhood and Adult Trauma Experiences of Incarcerated Persons and Their Relationship to Adult Behavioral Health Problems and Treatment. *International Journal of Environmental Research and Public Health, 9*(5), 1908–1926. https://doi.org/10.3390/ijerph9051908

Legislation

Children and Young Persons (Care and Protection) Act 1998 (NSW).

Part II

Part II: Trauma-Informed Responses in the Criminal Justice System

5

Trauma-Informed Criminal Justice Responses: Being "Sweet, Nice and Kind"?

5.1 Introduction

In 2014, I first heard the term "trauma-informed". However, the professionals who used it could not explain what they meant, alluding to the idea that it was simultaneously obvious and indeterminate. Having spoken to many victims of crime and people who have offended, I have reflected on the potential usefulness of "trauma-informed" criminal justice responses. This chapter includes examples of criminal justice practices labelled as "trauma-informed", which are, in some cases, either practices that reflect requisite, base-level practice or simply being "sweet, nice and kind" to victims of crime. Trauma-informed criminal justice must be more than just goodwill or being "sweet, nice and kind". It requires the application of a clear practice framework. The Substance Abuse and Mental Health Services Administration (SAMHSA, 2014) offers such a framework, such that justice agencies should ensure that workers realise and recognise the relevance and prevalence of trauma and respond in a way that promotes safety, trust, and empowerment of all people who encounter their service and resists re-traumatisation. The

K. J. McLachlan, *Trauma-informed Criminal Justice*,
https://doi.org/10.1007/978-3-031-59290-4_5

purpose of the justice system is to promote community safety. Trauma-informed criminal justice offers a new way of thinking about how to better achieve this.

5.2 Trauma-Informed Practice

Trauma-informed practice requires that service providers understand and recognise adversity and its traumatic impacts, respond in an evidence-informed way that focuses on the individual and prevent further trauma. The concept of "trauma-informed" emerged in 2001 in the work of Maxine Harris and Roger Fallot (2001). Trauma-informed practice is not designed to treat trauma (which is the purpose of "trauma-focused" or "trauma-specific" practice). Rather, trauma-informed practice requires that service providers at all organisational levels understand the potentially traumatic effects of adversity on an individual's ability to function and interact with the world and promote service environments conducive to recovery and avoid further traumatisation (Kezelman & Stavropoulos, 2016).

Trauma-informed practice is core to the victims' rights movement, which emerged in the 1970s and 1980s. Its growth was driven by the increased awareness of post-traumatic issues faced by Vietnam War veterans and in support of women escaping domestic abuse (Herman, 2015). The term "trauma-informed" emerged simultaneously with the recognition of the broad and devastating impact of adverse childhood experiences (ACEs) on health and wellbeing (Felitti et al., 1998). Since then, trauma-informed practice has been refined, particularly by mental health and substance abuse professionals. In the last five years, there has been a substantial increase in 'trauma-informed' publications across various disciplines. Trauma-informed practice is expanding across health and therapeutic services, including forensic practice (Willmot & Jones, 2022), education, disability, and community services. In criminal justice, trauma-informed correctional care (TICC) is being applied in mainstream prisons, particularly with women and children, and trauma-informed lawyering and judicial practice are emerging (Gohara, 2018; Maki et al., 2023; Martin et al., 2019).

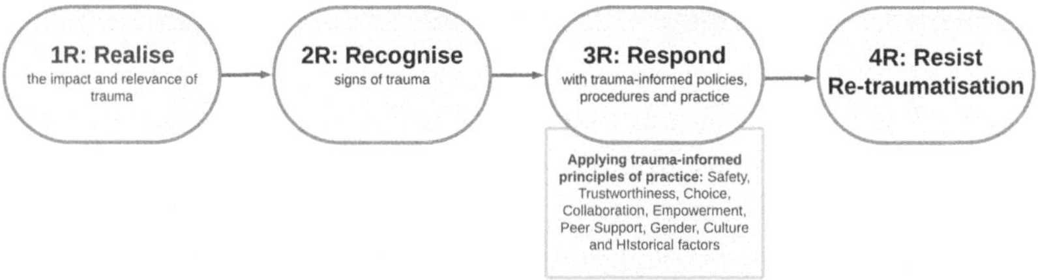

Fig. 5.1 The 4Rs trauma-informed practice framework (SAMHSA, 2014)

5.2.1 SAMHSA's (2014) 4Rs of Trauma-Informed Practice

To be trauma-informed, a service or sector must "recognize, understand and minimize" the long-term impact of trauma (Kubiak et al., 2017, p. 92). This approach has been articulated as four steps ("the 4Rs") by SAMHSA (2014), as per Fig. 5.1. Specifically, a service must:

- **1R: Realise** what trauma is and the potential impacts of adversity,
- **2R: Recognise** trauma symptoms experienced by the individual accessing the service,
- **3R: Respond** appropriately to the individual's unique trauma, and
- **4R: Resist re-traumatisation** by avoiding insensitive or inappropriate responses when providing services (SAMHSA, 2014).

It is relatively easy to see how the 4Rs could be applied by drug and alcohol services, which take a harm-reduction approach or a domestic abuse support service driven by feminist ideology. However, it is more challenging to reconcile trauma-informed practice principles in the criminal justice system when incarcerating an individual.

5.2.2 3R: Trauma-Informed Responses

The key to trauma-informed responses (the 3R in SAMHSA's 4Rs) is that they should be universal. Work from the US (e.g., Fallot & Harris, 2011; SAMHSA, 2014), UK (e.g., Covington, 2016), and Australia (e.g.,

Kezelman & Stavropoulos, 2012) has established common principles that underpin trauma-informed responses (although the actual number may vary from five to eight principles). Blue Knot, a not-for-profit organisation in Australia that supports adult survivors of child sexual abuse, refers to "five foundational principles" of trauma-informed care: safety, trustworthiness, choice, collaboration, and empowerment (Kezelman & Stavropoulos, 2012, p. 12).

- **Safety** aims to provide effective and consistent physical and emotional safety to service users when they access services; ensure service users feel welcome, included, and heard by the service provider; and educate users and workers regarding client rights, feedback processes, and protective policies and practices.
- **Trustworthiness** refers to establishing mutually understood, clear, consistent expectations and boundaries, enabling trust between the service provider and the service user.
- **Choice** involves providing service users with control regarding their service preferences through information, options, and an awareness of users' rights and responsibilities.
- **Collaboration** requires that service users can participate in the planning and shared decision-making around activities and settings related to service provision.
- **Empowerment** aims to promote the skills development of service users through a strengths-based approach. Empowerment recognises the importance of individual characteristics, such as culture, history, and gender, when designing an effective service to promote change and recovery (Covington, 2016; Fallot & Harris, 2011; Kezelman & Stavropoulos, 2012; McLachlan, 2022).

The SAMHSA (2014) model also prioritises **peer support** and **historical, cultural, and gender issues** as separate principles rather than embedding them in the five principles above (as shown in Chapter 7). Chapters 4 and 10 talk a lot about "culture", in the context of First Nations peoples and communities. However, culture (like trauma) has no single definition. ***Culture*** "encompasses many shared and intersecting experiences and identities, such as traditions, dress, rituals, norms, and daily behaviours" (Workman et al., 2023, p. 4). Chapter 7 discusses organisational cultures, such as police culture, in the context of secondary traumatisation.

5.3 Trauma-Informed Criminal Justice

Despite SAMHSA's (2014) 4Rs model of trauma-informed practice, there is currently no agreed approach to operationalise trauma-informed practice and care within criminal justice agencies. The phrase "trauma-informed" has been overused without clarification and often refers to practices that are merely well-intentioned. There is no accreditation process required for organisations to claim trauma-informed status. While there are isolated examples of agencies and individuals striving to become more trauma-informed, most examples are piecemeal (as shown later in this chapter), aiming to achieve greater realisation (1R) and recognition (2R) of trauma but rarely applying a structured practice response (3R) or actively resisting re-traumatisation (4R).

5.3.1 Compassionate Justice

"Trauma-informed criminal justice" has no accepted meaning. In the context of criminal justice (specifically corrections), it has been defined as:

> ... a harm reduction approach where we recognise the harms that can occur to people in the system, either because of past or present experiences, and work to reduce the likelihood that our current practice adds to that harm... Being trauma informed in the criminal justice system is different to being trauma informed in other sectors; instead of being sympathetic or empathic, there is a need to be compassionate. (Senker et al., 2023, p. 7)

As discussed in Chapter 1, ***compassionate justice*** aims to understand and better respond to the commission and impact of crime through a lens of empathy and humanity. Compassionate criminal justice focuses on the broader community, including but not limited to victims of crime. Jo-Anne Wemmers (2012) emphasises that often, the criminal justice system overlooks the human rights—and indeed the humanity—of victims of crime. The same is true for victims (and others) who offend. Anthony Hopkins et al. (2022) focus on humanising the people who offend "to understand the individual and systemic causes of their criminality…" (p. 2). Thus, a compassionate approach includes a focus on addressing the drivers of crime for individuals who offend, aiming to improve community safety.

5.3.2 Universal Organisational Responses

True trauma-informed responses (3R in the SAMHSA model) offer compassion to victims of crime, people who offend, and the criminal justice workforce. If we consider the relevance of the 4R SAMHSA (2014) framework, realising and recognising the relevance and significance of trauma in the justice system helps workers understand why some people may present and act the way they do. While this is vitally important to contextualising people's behaviour, implementing policies and practices that reflect trauma-informed responses and aim to resist re-traumatisation can and should exist independently (or additionally) as organisational and sector priorities. Trauma-informed approaches are not just about individuals and their actions; they also relate to the environment or organisational context (Senker et al., 2023).

The NHS Education for Scotland (NES, 2023) and SAMHSA (2014) both acknowledge that trauma-informed practice should be entry-level and universal, with certain workers in advocacy and support positions, evidence gathering, presentation, and interpretation roles or who are managers required to have knowledge and skills at a more advanced level. In addition to people in client-focused or leadership roles, trauma-informed practice requires that all workers know and apply trauma-informed ways of working with all clients. Additionally, there is increasing recognition of secondary trauma: the impact of working in criminal justice on the social and emotional wellbeing of police officers, correctional staff, lawyers, and the judiciary (as per Chapter 7).

Trauma-informed practice has also been shown to promote safety and job satisfaction for workers in the criminal justice system.

Building on the 4Rs trauma-informed framework (SAMHSA, 2014), trauma-informed organisational practice requires:

- a commitment to a trauma-informed approach,
- staff training,
- proactive use of trauma-informed language and communication,
- safe physical environments and procedures that minimise trauma triggers,
- a culture of continuous improvement,
- the promotion of trauma-focused practice to enhance recovery, and
- the establishment of a trauma-informed community of both staff and service users (Benedict, 2014; Kubiak et al., 2017).

Further, organisations and professionals must also acknowledge that the criminal justice system can be trauma-inducing for staff, victims of crime and people who have offended (Senker et al., 2023).

5.3.3 Being "Sweet, Nice and Kind"?

Often, international examples of trauma-informed criminal justice are based on being "sweet, nice and kind" (Treisman, 2022). Being "sweet, nice and kind" in an inherently traumatic system may mean that for people who have been hurt and betrayed by people they love, the criminal justice system is "systemically… doing the same thing… doing something that's harmful but… putting the smile on it [resulting in further] confusion and then the shame and the blame and all the stuff that people take on" (Davis in Treisman, 2022, 8.55–9.06 mins). Trauma-informed criminal justice also tends to be equated with ethical practice by organisations who self-congratulate for offering a baseline of professional or corporate responses that uphold fundamental human rights, reflect legislated victims' rights, or are behaviours consistent with professional codes of conduct.

In fact, trauma-informed practice should strive to enact the trauma-informed principles of practice (i.e., safety, trust, choice, collaboration and peer support, empowerment, and acknowledging gender, culture, and historical issues) in professional practice rather than simply being "sweet, nice and kind". For some people, such as people working in the reception area of a service, being nice to everyone they encounter may be appropriate. However, this is not true for all criminal justice professionals. Karen Treisman and Mandy Davis challenge the idea that trauma-informed practice is just being "sweet, nice and kind" (Treisman, 2022), stating:

> [W]hen we talk about "trauma-informed", the clue is in the word "trauma". We are using the theories, the models, the concepts, the ideas of dissociation, of dysregulation, of brain development, of neurobiology, of sensory integration and processing. We're using that evidence base and theoretical background to apply that lens to the work that we do... When we use the words "sweet, nice, kind", it kind of dilutes it and takes away from the knowledge base and the values. (1.35–2.19 mins)

For criminal justice agencies and workers, to be trauma-informed requires consideration of how to promote safety in their workplace as well as humanise people who offend and victims of crime.

> When I first arrived in prison I was afraid of everyone, especially those who seemed too kind. How could I fear kindness? I knew from TV shows, fake news and articles that in prison kindness comes at a cost. I feared what I would have to do to repay that kindness. (Birungi, 2020, p. 26).

5.4 Agency-Specific Self-Identified "Trauma-Informed" Responses

The criminal justice system is not a system but a group of allied agencies with a common goal to reduce future crime and promote community safety. Later, in Chapter 6, responses to victims of crime will be expressly considered, and in Chapter 9, the degree to which sentencing is trauma-informed is examined using a case study example. This chapter specifically focuses on current practices in the criminal justice system that are self-described as "trauma-informed".

Much of the work related to trauma-informed criminal justice is highly influenced by the idea of individualised criminal responsibility (rational choice theory) and the myths of the "ideal victim" and "ideal offender" (Christie, 1986). The justice system and potentially the public tend to support trauma-informed approaches for people who "deserve" to receive them (see Jewkes et al., 2019, p. 10). A survey of Scottish police officers found:

> ... a perception that the appropriateness of trauma-informed practices was partly dependent on what level of responsibility an individual could take for their own actions. Thus, although participants asserted that they were aware of the link between childhood adversity and later behaviour, the issue of personal responsibility was more dominant than the link between ACEs and impulsivity, poor decision making or limited life choices. (Gillespie-Smith et al., 2020, p. 21)

Agencies often equate trauma-informed practice with victim-focused practice or compassionate practice with vulnerable people who have offended, particularly women and children (e.g., Ministry of Justice, 2018).

5.4.1 Trauma-Informed Police

"Trauma-informed policing" is emerging in the UK (e.g., Gillespie-Smith et al., 2020; Youansamouth et al., 2020), Europe (e.g., Warth et al., 2022), Canada, and the US (e.g., Lathan et al., 2019). Most examples of trauma-informed policing focus on raising police officers' awareness (i.e., realising and recognising the relevance of trauma), specifically, the traumatic impact of crime for victims, the link between trauma and crime perpetration, and the secondary trauma experienced by some police officers. For example, policing services often offer different services for victims of sexual violence or domestic abuse, recognising that a police response informed by the likely trauma experienced by victims will be necessary to pursue a successful arrest and prosecution.

Trauma-informed police practices lack a universal model. Trauma-informed responses tend to apply to a specific population (e.g., victims of crime), for certain crimes (e.g., sexual assault), for some people who offend (e.g., children and women; Bateson et al., 2020; Blue et al., 2016; Gillespie-Smith et al., 2020). For example, in 2018, the Ayrshire Division of Police Scotland announced its aim to become trauma-informed, specifically focusing on enhancing officers' skills when responding to the increase in welfare-related policing jobs (Gillespie-Smith et al., 2020). However, Bateson et al. (2020) emphasise that police responses must be more than just based on the recognition that many people who encounter the justice system have been exposed to adverse events in childhood. Responding to trauma, in terms of the mechanisms and practices to achieve trauma-informed policing, remains a combination of individually driven compassionate practice and top-down training and directives.

There are international examples of top-down police commitment to trauma-informed practice. For example, the Lancashire Violence Reduction Network in the UK has developed an evaluation toolkit to assist organisations in becoming trauma-informed using a staged approach (Youansamouth et al., 2020). Tasmania Police in Australia is fostering a culture of wellbeing that supports and responds to "each other and the communities they serve" (Adams, 2024). They have created audiovisual resources featuring commissioned officers discussing their lived experiences of secondary trauma to help normalise the adverse impact of policing on police officers (Adams, 2024). Other emerging examples of trauma-informed support for police officers include BlueHub, established by the Police Association of Victoria (TPAV) in association with

Phoenix Australia, to provide timely, confidential mental health support and treatment to serving police officers (BlueHub, 2021).

Trauma-informed police responses often aim to promote procedural justice for victims of crime. Research consistently shows that victims of crime prioritise procedural justice over outcome justice (McLachlan, 2021b). ***Procedural justice*** occurs when people are treated with compassion by workers, where their humanity is recognised, and their rights (e.g., to be informed and consulted) are upheld (Samuels, 2020). Similarly, this is indicative of a trauma-informed response. The same compassion should be afforded to people who offend, who themselves are often also victims of crime. A trauma-informed response—characterised as procedural justice—can occur without an outcome that a person might perceive as just (such as being arrested). As highlighted by Treisman (2022), police are:

> ... going to have to arrest people at times. That's not being sweet and nice, arresting someone. But how you arrest someone, how you link someone's feelings, the language that you use, the body language that you do, the information you give to people, the understanding and treating people in a human way, that is the part that is [trauma-informed]. So much more than just being sweet, nice, and kind. (7.45–8.12 mins)

There are few specific examples of trauma-informed police responses that reflect trauma-informed practice principles for people who have been criminalised. One example from Norway focuses on situations where police arrest and deport children who lack legal residency (Warth et al., 2022). The authors highlighted that police are guided by principles of safety, understanding, and predictability (i.e., trust), and involvement (which broadly reflect the trauma-informed principles of collaboration, choice, and empowerment). Arguably, the process of being deported is inherently traumatic. The strategy aims to reduce re-traumatisation and promote procedural justice rather than empower the children or offer any sense of choice in the outcome. Nevertheless, this is a true example of a police service aspiring to offer trauma-informed responses for a specific cohort in a system that is most often trauma-inducing.

5.4.2 Trauma-Informed Courts

There has been international literature emphasising the importance not just of trauma-focused judicial education to enhance the realisation of trauma and recognition of its relevance but also judicial responses in problem-solving and mainstream courts to promote trauma-informed principles of practice (McKenna & Holtfreter, 2021; Murphy & Lumley, 2022). Trauma-informed responses exist in problem-solving courts and courts that focus on applying therapeutic jurisprudence principles (McKenna & Holtfreter, 2021; McLachlan, 2021a). Therapeutic jurisprudence aims to enhance mental health and emotional wellbeing through legal processes and outcomes (McLachlan, 2021a; Wexler, 2000). Community Courts in the US (e.g., Red Hook Court in New York), Canada (e.g., Vancouver's Downtown Community Court), the UK, and Australia (e.g., Neighbourhood Justice Centre, Melbourne) are examples of problem-solving courts. Although there is no single model for community courts (Ross, 2015), these courts often combine a focus on the safety and engagement of the local community, the targeting of an individual's support needs, and judicial oversight (Samuels, 2020). While evaluations are complex and mixed, these models have been found to be cost-effective examples of justice reinvestment—costing more upfront but reducing victimisation costs in the longer term due to reduced recidivism (Halsey & de Vel-Palumbo, 2018).

Chapter 6 outlines court practices that aim to provide trauma-informed services to victims of crime. Chapters 8 and 9 focus on trauma-informed sentencing, which, in practice, is the application of the trauma-informed principles of practice to the court process and imposing a sanction that considers the role trauma may play in the offending trajectory and seeks to resist re-traumatisation. Trauma-informed mainstream courts are not yet commonplace.

5.4.3 Trauma-Informed Correctional Services

The purpose of correctional service agencies is "to improve outcomes for the community through determined efforts to reduce offender recidivism and provide for successful reintegration back into the community" (DCS, 2023, p. 6). Programs designed to reduce re-offending may include treatment, rehabilitation, behaviour management, or support services and often focus on reducing the risk of violence, sexual offending, general offending, and drug and alcohol misuse (Heseltine et al., 2011). While trauma might be implicated as influencing the onset of criminality and as a cause of specific criminogenic needs (as per Chapter 3), it does not follow that it is also a criminogenic need that should be the focus of rehabilitation (Casey et al., 2013). Thus, trauma may help understand why the person committed offences and may inform (but not need to be the target of) intervention strategies designed to reduce the risk of future offending. For example, developmental trauma may result in self-medication in the early teenage years with illicit substances. However, antisocial peer associations and pro-criminal attitudes may be the maintenance factors in criminality and a much more relevant focus of evidence-informed sentencing sanctions.

5.4.3.1 Trauma-Informed Correctional Care

A key function of correctional service agencies is managing prisons. Punishment and incapacitation through imprisonment are common elements of justice systems internationally. As stated in Chapter 1, despite calls for decarceration and the abolition of prisons, we are far from this becoming a reality. However, this is no excuse for prisons to be excessively punitive beyond the deprivation of liberty. Prisons should not result in a loss of human rights and dignity. Nick Moss (2020) argues that a "kind prison" would seek to address the harms caused by incarceration (and society more broadly) by equipping people on release with the internal and external resources to lead a "good life". Currently, people can be released from prison in Australia and the UK without foundational supports such as stable accommodation. At best, prisons may offer a break from domestic abuse, an opportunity to detoxify from substances, and self-reflect (Crewe & Ievins, 2020). However, "…there are more effective ways of rehabilitating people, which do not require incarceration, with all of its attendant injuries, and are not precipitated by an initial trauma" (Crewe & Ievins, 2020, p. 16).

Nevertheless, trauma-informed responses can exist within prison walls. TICC promotes compassionate practices and therapeutic environments to achieve higher levels of safety for clients and corrections staff (Benedict, 2014). TICC can facilitate trauma-focused interventions to treat the manifestations of trauma, but this is not its fundamental purpose. For:

> [t]he over-arching goal of [TICC] is to incorporate knowledge about the neurobiological, social, and psychological effects of trauma into policies, procedures, and practices that guide a safe, compassionate, respectful service delivery environment. (Levenson & Wallis, 2019, p. 482)

TICC has emerged as a therapeutic approach in prisons and the community, a behaviour management strategy, and a safety strategy for correctional staff and clients (Jones, 2018; Miller & Najavits, 2012). At a minimum, TICC requires that employees recognise that engagement with correctional services need not be fundamentally traumatic. TICC requires that staff apply trauma-informed principles of practice to their daily work. Programs and interventions delivered by or on behalf of Corrections are designed explicitly to be trauma-informed, particularly for women (e.g., Benedict, 2014; Miller & Najavits, 2012) and children who have offended (Webb, 2016) with "male correctional populations… among the last frontier for [trauma-informed care] implementation" (Levenson & Willis, 2019, p. 482).

Many principles for developing a trauma-informed organisation are embedded in, or at least enabled by, the *Guiding Principles for Corrections in Australia* (Government of Australia, 2018). The Guiding Principles endorse continuous improvement, staff education, respectful searches (Principle 2.3.12.), and emphasise "[i]ndividual prisoners/offenders are managed and supervised in a manner that responds to their particular risk and needs, including the impacts of victimisation and trauma" (Principle 2.1.3.). While there is a clear top-down commitment to values that reflect TICC in Australia, it is unlikely that sufficient steps have been taken to ensure the implementation of trauma-informed responses across and within all correctional services in Australia or, indeed, more broadly. This is supported by a recent systematic review undertaken by a US scholar, which identified the limited effectiveness of staff training in promoting trauma-informed practice and generating positive, tangible client outcomes (Purtle, 2020).

One example of TICC is HMP Grendon in the UK. HMP Grendon is a high-security (Category B) prison that functions as a democratic ***therapeutic community*** (TC). HMP Grendon has up to six TCs with 40 residents, such that:

> [e]ach therapeutic community had a constitution, which sets out expected behaviour and outlines the consequences for transgression. Most inappropriate behaviour and disputes were dealt with by referring those involved to a group meeting. Repeated or more serious breaches of the constitution may lead to a commitment vote by other prisoners that determines whether the individual can remain a part of the therapeutic community. Acts of violence invariably led to a transfer out of the prison. (Taylor, 2021, p. 10, para 2.5)

This model demonstrates that empowering people in prison and offering trust and choice results in a safer space for both residents and workers, with low levels of violence and self-harm (Taylor, 2021) and the potential for greater behaviour change (Jones, 2015) and a reduction in recidivism (Beaudry et al., 2021).

5.4.4 Trauma-Informed Youth Justice

The implementation of trauma-informed criminal justice practices and care is more highly prioritised in youth justice than adult justice systems, given that most children who are justice-involved have extensive histories of adversity and youth justice systems are based on a strong philosophy of diversion and early intervention (Branson et al., 2017; Day et al., 2023; Malvaso et al., 2022). Courts also recognise and work to resist re-traumatisation by diverting children and young people away from formal justice processes and custodial sanctions (Bouhours & Daly, 2007). Youth and Children's Courts often impose sanctions that promote treatment and other evidence-informed interventions, hoping that young people will desist from crime (Skuse & Matthew, 2015). In other situations, young people are diverted from the system before reaching the courts. However, there continue to be examples of highly traumatic practices in youth justice facilities, including strip searches, physical restraints, and removal from family and community supports, all breaches of children's foundational human rights (Branson et al., 2017; Day et al., 2023).

Christopher Branson et al. (2017) systematically reviewed the core components of a trauma-informed youth justice system. They highlighted 10 domains relating to screening and assessment for adversity and trauma, trauma-informed and trauma-focused interventions, services responsive to people from diverse cultures, sexualities, and genders, collaborative family supports, organisation and systemic commitment to trauma-informed ways of working, a focus on diversion from the justice system, and workforce development. When working with children, the youth justice system has focused on the latter, particularly "staff training, reducing coercive practices, improving physical environments and providing access to sensory and other interventions" (Day et al., 2023, p. 109).

The biggest barrier to trauma-informed youth justice is the age of criminal responsibility, which is as low as 10 years in many Australian jurisdictions, Aotearoa New Zealand, England, Wales, and Northern Ireland, and 12 in Scotland and Canada. In 32 US states there is no minimum age of criminal responsibility, and where specified, the age of criminal responsibility ranges from 6 to 12 years (JJGPPS, 2024). In Australia and Aotearoa New Zealand, a common law principle (doli incapax) exists such that children under 14 lack the cognitive capacity to understand the criminal nature of their behaviour and thus be held criminally responsible. The prosecution must show beyond reasonable doubt that a child under 14 has actual knowledge that their behaviour is wrong or the capacity to know that their behaviour is wrong (depending on the jurisdiction). For children to have the capacity to know their behaviour is wrong, they need to have the neurological, psychological, and emotional maturity to form the knowledge and understanding of the criminal nature of their behaviour (McLachlan, 2023). Developmental age should not necessarily be equated with chronological age, particularly for children whose neuropsychological and emotional development has been negatively impacted by developmental trauma, such that there is a gap between chronological age and developmental age.

5.5 Achieving the Purpose of the Criminal Justice System Through Trauma-Informed Practices

As noted by Sarah Senker et al. (2023), "[t]rauma-informed practices can only be implemented with appropriate training but also within an environment that is supportive of the care and compassion that is required to deliver and sustain the therapeutic nature of the practice" (p. 12). Research undertaken with Police Scotland members highlighted that while officers recognised that trauma-informed policing is more compassionate than a traditional policing approach, they did not recognise that it could also help to address the underlying causes of crime. Instead, they:

> felt that there was an inherent conflict in public attitudes towards the police becoming more trauma-informed, with the public often still prioritising individuals who offend being dealt with in a way that they consider appropriate in order to protect their safety. (Gillespie-Smith et al., 2020, p. 23)

This is problematic because it supports the myths that "tough on crime" approaches are the most effective (they're not) and that the general public is fundamentally punitive (it's not; Day et al., 2021). Further education of both practitioners and the broader community is required to highlight that current criminal justice system responses are not particularly effective in reducing re-offending and that protecting community safety may be better achieved through cohesive trauma-informed criminal justice strategies and multiagency approaches.

Factors that decrease the risk of offending include connection to family and community and engagement in education and employment. Desistance from crime is often achieved through individuals developing (and finding pride in) a new self-identity. None of this can be easily achieved through current justice responses. Incarceration is an expensive, overused and criminogenic option. Focusing on specific deterrence through punishment will not address social risk factors such as poverty, social exclusion, and a lack of meaningful life opportunities. However, by humanising people who offend and applying trauma-informed practice principles, it may be possible to assist in reducing future crime. This chapter includes examples of justice practices labelled as "trauma-informed", which are, in some cases, either practices that reflect requisite, base-level practice or simply being "sweet, nice and kind" to victims of crime.

5.6 Conclusion

The examples of current "trauma-informed" practice across the criminal justice system show that agencies tend to focus on improving the realisation and recognition of trauma. Little work has been done on how to offer universal, trauma-informed responses characterised by trauma-informed principles of practice across justice agencies. Trauma-informed policing is in its infancy and is not very ambitious, focusing on practices that uphold victims' rights. Youth justice and correctional services have designed trauma-informed approaches for detained populations, such as children and women in prisons. However, holistic approaches remain theoretical at best. Trauma-informed judicial practices build on therapeutic jurisprudence models, which have been present in the US and Australia for many years. The idea of a wholly trauma-informed criminal justice system remains unlikely for some time yet.

Key Points

- Trauma-informed practice and care in the criminal justice system is in its infancy.
- Trauma-informed policing tends to focus on victim services, particularly for sexual violence offences.
- Existing trauma-informed correctional care focuses on women in custody and children in detention, but not men in custody.
- Many of the practices claimed to be trauma-informed are, in fact, just professional and appropriate practices.
- Universal trauma-informed criminal justice for everyone does not yet exist.

References

Adams, D. (2024, February 12). *The Leadership Role of Police Commissioners in Creating Trauma-Informed Organisations.* [Conference Presentation] 2024 Trauma Informed Policing and Law Enforcement Conference, Melbourne.

Bateson, K., McManus, M., & Johnson, G. (2020). Understanding the Use, and Misuse, of Adverse Childhood Experiences (ACEs) in Trauma-Informed Policing. *The Police Journal: Theory, Practice and Principles, 93*(2), 131–145. https://doi.org/10.1177/0032258X19841409

Beaudry, G., Yu, R., Perry, A. E., & Fazel, S. (2021). Effectiveness of Psychological Interventions in Prison to Reduce Recidivism: A Systematic Review and Meta-Analysis of Randomised Controlled Trials. *Lancet Psychiatry, 8*, 759–773.

Benedict, A. (2014). *Using Trauma-Informed Practices to Enhance Safety and Security in Women's Correctional Facilities.* National Resource Center on Justice Involved Women.

Birungi, B. (2020). Kindness, Hope and Compassion: A Matter of Life and Death for Those in Prison. In L. Rowles & I. Haji (Eds.), *Humane Justice: What Role Do Kindness, Hope and Compassion Play in the Criminal Justice System?* (pp. 26–28). The Monument Fellowship.

Blue, K., Donovan, A., Fleck-Henderson, A., Fulambarker, A., Neyland, K., Speakman, E., Warnick, J., & Weiner, A. (2016). *Guide for a Trauma-Informed Law Enforcement Initiative.* Cambridge Police Department.

BlueHub. (2021). *Helping Police Safely Move Through Trauma*. https://www.bluehub.org.au/

Bouhours, B., & Daly, K. (2007). Youth Sex Offenders in Court: An Analysis of Judicial Sentencing Remarks. *Punishment & Society, 9*(4), 371.

Branson, C. E., Baetz, C. L., Horwitz, S. M., & Hoagwood, K. E. (2017). Trauma-Informed Juvenile Justice Systems: A Systematic Review of Definitions and Core Components. *Psychological Trauma: Theory, Research, Practice, and Policy, 9*(6), 635–646. https://doi.org/10.1037/tra0000255

Casey, S., Day, A., Vess, J., & Ward, T. (2013). *Foundations of Offender Rehabilitation*. Routledge.

Christie, N. (1986). The Ideal Victim. In M. Duggan (Ed.). (2018). *Revisiting the 'Ideal Victim': Developments in Critical Victimology* (pp. 11–23). Policy Press.

Covington, S. S. (2016). *Becoming Trauma Informed: Tool Kit for Women's Community Service Providers*. Center for Gender and Justice.

Crewe, B., & Ievins, A. (2020). The Prison as a Reinventive Institution. *Theoretical Criminology, 24*(4), 568–589. https://doi.org/10.1177/1362480619841900

Day, A., Malvaso, C., Butcher, L., O'Connor, J., & McLachlan, K. (2023). Co-Producing Trauma-Informed Youth Justice in Australia? *Safer Communities, 22*(2), 106–120. https://doi.org/10.1108/SC-08-2022-0030

Day, A., Ross, S., & McLachlan, K. (2021). *The Effectiveness of Minimum Non-parole Period Schemes for Serious Violent, Sexual and Drug Offenders and Evidence-Based Approaches to Community Protection, Deterrence, and Rehabilitation*. Queensland Sentencing Advisory Council.

Department for Correctional Services (DCS). (2023). *Annual Report 2022–2023*. Government of South Australia.

Fallot, R. D., & Harris, M. (2011). *Creating Cultures of Trauma-Informed Care (CCTIC): A Self-Assessment and Planning Protocol*. Community Connections.

Felitti, V. J., Anda, R. F., Nordenberg, D., Williamson, D. F., Spitz, A. M., Edwards, V., Koss, M. P., & Marks, J. S. (1998). Relationship of Childhood Abuse and Household Dysfunction to Many of the Leading Causes of Death in Adults: The Adverse Childhood Experiences (ACE) Study. *American Journal of Preventative Medicine, 14*(4), 245–258. https://doi.org/10.1016/s0749-3797(98)00017-8

Gillespie-Smith, K., Brodie, Z. P., Collins, K., Deacon, K., & Goodall, K. (2020). *Moving Towards Trauma-Informed Policing: An Exploration of Police*

Officer's Attitudes and Perceptions Towards Adverse Childhood Experiences (ACEs). Scottish Institute for Policing Research.

Gohara, M. S. (2018). In Defense of the Injured: How Trauma-Informed Criminal Defense Can Reform Sentencing. *American Journal of Criminal Law, 45*(1), 1–53.

Government of Australia. (2018). *Guiding Principles for Corrections in Australia.* Government of Australia.

Halsey, M., & de Vel-Palumbo, M. (2018). Courts as Empathic Spaces: Reflections on the Melbourne Neighbourhood Justice Centre. *Griffith Law Review, 27*(2), 182–201. https://doi.org/10.1080/10383441.2018.1500081

Harris, M., & Fallot, R. D. (2001). Envisioning a Trauma-Informed Service System: A Vital Paradigm Shift. *New Directions for Mental Health Services, 2001*(89), 3–22. https://doi.org/10.1002/yd.23320018903

Herman, J. L. (2015). *Trauma and Recovery: The Aftermath of Violence—From Domestic Abuse to Political Terror.* Basic Books.

Heseltine, K., Sarre, R., & Day, A. (2011). *Prison-Based Correctional Offender Rehabilitation Programs: The 2009 National Picture in Australia.* Australian Institute of Criminology.

Hopkins, A., Dodd, S., Nolan, M., & Bartels, L. (2022). At the Heart of Sentencing: Exploring Whether More Compassionate Delivery of Sentencing Remarks Increases Public Concern for People Who Offend. *Psychiatry, Psychology and Law, 30*(4), 459–485. https://doi.org/10.1080/13218719.2022.2040398

Jewkes, Y., Jordan, M., Wright, S., & Bendelow, G. (2019). Designing 'Healthy' Prisons for Women: Incorporating Trauma-Informed Care and Practice (TICP) into Prison Planning and Design. *International Journal of Environmental Research and Public Health, 16*(3818), 1–15. https://doi.org/10.3390/ijerph16203818

Jones, L. (2015). The Peaks Unit: From a Pilot for "Untreatable" Psychopaths to Trauma Informed Milieu Therapy. *Prison Service Journal, 218*, 17–23.

Jones, L. (2018). Trauma-Informed Care And "Good Lives" In Confinement: Acknowledging and Offsetting Adverse Impacts of Chronic Trauma and Loss of Liberty. In G. Akerman, A. Needs, & C. Bainbridge (Eds.), *Transforming Environments and Rehabilitation: A Guide for Practitioners in Forensic Settings and Criminal Justice* (pp. 92–114). Routledge.

Juvenile Justice Geography, Policy, Practice and Statistics (JJGPPS). (2024). *Jurisdictional Boundaries.* National Center for Juvenile Justice.

Kezelman, C., & Stavropoulos, P. (2012). *"The Last Frontier": Practice Guidelines for Treatment of Complex Trauma and Trauma Informed Care and Service Delivery*. Adults Surviving Child Abuse.

Kezelman, C., & Stavropoulos, P. (2016). *Trauma and the Law: Applying Trauma-Informed Practice to Legal and Judicial Contexts*. Blue Knot Foundation.

Kubiak, S. P., Covington, S. S., & Hillier, C. (2017). Trauma-Informed Corrections. In D. Springer & A. Roberts (Eds.), *Social Work in Juvenile and Criminal Justice Systems* (4th ed., pp. 92–104). Charles C. Thomas.

Lathan, E., Duncan, J., Langhinrichsen-Rohling, J., & Stefurak, J. T. (2019). The Promise Initiative: Promoting a Trauma-Informed Police Response to Sexual Assault in a Mid-Size Southern Community. *Journal of Community Psychology, 47*, 1733–1749. https://doi.org/10.1002/jcop.22223

Levenson, J. S., & Willis, G. M. (2019). Implementing Trauma-Informed Care in Correctional Treatment and Supervision. *Journal of Aggression, Maltreatment & Trauma, 28*(4), 481–501. https://doi.org/10.1080/10926771.2018.1531959

Maki, H., Florestal, M., McCallum, M., & Wright, J. K. (Eds.). (2023). *Trauma-Informed Law: A Primer for Practicing Lawyers and a Pathway for Resilience and Healing*. American Bar Association.

Malvaso, C. G., Cale, J., Whitten, T., Day, A., Singh, S., Hackett, L., Delfabbro, P. H., & Ross, S. (2022). Associations Between Adverse Childhood Experiences and Trauma Among Young People Who Offend: A Systematic Literature Review. *Trauma, Violence & Abuse, 23*(5), 1677–1694. https://doi.org/10.1177/15248380211013132

Martin, N., Woodhouse, A., & Burke, C. (2019). Being Trauma-Informed-in Practice. *Law Society of Scotland Journal, 64*(10), 1.

McKenna, N. C., & Holtfreter, K. (2021). Trauma-Informed Courts: A Review and Integration of Justice Perspectives and Gender Responsiveness. *Journal of Aggression, Maltreatment & Trauma, 30*(4), 450–470.

McLachlan, K. J. (2021a). Same, Same or Different? Is Trauma-Informed Sentencing a Form of Therapeutic Jurisprudence? *European Journal of Current Legal Issues, 25*(1), 1–20.

McLachlan, K. J. (2021b). "Whether the Victim Wishes the Offender to be Released or Not Is Unimportant": Australia and New Zealand Parole Board Members' Views of the Role of Victims of Crime. *Criminal Law Journal, 45*, 122–133.

McLachlan, K. J. (2022). Trauma-Informed Sentencing in South Australian Courts. *Journal of Criminology, 55*(4), 495–513. https://doi.org/10.1177/26338076221113073

McLachlan, K. J. (2023). Using a Trauma-Informed Practice Framework to Operationalise the #raisetheage Campaign. *Current Issues in Criminal Justice*. https://doi.org/10.1080/10345329.2023.2196099

Miller, N. A., & Najavits, L. M. (2012). Creating Trauma-Informed Correctional Care: A Balance of Goals and Environment. *European Journal of Psychotraumatology, 3*, 1–8. https://doi.org/10.3402/ejpt.v3i0.17246

Ministry of Justice. (2018). *Female Offender Strategy*. Crown.

Moss, N. (2020). A Kind Prison. In L. Rowles & I. Haji (Eds.), *Humane Justice: What Role Do Kindness, Hope and Compassion Play in the Criminal Justice System?* (pp. 29–35). The Monument Fellowship.

Murphy, A., & Lumley, K. (2022). *Trauma-Informed Courts: Guidance for Trauma-Informed Judicial Practices*. Judicial Commission of New South Wales.

NHS Education for Scotland (NES). (2023). *Trauma-Informed Justice: A Knowledge and Skills Framework for Working with Victims and Witnesses*. NHS Education for Scotland.

Purtle, J. (2020). Systematic Review of Evaluations of Trauma-Informed Organizational Interventions That Include Staff Trainings. *Trauma Violence & Abuse, 21*(4), 725–740. https://doi.org/10.1177/1524838018791304

Ross, S. (2015). Evaluating Neighbourhood Justice: Measuring and Attributing Outcomes for a Community Justice Program. *Trends & Issues in Crime and Criminal Justice, 499*, 1–8.

Samuels, J. (2020). Casting Off the Gilded Blindfold: The Role of Judges in Creating a Fairer, More Rehabilitative, Justice System. In L. Rowles & I. Haji (Eds.), *Humane Justice: What Role Do Kindness, Hope and Compassion Play in the Criminal Justice System?* (pp. 75–82). Monument Fellowship.

Senker, S., Eason, A., Pawson, C., & McCartan, K. (2023). *Issues, Challenges and Opportunities for Trauma-Informed Practice*. HM Inspectorate of Probation.

Skuse, T., & Matthew, J. (2015). The Trauma Recovery Model: Sequencing Youth Justice Interventions for Young People with Complex Needs. *Prison Service Journal, 220*, 16–25.

Substance Abuse and Mental Health Services Administration. (SAMSHA). (2014). *SAMHSA's Concept of Trauma and Guidance for a Trauma-Informed Approach*. US Department of Health and Human Services.

Taylor, C. (2021). *Report on a Scrutiny Visit to HMP Grendon, 2 and 9–10 March 2021*. HM Chief Inspector of Prisons.

Treisman, K. (2022, 28 May). "*Is Trauma-Informed Just About Being Sweet, Nice, & Kind"—Karen Treisman & Mandy Davis Discuss.* [Video]. YouTube. https://www.youtube.com/watch?v=vFR1MyznXW4

Warth, L. L., Langballe, Å., & Schultz, J.-H. (2022). A Trauma-Informed Approach to Arresting Migrant Families for Deportation: New Policing Practice. *European Journal of Policing Studies, 6* (Online First), 1–22. https://doi.org/10.5553/EJPS/2034760X2022001008

Webb, T. (2016). Children Exposed to Violence: A Developmental Trauma Informed Response for the Criminal Justice System. *Journal of Child and Adolescent Trauma, 9*(3), 183–189. https://doi.org/10.1007/s40653-015-0069-5

Wemmers, J. A. (2012). Victims' Rights Are Human Rights: The Importance of Recognizing Victims as Persons. *Temida*. https://doi.org/10.2298/TEM1202071W

Wexler, D. B. (2000). Therapeutic Jurisprudence: An Overview. *Thomas M. Cooley Law Review, 17*(1), 125–134.

Willmot, P., & Jones, L. (Eds.). (2022). *Trauma-Informed Forensic Practice*. Routledge. https://doi.org/10.4324/9781003120766-1

Workman, A., Kaddour, R., & Griffin, P. M. (2023). Introduction to Culture, Diversity, and Criminal Justice. In A. Workman, R. Kaddour, & P. M. Griffin (Eds.), *Culture, Diversity, and Criminal Justice: Towards Culturally Safe Criminal Justice Systems* (pp. 3–16). Routledge. https://doi.org/10.4324/9781003258032-2

Youansamouth, L., Irwin, S., Srivastava, J., & Clarke, S. (2020). *A Trauma Informed Organisational Development Framework: A Self and Peer Evaluation Toolkit*. Lancashire Violence Reduction Framework.

6

Trauma-Informed Responses to Victims of Crime

6.1 Introduction

There is an emerging scholarship regarding trauma-informed justice responses to people who are victims of crime, with most emerging from the US and generated by practitioners. Often, victim support agencies are assumed to apply trauma-informed care and practice approaches already. Nevertheless, in my experience working with a victim support agency, trauma-informed services for victims of crime tend to be implicit and assumed through goodwill and a commitment to be trauma-informed rather than being informed explicitly by scientific information about trauma or an articulated trauma-informed practice framework. This chapter will highlight the importance of trauma-informed criminal justice responses to victims of crime in terms of ethical, legal, and procedural outcomes. The chapter will further examine how trauma-informed principles of practice may inform justice system responses to victims of crime. Work that emphasises the importance of trauma-informed responses to victims of crime is not universal: it has focused on violence against women and children, particularly sexual violence and people trafficking. This chapter will demonstrate how the SAMHSA (2014) 4Rs trauma-informed framework could be used to ensure appropriate and

K. J. McLachlan, *Trauma-informed Criminal Justice*,
https://doi.org/10.1007/978-3-031-59290-4_6

consistent responses to victims of crime at any point of contact with the criminal justice system.

6.2 The Potentially Traumatic Impact of Crime

A victim of crime is someone who has experienced a loss or injury (which may be physical, financial, or psychological) due to crime. Some—but not all—people will be traumatised by their experience as a victim of crime. Crime is an adverse experience that is potentially traumatic. Trauma, rather than being an event or experience itself:

> … results from an event, series of events or set of circumstances that is experienced by an individual as physically or emotionally harmful or life threatening and that has lasting adverse effects on the individual's functioning and mental, physical, social, emotional or spiritual wellbeing. (SAMHSA, 2014, p. 7)

Crime victims are not homogenous; they can represent a broad cross-section of the community. Experiences of crime and its impact are also individualised and subjective. Whether a crime is traumatic depends on a range of factors, including the nature and characteristics of the offending, the relationship between a victim and the person who committed the crime, and the victim's access to internal and external supports.

As outlined in Chapter 2, when victims of crime experience trauma, it may manifest as psychological, emotional, physical, and social harm to the individual. Psychological trauma is often associated with various psychiatric diagnoses, including diagnoses relating to psychosis, dissociation, anxiety and depression, and personality disorders. If the crime experienced is particularly threatening (e.g., attempted murder), an individual may meet the diagnostic criteria for Post-Traumatic Stress Disorder (PTSD). Some victims may be diagnosed with complex trauma or complex PTSD if the crime they have experienced is chronic or a significant betrayal of trust (e.g., child sexual abuse or domestic abuse).

Prolonged experiences of crime victimisation may also result in neurological trauma, changing the physical structure of a person's brain. This may lead to an increase in impulsive, unpredictable, or violent behaviour due to changes in the volume and functioning in areas of the brain associated with emotional regulation and problem-solving (Rinne-Albers et al., 2017).

Given the diversity of victims of crime and their experiences, some people may require formal support (e.g., counselling), with many relying on informal support from family and friends to deal with the impacts of crime (Silk, 2023). Trauma-focused (or trauma-specific) therapeutic practices are outlined in Chapter 2 and include long-term, trauma-focused cognitive behavioural therapy (TF-CBT), contextual behaviour trauma therapy, and reprocessing therapies such as Eye Movement Desensitisation and Reprocessing (EMDR). Some of these treatment approaches are less appropriate for victims of crime who have complex trauma, who instead require "treatments for these disorders [that] seek to heal attachment-related injuries, to rehabilitate developmental competencies, and to revise ongoing emotional reactivity, maladaptive interpersonal patterns, and negative social perceptions" (Cloitre et al., 2009, p. 406). Despite the established evidence for individualised support for people with trauma, services for crime victims tend to be "one-size-fits-all" (Ellard & Campbell, 2020, p. 7).

6.3 Terminology: Victims, Survivors and Victims/Offenders

6.3.1 Victims/Survivors

For many people who have been victimised—especially victims of gendered crimes—they may identify as survivors rather than victims. The term "victim" implies passivity and powerlessness (McCarthy, 1997) and is loaded with blame, guilt, shame, and weakness. Further, it has been suggested "when one becomes a 'victim' and not a person who has experienced [crime] the rest of one's identity is obscured" (Spangaro, 1993, p. 15). Conversely, "survivor" is associated with re-empowerment and the recovery process (McCarthy, 1997). Additionally, the labels "victim" and "survivor" have been described as existing on a continuum, such that a person begins as a victim and becomes a survivor over time, as they cope and recover from their experience. Yet, as Jan Jordan (2001) notes: "an unintended consequence resulting from overemphasis of the survival aspects can be a silencing of the victim's voice, and a minimising by some women of the effects of [the victimisation]" (p. 9). "Victim" is a legal term that emphasises that a person has been criminally offended against and, in some cases, re-victimised through their experiences throughout the criminal justice process (Easteal, 1994). In this chapter, people who have experienced crime are referred to as victims rather than victims/survivors for ease of reading and in line with systemic terminology (acknowledging that the terminology may be problematic for some readers).

6.3.2 Victim-Offenders

There is a false dichotomy in the law that people cannot be both "victims" and "offenders". In the past 40 years or so, there has been growing recognition that many people who offend are also victims of crime. Often the media and the general public focus on blameless or "ideal victims" as those worthy of our support and sympathy (Christie, 1986). Victims who offend, as non-ideal victims, do not garner much sympathy at all. However, the "***victim-offender overlap***" is not uncommon. People who are both victims and offenders exist in certain populations with an increased risk of both offending and victimisation (Hass & Hannis, 2017) and are an international phenomenon (Berg & Schreck, 2022). As examined in Chapter 4, many adults who are victims of child maltreatment also have an offending history. Indeed, the association between trauma and offending discussed in Chapter 3 acknowledges that trauma may be the product of adversity associated with crime victimisation. While many people may be victims of crime and never offend, being a victim of crime increases the risk of further victimisation and offending.

Consider the examples in the textbox of victimisation taken from a South Australian (SA) sample of people who were convicted of drug trafficking. Do these people deserve less support and sympathy simply because they went on to offend after being victims of crime? If you have read Chapter 3, you should understand how such adverse experiences might result in trauma and criminality, such as illicit drug use. I ask you to keep this in mind as you read on.

You had a very dysfunctional and difficult relationship with your biological mother who was a drug addict and who was absent and neglectful of you during your childhood. On two occasions she left you as what you would describe as 'collateral' with a drug dealer for debts owed and you were subjected to abuse during those times. You also perceive that your mother sold your younger sister in prostitution to support your mother's drug habit and your other siblings were also subjected to abuse and neglect. (R v KJB)

At the age of 13, she used illicit drugs for the first time when her boyfriend held her down and injected her with methylamphetamine against her will. (R v TLI)

You were together for about 10 years. Although you had a good relationship at first, things began to change and he became physically violent towards you and quite manipulative. You found yourself trapped in a cycle of violence. You tried to force him to leave the house but he refused. In desperation, you started to sleep in your own car after work rather than going home. (R v TLS).

6.4 What Is Trauma-Informed, Victim-Centred Practice?

A recent literature review of 54 empirical studies that examined the experiences and support needs of adult survivors of sexual violence found that victims of crime require trauma-informed responses (Silk, 2023). Trauma-informed practice does not aim to resolve trauma. According to SAMHSA (2014):

> A program, organization, or system that is trauma-informed realizes the widespread impact of trauma and understands potential paths for recovery; recognizes the signs and symptoms of trauma in clients, families,

> staff, and others involved with the system; and responds by fully integrating knowledge about trauma into policies, procedures, and practices, and seeks to actively resist re-traumatization. (p. 9)

A trauma-informed service or organisation requires an explicit trauma-informed care framework. Furthermore, trauma-informed organisations and service providers must acknowledge the impact of inherent power imbalances between the agency and the individual client (DePrince & Gagnon, 2018, p. 27).

The pioneers of trauma-informed work, Maxine Harris and Roger Fallot (2001) identified four principles underpinning any interaction with a potentially traumatised individual: respect, information, connection, and hope ('RICH'). They later refined ***trauma-informed principles of practice*** to incorporate safety, trustworthiness, choice, collaboration, and empowerment (Fallot & Harris, 2011). In operationalising the 4Rs framework (i.e., to realise, recognise, respond to trauma, and resist re-traumatisation), SAMHSA (2014) identified six trauma-informed principles of practice:

1. Safety,
2. Trustworthiness and transparency,
3. Peer support,
4. Collaboration and mutuality,
5. Empowerment, voice, and choice, and
6. Cultural, historical, and gender issues.

These six principles extend the five trauma-informed principles outlined in Chapter 5 (re Kezelman & Stavropoulos, 2012).

If the SAMHSA (2014) trauma-informed practice principles and framework are applied to services for victims of crime, this means that everyone within the service agency must:

- **realise** the ways that crime victimisation may be traumatic,
- **recognise** the signs and symptoms of unresolved trauma,

- **respond** in a way that seeks to promote a sense of safety, trust, collaboration, empowerment, and choice, as well as reflect the personal characteristics and needs of the individual, and
- **resist** re-traumatisation.

Recent research with victims of crime and practitioners in Scotland has highlighted the importance of all the elements of the 4Rs process to promote the best outcomes for victims of crime (NES, 2021b). The next section will explain why a trauma-informed approach is necessary before examining the 4Rs SAMHSA (2014) victim-focused process in detail.

6.5 The Importance of a Trauma-Informed Response for all Victims of Crime

Government and academic work from Australia (Ombudsman WA, 2022) and the US (Gjika & Marganski, 2020) highlights the importance of trauma-informed service responses to victims of various types of crime. There are three main reasons for criminal justice agencies to provide trauma-informed services to victims of crime:

1. First, trauma-informed victim-focused responses are ethically appropriate.
2. Second, trauma-informed victim-focused responses are legally required.
3. Third, trauma-informed victim-focused responses promote better outcomes regarding reduced attrition and increased convictions.

Each of these will be examined in turn.

6.5.1 Ethical Reasons to be Trauma-Informed: Avoid Re-traumatisation

How criminal justice agencies respond to victims of crime can exacerbate the impact of crime. Evidence suggests that if victims of crime have positive experiences with justice agencies, where they feel respected, involved, and informed, the criminal justice system can validate and empower victims (Werner, 2021). As stated by Eric Werner (2021), a US attorney, "[w]hen victims are left out of the system, they are disempowered and disconnected. When victims refuse to participate in the criminal justice system by not reporting a crime or refusing to testify—it is *justice* that suffers" (p. 578, references removed). It is the ethical obligation of justice agencies to support victims of crime in a way that is "trauma-reducing rather than trauma-inducing" (Gjika & Marganski, 2020, p. 170). However, as outlined later in this chapter, there is significant evidence that contact with the justice system may result in additional or compounded trauma, especially if the victim of crime feels they have received neither procedural justice (i.e., fair, decent, appropriate treatment; CVWEW, 2011) nor outcome justice (i.e., a finding or admission of guilt, a type or length of sentence; CVWEW, 2011). Secondary traumatisation may occur when people feel disempowered, silenced, or disbelieved, or their experiences are minimised. This can occur when the individual experiences of victims are overlooked, for example, when it is assumed that specific crime victimisation experiences are always more traumatic than other types of crime victimisation for all victims, all the time (Ellard & Campbell, 2020).

6.5.2 Legal Obligation to be Trauma-Informed: Victims' Rights

Victims of crime have rights articulated by the United Nations in the *Declaration of Basic Principles of Justice for Victims of Crime and Abuse of Power* (1985), which include:

- being "treated with compassion and respect for their dignity" (Principle 4),
- being informed, having a voice and having the opportunity to participate (Principle 6),
- receiving individualised "necessary… assistance" (Principle 14),

- receiving "proper and prompt aid" from criminal justice agencies (Principle 16),
- access to redress, restitution, or reparation where possible.

Victims' rights are typically also embedded in local legislation (McLachlan, 2021b). Re-traumatisation by the criminal justice system often occurs when these rights are overlooked or breached. In some jurisdictions (e.g., England and Wales), service agencies are legally bound to recognise victims' rights (McLachlan, 2021b). In other jurisdictions, such as Australia, rights are legislated but not enforceable. Victims also have rights under the Universal Declaration of Human Rights (UDHR; UN, 1948; refer Wemmers, 2012), namely:

- recognising victims as "equal in dignity and rights" (i.e., deserves dignity and respect; Article 1),
- acknowledging crime as a violation of victims' "right to life, liberty and security of person" (Article 3),
- victims have "the right to recognition as a person before the law" (i.e., victim participation and procedural rights; Article 6), and
- "equal protection of the law" (Article 7).

Often, secondary traumatisation by the criminal justice system occurs through a lack of procedural justice, which undermines any benefit they may have otherwise felt regarding outcome justice (Ellard & Campbell, 2020). By embedding trauma-informed principles of practice in criminal justice responses to victims of crime, victims' rights are also upheld.

6.5.3 Better Outcomes Through Trauma-Informed Victim Support

Secondary trauma caused by the criminal justice system can exacerbate crime-induced trauma (DePrince, & Gagnon, 2018). Procedural justice can be aided by a trauma-informed approach that reflects victims' rights (CVWEW, 2011). Consistent and respectful support for victims of crime can result in better long-term health outcomes, more effective evidence-collection, and positive ongoing relationships between victims and justice agencies. This can assist police and prosecutors in achieving successful prosecutions based on strong evidence from victims of crime who are also witnesses. Trauma-focused training is key to embedding trauma-informed practices in criminal justice agencies.

Trauma-informed victim support should exist across all criminal justice agencies and entities. Police are the gatekeepers of the justice system, and their responses are pivotal to the likelihood and success of a victim's journey into court and beyond (Ellard & Campbell, 2020). There is considerable grey literature (often developed or commissioned by policing organisations) encouraging police to use trauma-informed interview techniques when taking statements from victims of crime (IACP, 2017; Lonsway et al., 2020). Such approaches are characterised by recognising victims' rights and avoiding statements or behaviour that may be perceived as victim blaming. For example, when interviewing victims, rather than asking victims "why" they did or did not do something during the crime, questions should be framed in a way that is non-judgmental and aims to understand their experiences, their reactions, and (often automatic) decisions, e.g., "Tell me what you were thinking/ feeling/ experiencing…?" (IACP, 2017; Lonsway et al., 2020).

Trauma-informed support of victims of crime (and others) during the court process is not a new idea either. The legal concept of therapeutic jurisprudence was introduced more than 30 years ago (Wexler, 2000) and is based on the premise that the law (i.e., legislation, legal rules, legal procedures, and legal roles) should promote therapeutic consequences and avoid anti-therapeutic consequences for individuals (Stobbs et al., 2019). The foundational purposes of therapeutic jurisprudence and trauma-informed court practices are similar: "to recognise the importance of therapeutic (trauma-informed) interactions in promoting recovery and desistance from crime, while also avoiding anti-therapeutic outcomes caused by interactions with the criminal justice system" (McLachlan, 2021a, p. 1).

Advocates for trauma-informed prosecutions emphasise that the benefits of trauma-informed victim treatment include prioritising the wellbeing of victims (ethical and legal obligations) and maximising prosecutorial success (better outcomes). Werner (2021) acknowledges:

> The purpose of trauma-informed prosecution is to empower and engage people that have experienced trauma. These practices are designed to help people recover from the fear, anxiety, and damage to their sense of self-worth caused by their experience. The purpose of trauma-informed prosecution is not to guarantee success at trial. (p. 577)

There is also pragmatism in recognising how trauma-informed responses to victims of crime can assist in success at trial. Victims of crime are often central witnesses who provide the evidence required to convict an alleged offender. While victims of crime are not technically a party to criminal law proceedings in adversarial justice systems, victims are integral to a strong case. To maintain victim engagement, justice practitioners must be able to realise and recognise trauma and its manifestations.

6.6 Realising and Recognising Trauma

To provide trauma-informed care and responses to victims of crime, the criminal justice system and its agencies must apply the 4Rs: **realising** how crime victimisation may be traumatic, **recognising** signs and symptoms of unresolved trauma, **responding** in a trauma-informed manner, and **resisting** re-traumatisation (SAMHSA, 2014). Trauma-informed care occurs when service providers ensure they understand:

> the prevalence and nature of trauma arising from interpersonal violence and its impacts on other areas of life and functioning. Practices should ensure the physical and emotional safety of survivors and recognise and be responsive to the lived social and cultural contexts which shape victims' needs and healing pathways. (Silk, 2023, p. III)

Two key issues continually emerge in the literature that are rarely reflected in criminal justice professionals' knowledge or practice: first, that trauma may manifest in different ways for different people, and second, that memory and recall can be impacted by trauma. Thus, developing practitioner knowledge through training is imperative to promote trauma-informed responses by justice agencies. For example, a training bulletin created by Lonsway et al. (2020) for US police officers when interviewing victims of crime advises police officers about how a continuum of reactions to crime victimisation is to be expected. People respond differently to trauma and the adversity of being a crime victim, not just in the ways that police officers may assume "real" victims act and express their distress, e.g., a "victim's lack of engagement [may be taken to be] a sign that they are uncooperative, rather than a result of being emotionally overwhelmed and/or shut down" (Lonsway et al., 2020, p. 6).

6.7 Responding to Trauma: Operationalising Trauma-Informed Principles of Practice

Trauma-informed practice in the criminal justice system should be universal, individual, and systemic (NES, 2021a). Any time an individual or agency responds to a person who is a victim of crime, they should act in a way that upholds the victim's rights and reflects trauma-informed principles of practice. Trauma-informed service responses should not be only available for certain crimes or specific individuals or solely from victim-focused agencies. An organisation claiming to offer trauma-informed services must shift from not just realising trauma may be present and recognising its impacts to responding with a systemic, organisation-wide approach that consistently reflects the trauma-informed practice principles.

Most of the analyses of trauma-informed service responses for victims of crime have come from the US and the UK, focusing primarily on gender-based violence (i.e., sexual violence, domestic abuse, and people trafficking). That research has concentrated on first responders, namely police and health organisations (e.g., Jain et al., 2022), rather than holistic trauma-informed experiences throughout all contact points with criminal justice agencies. Very little work has been done in Australia focusing on trauma-informed criminal justice practices. The good news is that this work is emerging. The bad news is that victims' experiences with the criminal justice system, especially vulnerable and highly traumatised victims, have remained (at best) inconsistent for decades (refer McLachlan, 2007). There are current examples of ad hoc trauma-informed practice in police, courts, and corrections. This indicates an awareness of the benefits of trauma-informed practice in terms of ethical and legal obligations and better outcomes.

Trauma-informed responses to victims of crime by criminal justice agencies should be characterised by the six key principles of practice (SAMHSA, 2014), as outlined above. However, there is a dearth of information about how this might occur. The following section provides an overview of international examples of how trauma-informed practice principles may be operationalised by justice agencies to inform the development of consistent responses to victims of crime.

6.7.1 Demonstrations of Safety by Criminal Justice Agencies

Safety is a basic human right (Tucci et al., 2020). As outlined earlier in this chapter, if justice agencies assure the safety for victims of crime, this will assist in meeting legal and ethical obligations and promoting better outcomes for everyone involved. Safety is relational and exists in interpersonal connections (Tucci et al., 2020). Tucci et al. (2020) suggest that:

> In order to offer safety, it is our belief that adults need to orient themselves to its feel, its dimensions, its reverberations… They need to find the experiences in themselves and their relationships of moments of shared safety that have given way to a sense of relief, comfort and restoration. (p. 9)

Workers must consider how personal responses and systemic functions may provide safety. At a personal level, a person's language and tone, body language, and self-regulation can assist in establishing an environment of psychological safety. Victims of crime may be hypervigilant and instinctively rather than rationally assess their safety in different social situations (Tucci et al., 2020). Safety requires that a worker bears witness to a victim's experiences and concerns or fears without judgement. If someone feels that they are being judged or disbelieved, they are unlikely to feel safe.

To promote safety, professionals must be respectful and supportive when dealing with people who are victims of crime. However, even more than this, they need to be aware of the relevance of their own experiences and triggers and work to neutralise or manage responses that may be unhelpful or misconstrued by the victim as an adverse and judgmental reaction. Professionals must reassure individuals that all reactions to crime and crime victimisation are normal and valid. System issues that can promote or undermine safety include the design of the physical space in which victims receive services, delays, and attrition throughout the criminal justice process, and the requirement to repeatedly describe their experience to multiple police officers, prosecutors, and sometimes in open court, with no warm referrals or single point of contact. To promote safety, agencies can take a "'no wrong-door' entry to services… in which victims receive fully coordinated, comprehensive services no matter where or how they enter the system" (OCVA, 2010).

6.7.2 Trustworthiness and Transparency in the Actions of Criminal Justice System Agencies

Trust is related to safety, with transparency more closely related to workers being honest about the availability of victim services and the limitations or scope of victims' spheres of influence. Workers may be inclined to overstate the influence a victim of crime can have on a justice outcome to make them feel more empowered or involved (or respected). Trust and transparency are better achieved through an honest disclosure of the limitations of a victim's influence on a justice process or outcome. Continuity of care, with a single point of contact and predictability, is a simple way of promoting safety and trust (refer to Ellard & Campbell, 2020) but may be challenging to implement in practice due to organisational practices, such as police shift work, workloads, and role descriptions. To build trust in the court process, a judicial officer should ensure that victims of crime understand what is happening in the court. Trust can be promoted by clearly explaining what is happening in court and the person's role in the courtroom, explaining the sanction or outcome of the court process, explaining why a conversation with legal representatives is happening, and using language that is not threatening (SAMHSA, 2013).

6.7.3 Peer Support

Peer support can be key in ensuring that victims feel and are understood and have their experiences acknowledged. In practice, peer support may be either direct or indirect. Direct peer support might occur when professionals refer victims to support provided by people who themselves have been victims of crime (such as Homicide Support Groups). For the minority of victims of crime whose matter progresses to court, peer support may be available through volunteer court companions who have been victims of crime. Court companions can help demystify the court process and be physically present during the court hearing. Indirect peer support may be achieved by ensuring that advisory committees and improvement processes involve people with lived experience of crime victimisation. While professionals may also have their own experiences of adversity, workers in the justice system must be honest and empathic while remaining self-regulated. A professional, such as a police officer or social worker, who is burnt out by their own experiences of adversity or secondary trauma can rarely provide empathetic and supportive care to victims of crime.

6.7.4 Collaboration in Decision-Making

Collaborating with a victim of crime requires working with them to minimise re-traumatisation and achieve the best outcomes within the scope of the criminal justice process (DePrince & Gagnon, 2018). This may occur, for example, by offering to collect and store forensic evidence even if the victim is unsure at the time whether to formally report a crime (so that the option remains open to them later) and assisting victims in providing impact statements or submissions to courts or parole authorities, to influence decision-making (McLachlan, 2021b).

Correctional services organisations have obligations to provide victims of crime with information and services about the crime and the person who committed the crime. Often, victims are required to be registered to be kept informed, and there may be limitations to registration (e.g., nature of the offence, direct victim as opposed to secondary victim except in the case of homicide). Correctional service agencies may also have Victims Service Charters, which set out what people can expect and typically reflect victims' legislative rights. Victims of crime also have rights embedded in legislation relating to participation in justice processes, such as Parole Board proceedings (McLachlan, 2021b). Victims of crime are given a voice to share their views and concerns about the offence or the person who has applied for parole. This is most often done in writing, but in some jurisdictions may also be able to be provided in person (McLachlan, 2021b). The content of such a submission is not prescriptive, and victims often outline the trauma they have experienced regarding the impact on their social and emotional wellbeing.

6.7.5 Prioritising Empowerment, Voice, and Choice

Victims have the right to be informed and have a voice and opportunity to participate in justice processes (UN, 1985, Principle 6). Some victims of certain types of crimes, such as sexual violence, are more likely to feel disempowered by their experiences reporting the crime than victims of other crimes (Silk, 2023). As highlighted by Anne DePrince and Kerry Gagnon (2018), "if someone's car is stolen, we would not begin an interaction by questioning whether it was really stolen and then suggest that the person asked for the car to be stolen" (p. 19). When victims in the UK, US, Canada, and Australia were asked what they most needed, they indicated they needed more choices. Victims wanted to choose how, when, and what kinds of emotional support (e.g., group or individual therapy, online or face-to-face, open-ended, or time-limited, available without engaging with the criminal justice system, at a time and in a suitable language), appropriate and relevant practical supports, as well as whether and how to engage with the criminal justice system (Silk, 2023). They are also keen to identify opportunities to empower themselves and others (Silk, 2023).

Staff should have the enthusiasm and the skills to engage with victims effectively. One way to ensure that victims of crime receive a supportive response is to have victim advocates/counsellors work alongside patrol officers (Dean et al., 2000). At a more basic level for all policing agencies, when taking a statement or evidence from a victim of crime, police must be cognizant of the legal rights of victims of crime. However, it is also essential to understand the science of traumatic memory and recognise that traumatic memories may be "vague, inaccurate, or incomplete" (Werner, 2021, p. 583). Lonsway et al. (2020) promote the education of police officers about memory. They encourage police to move away from assumptions that recall is linear and instead suggest that other cues and prompts (e.g., sensory experiences such as smells, sounds, or a location) may encourage a victim to remember additional details. All victims of crime (whether they appear to be traumatised or not) benefit from a sensitive statement-taking approach that both acknowledges that recall is not perfect, communicates this fact to the individual, and offers opportunities for additional evidence to be provided in due course to supplement their original statement, should the victim remember additional details, later.

Milam et al. (2017) demonstrate how trauma-informed practice principles can assist prosecutors to:

> restore feelings of self-efficacy and control to the victims by providing them with opportunities for choice and consistency. Allowing them to meet with an agent whose gender puts the victim at ease, or allowing them to select the location for meetings, greatly empowers victims. Also, to the extent possible, minimize unexpected changes in meeting times or locations. It is most important to demonstrate honesty and respect. The nature and location of the victim interview is vital to the success of any agent-victim relationship. The agent's attitude and behavior during the interview are critical. It is essential to monitor your own comportment to guard against actions that can be interpreted as biased or judgmental. Remain honest and respectful, and strive to honor all commitments. A familiarity with and keen attention to the meaning of both verbal

> and nonverbal cues are also essential. Crossed arms, lack of eye contact, and changes in facial expression can all indicate shifts in victim comfort during the interview. Also, consider the location and timing of the interview. (p. 40)

Australia has provisions for vulnerable witnesses, such as giving pre-recorded evidence, having a support person or support dog, and using screens or CCTV to distance the victim from the defendant. However, many of these options are only available with judicial approval. The victim has no choice or voice in terms of whether it will be available or not. The US is more advanced than Australia in thinking about how courtrooms can be trauma-informed for victims of crime. The US Office for Victims of Crime (OVCTTAC, n.d.) recommends accepting reasonable individual requests to modify court proceedings, reducing court formalities wherever possible, adjusting (dimming) court lighting where required, and providing tissues, water, and snacks.

6.7.6 Acknowledgement of the Importance of Cultural, Historical, and Gender Issues

A person's cultural background, gender identity and sexuality, and personal and intergenerational experiences of past adversity and trauma are all relevant considerations for justice agencies. Stereotypes about "ideal victims" (Christie, 1986) and rape myths mean that specific populations who are at high risk of victimisation and re-victimisation (such as women from culturally and linguistically diverse backgrounds, sex workers, First Nations women, people who identify as LGBTQIA+) are also at risk of marginalisation and negative experiences with justice agencies (Daley, 2022; Dwyer et al., 2017). There are high rates of unreported sexual violence for women, especially those who identify as LGBTQIA+ (DePrince & Gagnon, 2018). This indicates that far more work needs to be done to promote trauma-informed justice responses which offer tangible benefits for high-risk victims of crime in terms of procedural and outcome justice.

Some people may distrust justice agencies such as the police due to past experiences or the experiences of significant others. Often, this relates to race, culture, or gender identity. There is significant research demonstrating poor police responses to women who have experienced violence (McLachlan, 2007), to LGBTQIA+ people (Dwyer et al., 2017), to Aboriginal people (Daley, 2022) or to people who are displaced, refugees, and/or of African (Shepherd, 2021) backgrounds. People who have previously been criminalised are unlikely to expect supportive police responses if they are also victimised (which is statistically likely). This mistrust of the police must be recognised as a reasonable response given many victims' reference points. Other issues, such as language barriers and religious views, make it difficult for people from culturally and linguistically diverse communities to know how to report crimes, recognise gender-based violence as a crime, or understand how a justice response may be helpful.

6.8 Resisting Re-traumatisation

Individuals report that experiences with the justice system may be more traumatic than the crime itself (CVWEW, 2011). Given that a foundational purpose of the criminal justice system is to promote community safety, this is sadly ironic. Thus, an essential consideration for all criminal justice agencies is not just to respond in a way that reflects an understanding of the potentially traumatic impact of crime but also to ensure that experiences with the criminal justice system are not re-traumatising.

International research has found that contact with police has the potential to be traumatic, particularly for (but not limited to) victims of sexual violence (Rich, 2019) and domestic abuse.

> Historically, officers have been taught effective investigative strategies for suspect-based crimes (i.e., homicide, burglary), which encourages skepticism, the discovery of inconsistencies, and reliance on physical evidence to determine the truth. (Lathan et al., 2019, p. 1735f)

In responding to victims of crime, police officers often defer to their (overestimated) skills of deception detection and rely on myths about the typical behaviours of "real" victims of sexual assault and domestic abuse to determine the veracity of victims' reports (Rich, 2019). Police overestimate the rate of false reports and are often more sympathetic to the emotional (e.g., hysterical, despairing) victims than the victims with limited or flat affect (Franklin et al., 2020; Lathan et al., 2019) despite clinical research demonstrating that trauma may manifest in a range of behaviours across a continuum, both in the immediate aftermath of the crime and over time (Lonsway et al., 2020).

Research undertaken in the US has found that police responses that lead to secondary traumatisation are often due to a lack of training and understanding of the range of responses to trauma (Franklin et al., 2020; Lathan et al., 2019). In such cases, victims may face scepticism, disbelief, and blame. Even with training, police officers' responses remain inconsistent (Franklin et al., 2020). A Norwegian study found that even when police realised the presence and recognised the impact of trauma, they were unsure how to provide direct support and be empathic and professional. As a result of this internal struggle, police officers may inadvertently present as cold and disengaged (Jakobsen et al., 2017).

To achieve consistently trauma-informed victim treatment, ideally, all police officers and criminal justice professionals should be able to offer victims a trauma-informed response. Research across jurisdictions shows this is not the case (McLachlan, 2007; NHS, 2021b). Some people and personalities within policing agencies are better suited to "crime-fighting", with others better suited to community-facing roles. However, given that most policing tasks focus on the latter (White et al., 2019), it is not unreasonable to expect that all patrol officers have the skills and knowledge to respond to all community members in a trauma-informed manner. While Scottish and US research has found that female and older police officers may be more favourable towards victims and trauma-informed practices (Franklin et al., 2020; Gillespie-Smith et al., 2020, p. 13), training and policies should promote an expectation of consistent trauma-informed responses by police, that become the norm rather than the exception. That is the intention of the Ayrshire Division of Police Scotland, which is moving towards becoming a trauma-informed division (Gillespie-Smith et al., 2020).

6.9 Trauma-Informed Criminal Justice Policies and Practices

There is clear evidence that some justice agencies in some countries are looking to provide trauma-informed services to victims of crime. However, these approaches often lack an implementation framework. SAMHSA (2014) has developed a 10-step implementation approach. In addition to factors discussed in this chapter, such as providing safe physical spaces and ensuring staff are trained in the 4Rs, organisations must also ensure top-down leadership and bottom-up co-designed trauma-informed practice. SAMHSA (2014) emphasises that trauma-informed principles must be embedded in criminal justice policies and practices, with ongoing quality assurance and evaluative processes.

There are obvious challenges to consistently achieving trauma-informed justice for all crime victims. However, there are also many opportunities for trauma-informed practice principles to promote procedural justice even if "outcome justice" cannot be promised. Within an adversarial justice system, experiences such as cross-examining victims can be improved by not allowing questions relating to non-linear recall and memory to undermine victim/witness character. Court processes can remain adversarial without promoting myths and stereotypes about the dichotomy of victims and offenders. The argument that providing (trauma-informed) justice to victims of crime somehow takes away from just outcomes for people who have offended is nonsense. Many people who have offended are also victims of crime. A compassionate justice system uses scientific evidence to inform and improve how society responds to crime to promote community safety. A trauma-informed criminal justice system requires commitment from all people and agencies within it. With this commitment comes a stronger sense of justice for victims of crime and other participants.

6.10 Conclusion

Surprisingly, little has been written about holistic trauma-informed support and services for victims of crime as they navigate the criminal justice system. Trauma-informed victim services should underpin all contact with all victims of crime, regardless of the crime or the subjective impact of that crime. Many non-government support agencies and health services claim to be trauma-informed without articulating a clear framework or way of working. Criminal justice agencies have identified the procedural benefit of ensuring trauma-informed interviews and evidence-collection procedures (to promote successful prosecutions). However, there has been very little written about trauma-informed practices and ways of working that prioritise the fundamental rights of victims to feel respected, believed, engaged, and informed participants in the criminal justice system. Using the SAMHSA 4Rs framework, this chapter has demonstrated how a trauma-informed framework and practice principles can assist in ensuring that victims' rights are upheld and re-traumatisation by the justice system is avoided.

Key Points

- Trauma-informed responses to victims of crime help to reduce re-victimisation, uphold victims' legal and human rights, and can result in better criminal justice outcomes.
- Often criminal justice professionals lack the knowledge that trauma may manifest in different ways for different people and that memory and recall can be impacted by trauma.
- Myths about how "real" victims respond to trauma can negatively influence the way that criminal justice professionals respond to victims of crime.
- Trauma-informed practice in the criminal justice system should be universal, individual, and systemic such that any time an individual or agency responds to a person who is a victim of crime, they should act in a way that upholds the victim's rights and reflects trauma-informed principles of practice.
- For some victims of crime, experiences with the criminal justice system may be more traumatic than the crime itself.

References

Berg, M. T., & Schreck, C. J. (2022). The Meaning of the Victim–Offender Overlap for Criminological Theory and Crime Prevention Policy. *Annual Review of Criminology, 5*, 277–297. https://doi.org/10.1146/annurev-criminol-030920120724

Christie, N. (1986). The Ideal Victim. In E. A. Fattah (Ed.), *From Crime Policy to Victim Policy* (pp. 17–30). Palgrave Macmillan. https://doi.org/10.1007/978-1-349-08305-3_2

Cloitre, M., Stolbach, B. C., Herman, J. L., Kolk, B. V. D., Pynoos, R., Wang, J., & Petkova, E. (2009). A Developmental Approach to Complex PTSD: Childhood and Adult Cumulative Trauma as Predictors of Symptom Complexity. *Journal of Traumatic Stress, 22*(5), 399–408. https://doi.org/10.1002/jts.20444

Commissioner for Victims and Witnesses in England and Wales (CVWEW). (2011). *Victims' Views of Court and Sentencing: Qualitative Research with WAVES Victims*. CVWEW.

Daley, P. (2022, March 19). Police Interactions with Aboriginal People Are Scarred by Australia's Violent Frontier History. *The Guardian*.

Dean, C. W., Lumb, R., Proctor, K., Klopovic, J., Hyatt, A., & Hamby, R. (2000). *Social Work and Law Enforcement Partnerships: A Summons to The Village. Strategies and Effective Practices*. North Carolina Department of Crime Control and Public Safety.

DePrince, A. P., & Gagnon, K. L. (2018). Understanding the Consequences of Sexual Assault: What Does It Mean for Prevention to Be Trauma Informed? In L. M. Orchowski & C. A. Gidycz (Eds.), *Sexual Assault Risk Reduction and Resistance* (pp. 15–35). Academic Press. https://doi.org/10.1016/B978-0-12-805389-8.00002-5

Dwyer, A., Ball, M., Bond, C., Lee, M., & Crofts, T. (2017). *Exploring LGBTI Police Liaison Services: Factors Influencing Their Use and Effectiveness According to LGBTI People and LGBTI Police Liaison Officers*. Report to the Criminology Research Advisory Council. Grant: CRG 31/11–12. Australian Institute of Criminology.

Easteal, P. (1994). *Voices of the Survivors*. Australian Institute of Criminology.

Ellard, R., & Campbell, E. (2020). *Improving Support for Victims of Crime: Key Practice Insights*. RMIT University.

Fallot, R. D., & Harris, M. (2011). *Creating Cultures of Trauma-Informed Care (CCTIC): A Self-Assessment and Planning Protocol*. Community Connections.

Franklin, C. A., Garza, A. D., Goodson, A., & Bouffard, L. A. (2020). Police Perceptions of Crime Victim Behaviors: A Trend Analysis Exploring Mandatory Training and Knowledge of Sexual and Domestic Violence Survivors' Trauma Responses. *Crime and Delinquency, 66*(8), 1055–1086.

Gillespie-Smith, K., Brodie, Z. P., Collins, K., Deacon, K., & Goodall, K. (2020). *Moving Towards Trauma-Informed Policing: An Exploration of Police Officer's Attitudes and Perceptions Towards Adverse Childhood Experiences (ACEs).* The Scottish Institute for Policing Research.

Gjika, A., & Marganski, A. J. (2020). Silent Voices, Hidden Stories: A Review of Sexual Assault (Non)Disclosure Literature, Emerging Issues, and Call to Action. *International Journal for Crime, Justice and Social Democracy, 9*(4), 163–176. https://doi.org/10.5204/ijcjsd.v9i4.1439

Harris, M., & Fallot, R. D. (2001). Envisioning a Trauma-Informed Service System: A Vital Paradigm Shift. *New Directions for Mental Health Services, 2001*(89), 3–22. https://doi.org/10.1002/yd.23320018903

Hass, A. Y., & Hannis, C. (2017). In Their Words: A Qualitative Analysis of the Overlap in Victimization and Offending. *International Review of Victimology, 23*(1), 81–94. https://doi.org/10.1177/0269758016654238

International Association of Chiefs of Police (IACP). (2017). *Successful Trauma Informed Victim Interviewing.* US Department of Justice.

Jain, J., Bennett, M., Bailey, M. D., Liaou, D., Kaltiso, S.-A.O., Greenbaum, J., Williams, K., Gordon, M. R., Torres, M. I. M., Nguyen, P. T., Coverdale, J. H., Williams, V., Hari, C., Rodriguez, S., Salami, T., & Potter, J. E. (2022). Creating a Collaborative Trauma-Informed Interdisciplinary Citywide Victim Services Model Focused on Health Care for Survivors of Human Trafficking. *Public Health Reports, 137*(Supplement 1), 30S–37S. https://doi.org/10.1177/00333549211059833

Jakobsen, K. K., Langballe, Å., & Schultz, J.-H. (2017). Trauma-Exposed Young Victims: Possibilities and Constraints for Providing Trauma Support within the Investigative Interview. *Psychology, Crime & Law, 23*(5), 427–444. https://doi.org/10.1080/1068316X.2016.1269903

Jordan, J. (2001). *True 'Lies' and False 'Truths': Women, Rape and the Police.* [PhD Thesis, Victoria University].

Kezelman, C., & Stavropoulos, P. (2012). *"The Last Frontier": Practice Guidelines for Treatment of Complex Trauma and Trauma Informed Care and Service Delivery.* Adults Surviving Child Abuse.

Lathan, E., Duncan, J., Langhinrichsen-Rohling, J., & Stefurak, J. T. (2019). The Promise Initiative: Promoting a Trauma-Informed Police Response to Sexual Assault in a Mid-Size Southern Community. *Journal of Community Psychology, 47*, 1733–1749. https://doi.org/10.1002/jcop.22223

Lonsway, K. A., Hopper, J., & Archambault, J. (2020). *Becoming Trauma-Informed: Understanding and Appropriately Applying the Neurobiology of Trauma to Victim Interviews.* End Violence Against Women International.

McCarthy, T. (1997). Rethinking Theories of Victimology. In S. Cook & J. Bessant (Eds.), *Women's Encounters with Violence: Australian Experiences* (pp. 127–144). Sage.

McLachlan, K. (2007). *Grounds for Hope and Disappointment: Victims'/Survivors' Perceptions of South Australia Police Responses to Rape*. LLM, Flinders University.

McLachlan, K. J. (2021a). Same, Same or Different? Is Trauma-Informed Sentencing a form of Therapeutic Jurisprudence? *European Journal of Current Legal Issues, 25*(1), 1–20.

McLachlan, K. (2021b). 'Whether the Victim Wishes the Offender to be Released or Not Is Unimportant': Australia and New Zealand Parole Board Members' Views of the Role of Victims of Crime. *Criminal Law Journal, 45*(2), 122–133.

Milam, M., Borrello, N., & Pooler, J. (2017). The Survivor-Centered, Trauma-Informed Approach. *United States Attorneys'. Bulletin, 65*(6), 39–44.

NHS Education for Scotland (NES). (2021a). *The Knowledge & Skills Needed for a Trauma-Informed Justice Workforce: What Did Justice Leaders Tell Us?* NHS.

NHS Education for Scotland (NES). (2021b). *The Knowledge & Skills Needed for a Trauma-Informed Justice Workforce: What Did Victims and Witnesses Tell Us?* NHS.

Office for Victims of Crime Training and Technical Assistance Centre (OVCTTAC). (n.d.). *Human Trafficking Task Force E-Guide: Strengthening Collaborative Responses.* Office of Justice Programs.

Office of Crime Victims Advocacy (OCVA). (2010). *No Wrong Door: Commercial Sexual Exploitation of Children.* Washington State Department of Commerce.

Ombudsman Western Australia (WA). (2022). *Investigation into Family and Domestic Violence and Suicide. Volume 4: The Need for Trauma Informed Responses*. Ombudsman WA.

Rich, K. (2019). Trauma-Informed Police Responses to Rape Victims. *Journal of Aggression, Maltreatment & Trauma, 28*(4), 463–480. https://doi.org/10.1080/10926771.2018.1540448

Rinne-Albers, M. A., Pannekoek, J. N., van Hoof, M.-J., van Lang, N. D., Lamers-Winkelman, F., Rombouts, S. A., van der Wee, N. J., & Vermeiren, R. R. (2017). Anterior Cingulate Cortex Grey Matter Volume Abnormalities in Adolescents with PTSD After Childhood Sexual Abuse. *European Neuropsychopharmacology, 27*(11), 1163–1171. https://doi.org/10.1016/j.euroneuro.2017.08.432

Shepherd, S. (2021, March 25). *Too Many Young African-Australians Are in Jail. Some Blame Police, But the Data Tells a More Complex Story.* ABC News.

Silk, K. (2023). *Formal Support Needs of Adult Victim-Survivors of Sexual Violence: A Literature Review.* Ministry of Justice.

Spangaro, J. (1993). Rape and "Real Rape". In P. Easteal (Ed.), *Without Consent: Confronting Adult Sexual Violence: Proceedings of a Conference Held 27–29 October 1992.* Australian Institute of Criminology.

Stobbs, N., Bartels, L., & Vols, M. (2019). Therapeutic Jurisprudence-A Strong Community and Maturing Discipline. In N. Stobbs, L. Bartels, & M. Vols (Eds.), *The Methodology and Practice of Therapeutic Jurisprudence* (pp. 15–28). Carolina Academic Press.

Substance Abuse and Mental Health Services Administration (SAMHSA). (2013). *Essential Components of Trauma-Informed Judicial Practice.* SAMHSA.

Substance Abuse and Mental Health Services Administration (SAMHSA). (2014). *SAMHSA's Concept of Trauma and Guidance for a Trauma-Informed Approach.* US Department of Health and Human Services.

Tucci, J., Weller, A., & Mitchell, J. (2020). *Realising Deep Safety for Children Who Have Experienced Abuse: What Really Is Therapeutic Work with Traumatised Children and Young People?* Australian Childhood Foundation.

UN General Assembly. (1985, November 29). *Declaration of Basic Principles of Justice for Victims of Crime and Abuse of Power. A/RES/40/34*. United Nations.

United Nations (UN). (1948). *UN Universal Declaration of Human Rights.* https://www.un.org/en/about-us/universal-declaration-of-human-rights

Wemmers, J. A. (2012). Victims' Rights Are Human Rights: The Importance of Recognizing Victims as Persons. *Temida.* https://doi.org/10.2298/TEM1202071W

Werner, E. M. (2021). Avoiding the Second Assault: Guidebook for Trauma-Informed Prosecutions. *Lewis & Clark Law Review, 25*(2), 573–606.

Wexler, D. B. (2000). Therapeutic Jurisprudence: An Overview. *Thomas M. Cooley Law Review, 17*(1), 125–134.
White, R., Perrone, S., & Howes, L. (2019). *Crime, Criminality and Criminal Justice* (3rd ed.) Oxford University Press.

Sentencing Remarks

R v KJB (District Court of SA, Judge #4, 14 August 2019).
R v TLI (District Court of SA, Judge #6, 4 June 2019).
R v TLS (District Court of SA, Judge #13, 4 July 2019).

7

Responding to Secondary Traumatisation in the Criminal Justice System

7.1 Introduction

Despite a broad recognition that working in the criminal justice system can be stressful, there is limited evidence about how individuals and agencies work to avoid and address secondary traumatisation, vicarious trauma, and psychosocial harm. This chapter examines what is known about direct and secondary trauma in the criminal justice system and how to support workers better, drawing from broader protective workplace strategies, such as supervision and reflective practices. Factors such as organisational culture and poor management may reduce the likelihood of people acknowledging the potentially traumatic nature of their work and seeking help when necessary. The chapter finishes by discussing the merits of trauma-informed responses in promoting healthier workplaces.

K. J. McLachlan, *Trauma-informed Criminal Justice*,
https://doi.org/10.1007/978-3-031-59290-4_7

7.2 What is Secondary Traumatisation?

Crime often impacts professionals in the criminal justice system indirectly, with the effects referred to as compassion fatigue, burnout, secondary traumatic stress, or vicarious trauma.

- ***Compassion fatigue*** is a form of ***burnout***, i.e., a gradual emergence of "psychological and emotional exhaustion, associated with feelings of hopelessness and difficulties in dealing with work or in doing your job effectively" (Turgoose et al., 2022, p. 64). Compassion fatigue reduces a person's ability to be compassionate towards (i.e., "bear the suffering of") others but is easily treated if identified early (Figley, 2002, p. 1434).
- Although sometimes conflated (see Foley et al., 2022), ***secondary traumatic stress*** (STS) and ***vicarious trauma*** may be thought to exist on a continuum (Polak et al., 2019). ***Secondary Traumatic Stress*** is the acute stress (in terms of behaviour and emotions) associated with wanting to help someone who is traumatised (Figley, 1995, p. 7). ***Vicarious traumatisation*** is described as "a more pervasive, longer-lasting shift in a caregiver's inner experience that results from disrupted beliefs regarding themselves, relationships, and the world, which distinguishes it from the more acute phenomena of secondary traumatic stress" (Rauvola et al., 2019, p. 303; see also Ko & Memon, 2023).

For simplicity, this chapter primarily refers to ***secondary traumatisation*** as an overall term to describe the traumatic effects of working in the criminal justice system and being exposed to the adverse experiences and trauma of others (see Ko & Memon, 2023). This book advocates for a compassionate justice system that aims to *relieve* the pain and suffering of others. Compassion is different from empathy, which is when workers *feel* the pain and suffering of others (Gilmour, 2024). Empathy is often associated with the various forms of secondary traumatisation outlined above.

A final issue worthy of mention here is the potential of the justice system to cause moral injury. ***Moral injury*** is a form of psychological distress that occurs when an individual is involved in actions or practices that violate their personal ethical or moral code (Fenton & Kelly, 2017). The conflict between intentions and actions may result in guilt and shame (Fenton & Kelly, 2017). When the criminal justice system or justice organisation in which a person works fails to help others—or worse, results in the harm and re-traumatisation of others, this can be very distressing for workers who chose to work in the justice system to achieve positive outcomes for individuals and the community. For example, although the criminal justice system strives to keep the community safe, the churn of people in and out of custody demonstrates the system's limited success in achieving its fundamental goal. Moral injury is a form of stress or distress caused by the workplace itself rather than a result of exposure to people who have offended or been victims of crime (Edwards, 2024).

The manifestations of secondary traumatisation are the same for criminal justice practitioners, such as legal practitioners, correctional service workers, and police officers, as they are for victims of crime and people who have experienced direct trauma. As outlined in Chapter 2, manifestations of trauma include impacts on social and emotional wellbeing, such as psychological distress, avoidance behaviours, hypervigilance, irritability, and poor emotional regulation (Duran & Woodhams, 2022). While some research has focused on the impact of specific types of stressors, such as being exposed to child exploitation material (Perez et al., 2010; Polak et al., 2019) or audio-visual evidence of violent crimes (Birze et al., 2023), secondary traumatisation is more likely to occur in response to chronic and repeated exposure to practices within the criminal justice system, and knowledge of adversity associated with a broad range of offending behaviours or victimisation.

7.3 Secondary Traumatisation in the Criminal Justice System

Depending on a worker's role in the criminal justice system, they may be at risk of secondary traumatisation and trauma from direct experiences of adversity (which may relate to crime or organisational factors). This section demonstrates that psychosocial harms impacting criminal justice workers relate to the nature of the work and the level of perceived organisational support and services. Workplace trauma may be associated with psychiatric diagnoses, including anxiety, depression, and post-traumatic stress disorder (PTSD; Conn & Butterfield, 2013). ***Avoidant coping*** strategies, as discussed in Chapter 3, such as alcohol abuse, are also common for workers across the criminal justice sector.

7.3.1 Traumatised Police Officers

Police roles are diverse, with officers often the first responders at fatalities, regularly exposed to victims of domestic, sexual, and child abuse, and facing the risk of injury or potential harm themselves. Dealing with death can be particularly challenging when the victim is a child, the circumstances are horrific, or the officer must deliver the news to the family (Paterson, 2021). Police can also be exposed to adversity in the form of assaults or threats of assaults. Because police are at high risk of exposure to multiple adverse experiences in their work, they potentially experience both primary and secondary trauma as a result (Conn & Butterfield, 2013; Devilly & Varker, 2013; Foley et al., 2022). Some of the more challenging work experiences reportedly related to child and family abuse, shift work, and internal policies and practices perceived to be non-supportive (Foley et al., 2022).

In cases where police officers feel they must choose between their mental health and that of a victim of crime, they may demonstrate compassion fatigue. Canadian research with ten general duty police officers found that six of the officers actively avoided being emotionally engaged (i.e., "learning or paying attention to personal details about the victim that might create a personal connection or feelings of empathy or sympathy" (Conn & Butterfield, 2013, p. 280). This demonstrates the insidious nature of untreated complex trauma on workers' effectiveness in doing the job.

Furthermore, policing organisations themselves may cause trauma. The paramilitary, hypermasculine culture of policing is associated with the "encultured behaviours" (Paterson, 2021, p. 56) of bullying, sexual and gender harassment, and "predatory behaviour", i.e., "the misuse of authority or influence to exploit others for sexual or other personal gratification" (EOC, 2016, p. xiii). ***Organisational culture*** is:

> the set of shared norms in the organisation, a consensus about what things mean and how things get done. It is learned through a process of socialisation. These shared patterns identify the members of a culture group while also distinguishing them from other groups. (EOC, 2016, p. 7)

Significant research from Australia (Paterson, 2021), the US, the UK (Foley et al., 2022; Porter & Lee, 2024), and Canada (Conn & Butterfield, 2013) suggest that when police officers are identified as having PTSD and secondary traumatisation, they are not often well supported by their employers. A systematised review of 20 UK articles found mixed evidence of the presence of trauma in policing organisations, with some police assessed as having levels of trauma similar to or lower than the general population despite exposure to significant, adverse experiences (Foley et al., 2022). Jim Foley and colleagues proposed that this underreporting of trauma and stress may be due to organisational factors (see also Porter & Lee, 2024). There remains a stigma in policing agencies that can prevent people from acknowledging distress, trauma, or internal issues such as bullying and harassment and seeking help.

> They cannot speak openly about what they've dealt with and how it's impacted them because it's seen (1) as a weakness and (2) as not professional enough or suitable for the role. No doubt even these days there are police officers who are reluctant to speak about incidents they are involved with because it will be viewed negatively against them. (Retired UK police officer, Porter & Lee, 2024, p. 2221).

Interestingly, recent research based on Australian coronial data from 2001 to 2017 has found that the risk of suicide for police is no higher than other occupations, once controlling for gender and age (Petrie et al., 2023). Yet, intervention strategies to reduce the rates of suicide in policing organisations over the past two decades remain unsuccessful (Petrie et al., 2023). Further, data since 2007 shows that Australian police officers are more likely to die from suicide than be killed on duty, with the rate of police suicidality in Australia higher than in the US, England and Wales, Italy, and France (WAPU, 2023). The impact of a police officer's suicide on colleagues may be exacerbated by policing organisations' silence or lack of a clear strategy to support fellow officers (Paterson, 2021).

7.3.2 Trauma and Correctional Service Workers

Like police officers, prison officers may be exposed to "stressful situations, including, for example, violence between prisoners, prisoner deaths, challenging interactions with prisoners, prisoner self-harm and suicidal behaviors, and violence and interpersonal harm directed at staff" (McKendy et al., 2021, p. 2). Community corrections workers may also be exposed to threats of personal harm or the adversity of others, as well as organisational factors that lead to stress, such as high workloads and limited autonomy (Page & Robertson, 2022; Regehr et al., 2021). The term ***"corrections fatigue"*** has been developed to refer to "a collection of symptoms that includes negative personality changes, socially dysfunctional thinking, and declined health and functioning" (Regehr et al., 2021, p. 230). Interestingly, organisational factors have been cited as more influential on workers' mental health than stressors related to critical incidents or the job per se (Regehr et al., 2021). A recent Canadian survey of more than 1000 correctional service workers identified a culture that normalised the emotional and physical harm experienced by staff, as illustrated in the text box below (McKendy et al., 2021).

> [O]ne officer recalled after being stabbed with a reinforced pencil, "No charges were laid as I was told 'This is part of working here, if it bothers you then quit'." Others expressed a similar sense that staff assaults were treated as inherent to correctional work. (McKendy et al., 2021, p. 8)

A systematic review considering the extent and predictors of work-related distress in community correction officers examined 19 studies from Australia (n = 2), US (n = 15), China (n = 1), and Israel (n = 1). The review found levels of burnout akin to police officers and prison officers (Page & Robertson, 2022). Another systematic review of the prevalence of PTSD, depression, and anxiety disorders in correctional officers focused on seven studies from the Netherlands, Canada, the US (n = 2), France, China, and Ireland (Regehr et al., 2021). Overall, diagnoses of PTSD, depression, and anxiety were considerably higher in the correctional workforce than in the general population, indicating a significant and costly burden of disease. Personal injury and exposure to violence were closely associated with diagnoses of PTSD (Regehr et al., 2021).

7.3.3 Trauma and Legal Practitioners

Lawyers are not traditionally trained to recognise the precursors or acknowledge the risk of psychosocial harm or secondary traumatisation related to their work (Burton & Paton, 2021). As noted by Colin James (2020), "[a] conventional approach to trauma in the legal profession is to deny the problem and assert that lawyers should get used to it, be resilient, toughen up or 'grow a thick skin'" (p. 276). Stine Iversen and Noelle Robertson (2021) published a systematic review of secondary trauma in the legal profession. They considered ten studies from the US (n = 6), Canada (n = 1), and Australia (n = 3), of which four referred to vicarious and secondary trauma in judges and six studies focused on lawyers. They found that legal practitioners experienced higher levels of secondary trauma than people in other occupations, including mental health professionals and medical staff (Iversen & Robertson, 2021). An Australian study comparing lawyers with mental health professionals found the latter more resilient when faced with workplace adversity (Maguire & Byrne, 2017). Grace Maguire and Mitchell Byrne (2017) suggested that mental health workers may better manage the symptoms of trauma because they have received training regarding trauma and trauma-informed practice and have greater access to informed peer support.

Law and legal practice promote silence around struggles with mental health and wellbeing, driven by a professional culture characterised by "pessimism, scepticism, and perfectionism" (James, 2020, p. 279, references removed). Evidence from the UK (Collier, 2016) and Australia (Doyle, 2021) indicates that the culture of the legal profession also enables and condones sexual and gender harassment, resulting in (or exacerbating) psychosocial harm to lawyers. The stigma in the legal profession associated with not acknowledging weakness nor speaking out can also exacerbate trauma symptoms. A 2012–2013 Australian survey of nearly 1000 legal practitioners found that they reported moderate to severe symptoms of depression (higher than other professional groups), with the study's findings suggesting "that higher use of alcohol was associated with more serious depression, anxiety and stress symptoms and a higher self-reported stress level" (Chan et al., 2014, p. 1087).

7.3.4 Trauma and the Judiciary

Fewer than 100 published studies focus on judicial stress (Schrever et al., 2019). Two key Australian studies examined secondary traumatisation in judicial officers, one in Victoria (Vic; Schrever, 2019; Schrever et al., 2019) and one in NSW (O'Sullivan et al., 2022). The Vic study was based on data from 152 judicial officers from five Australian courts, the majority of whom dealt with criminal matters (81.6%), some exclusively (58.6%) (Schrever, 2019). Carly Schrever found that more than half the judicial officers (52.9%) scored moderate to very high levels of psychological distress, with 83.6 percent reporting at least one symptom of STS in the week before completing the survey (based on 125 responses to the STS Scale). The NSW study (O'Sullivan et al., 2022) surveyed 205 judicial officers. Again, reported secondary traumatisation was high, with judicial officers highlighting that the most disturbing cases they presided over related to child abuse and child fatalities and the associated indifference or cruelty of adults. More than half (n = 125) reported aggressive behaviour or receiving threats of harm to themselves, family, or property (O'Sullivan et al., 2022). Judges also reported large and unrelenting workloads and highlighted the stress associated with public and media condemnation of their decisions, given they had no opportunity for public recourse as independent arbiters (O'Sullivan et al., 2022). This negative public criticism can also compound the impact of other stressors.

Judges have a unique workplace with high independence and limited organisational support (O'Sullivan et al., 2022; Polak et al., 2019). In the Vic study, one-third of judicial officers (30.6%) had "problematic" levels of alcohol use (like lawyers, which was 32%, but higher than the general population, 18.8%, using the Alcohol Use Disorders Identification Test; Schrever, 2019). As noted by Schrever (2019), "[w]hether the use of alcohol among judicial officers and lawyers is principally to manage stress, or is simply a cultural feature of the profession, is not known" (p. 42). In NSW, judicial officers reported that peer support was key in managing distress, with court security staff/sheriffs and support from the court management also helpful (O'Sullivan et al., 2022; see also Skilnick, 2017). Very few raised their work-related distress with medical practitioners. Similarly, a survey of judicial officers in the UK found that judges would like more opportunities to debrief with colleagues and more organisational support to help address work-related stress and secondary traumatisation (Thomas, 2021a, 2021b).

7.4 Responding to Secondary Traumatisation

Little empirical research has focused on what works to prevent or reduce secondary traumatisation in the criminal justice system (Bercier & Maynard, 2015; Foley et al., 2022). Secondary trauma may be managed or avoided through both systemic and individual responses (Martínez et al., 2021). A significant issue for criminal justice workers, as noted above, is occupational cultures of not speaking out or seeking help, which can result in compounded or complex trauma (Conn & Butterfield, 2013; Foley et al., 2022; Skilnick, 2017). Social welfare and health sector workers, such as psychologists and social workers, recognise the risk of ongoing exposure to adversity and actively require professional supervision to identify and manage traumatic impacts on workers' social and emotional wellbeing. Interventions should focus on cognitive, behavioural, and emotional support to minimise secondary traumatisation within the criminal justice workforce (Conn & Butterfield, 2013).

7.4.1 Cognitive and Educational Strategies

Cognitive strategies, such as psychoeducation, could be provided across the criminal justice sector to help combat secondary traumatisation in professionals by managing expectations and attitudes towards victims of crime and people who offend (Conn & Butterfield, 2013; Foley et al., 2022) as well as the worker's sphere of influence. Stephanie Conn and Lee Butterfield (2013) note that:

> The literature on countertransference among therapists discusses overidentification and distancing from the trauma victim. There do not appear to be strategies designed to address this same dilemma with police officers. It is possible that the treatment for therapists' countertransference issues could be adapted to suit the needs of police officers who may be troubled by tendencies to over-identify with or distance from victims. (p. 289, references removed)

7.4.2 Behaviour Self-Care Strategies

To deal with secondary traumatisation, professionals may employ self-care strategies. A recent concept analysis based on 31 studies defined ***self-care*** as "the ability to care for oneself through **awareness**, **self-control**, and **self-reliance** in order to achieve, maintain, or promote optimal health and well-being" (Martínez et al., 2021, p. 422, emphasis added).

- ***Self-awareness*** helps to recognise personal responses to adversity experienced by others and directly and normalise and validate those responses (James, 2020).

- ***Self-control*** relates to effective emotional regulation (Martínez et al., 2021).
- ***Self-reliance*** is necessary to implement self-care strategies actively and relates to perseverance and resilience (Martínez et al., 2021).

Self-care involves a commitment, a plan, and action (James, 2020) and includes subjective and individualised strategies such as exercising, relaxation activities, prayer, meditation, socialising and spending time with family and friends, hobbies, sleeping and eating well and setting boundaries (Conn & Butterfield, 2013). Self-care can also involve reliance on co-workers (i.e., the trauma-informed principle of peer support, see below), for professionals often feel they cannot, and should not, bring work-related adversity and stress home.

7.4.3 Emotional, Therapeutic Strategies

Therapeutic strategies to support emotional regulation and strengths can be provided by and for individual workers. The self-care element of "awareness" involves the self-monitoring of symptoms that indicate an increase in secondary traumatic stress (Martínez et al., 2021). ***Mindfulness*** is an "awareness of one's internal states and surroundings" (APA, 2018). Mindfulness-based strategies have been shown to be effective in reducing psychological distress and promoting positive mental health in a randomised controlled trial involving 114 US police officers (Grupe et al., 2021). Mindfulness-based training includes strategies to promote self-regulation, connection to and compassion for others, and an awareness and acceptance of difficult emotions (Grupe et al., 2021).

> The self-awareness enabled through mindfulness practice can help to integrate and resolve ideas, memories and images (cognitive) and somatic (body-related) and affective (emotional) aspects of anxiety-related trauma. It also helps improve self-compassion and other adaptive outcomes such as 'post-traumatic growth', enabling a forward-thinking optimism and a greater appreciation of life and meaning at work. (James, 2020, p. 289, references removed)

Further, workplaces, such as police services, correctional service agencies, and courts, should offer access to free and confidential employee support programs and encourage staff to engage in therapeutic services as required and without fear of stigma or judgement by their colleagues. Finally, proactive professional supervision—akin to that required for social workers and psychologists—could assist in normalising emotional responses in the context of their work and the broader criminal justice system (James, 2020).

7.5 The importance of a Trauma-Informed Response

A trauma-informed response is protective of criminal justice workers even if their exposure to adversity does not result in trauma. This chapter has referred to secondary traumatisation—burnout, compassion fatigue, STS, and vicarious trauma. Addressing secondary traumatisation is particularly important because people with trauma (e.g., clients, victims of crime and others) are likely to perceive and identify trauma in others, which may undermine a person's ability to do their job well (Kezelman & Stavropoulos, 2016). Indeed:

> [t]rauma-informed training as part of professional development may help lawyers not only to protect themselves, but to improve their client skills and effectiveness through better understanding of the responses and decisions of clients who may have suffered childhood abuse or other complex trauma. (James, 2020, p. 284)

However, the identification of risk and early intervention by individuals and employers is the best strategy to minimise the likelihood of trauma.

As discussed in Chapter 5 (and illustrated in Fig. 5.1), a trauma-informed approach can be broadly applied across the criminal justice system to ensure the 4Rs, namely: that the potential for trauma is **realised**, risks are **recognised**, the sector **responds** in a way that prevents entrenched trauma and **resists** further traumatisation (Kezelman &

Stavropoulos, 2016; SAMHSA, 2014). James (2020) recognised that: "[i]ndirect trauma… is likely to be common; however, it is not inevitable, and the risk can be reduced by ensuring there are good protocols and giving [workers] appropriate information, training, preparation, and support" (p. 284). The 3R of SAMHSA's (2014) 4Rs (i.e., a trauma-informed response) is key to reducing the risk of work-related adversity and associated direct and secondary traumatisation.

Workers must not only be able to access cognitive, behavioural, and emotional support, but employers should provide these in a way that reflects trauma-informed principles of practice. As discussed in Chapter 5, these "foundational principles" of practice are often represented as safety, trustworthiness, choice, collaboration, and empowerment (Kezelman & Stavropoulos, 2012, p. 12; citing Fallot & Harris, 2011), but SAMHSA (2014) has developed six, as shown in Fig. 7.1.

If these principles of practice are applied to employers' responsibilities, then:

- **Safety** requires that workers feel safe through organisational policies, procedures, and supervision (James, 2020). Safety can be maximised

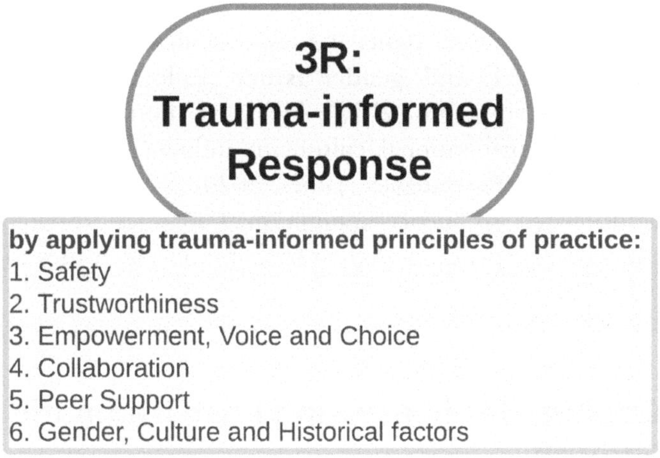

Fig. 7.1 The six principles of practice that underpin a trauma-informed response (SAMHSA, 2014)

through psychoeducation, awareness of the existing protective policies and practices, and the confidence to access services when required, knowing no judgement or penalty is attached to proactive self-care.

- **Trustworthiness and transparency** refer to establishing mutually understood, clear, and consistent expectations and boundaries, which could help workers know when it might be appropriate to access services and set professional boundaries.
- **Peer support** is key to avoiding and managing workplace-related stress and trauma (Foley et al., 2022). However, peer support alone is insufficient, for it is possible to have strong peer support but lack broader organisational support. Indeed, "[d]escriptions of camaraderie occurred in the context of an organization whose policies and practices may or may not have been conducive to employee mental health" (Conn & Butterfield, 2013, p. 281).
- **Collaboration** requires that workers can participate in the planning and shared decision-making around service provision with employers.
- **Empowerment and voice** aim to promote the skills development of workers through a strengths-based approach. This should include supervision where workers can share thoughts and emotions about their work and concerns (James, 2020). **Choice** involves allowing workers to decide when and how they access support and information and an awareness of their rights and responsibilities.
- **Culture, historical, and gender issues** (Fallot & Harris, 2011; Kezelman & Stavropoulos, 2012), including the recognition of the importance of organisational culture in influencing effective help-seeking and self-care strategies (James, 2020), as well as recognising that work-related secondary trauma may manifest differently for different people, depending on their backgrounds, identities and other personal factors.

7.6 Coping, Resilience, and Post-Traumatic Growth

As defined by Andrew Paterson (2021):

> Resilience is the capacity to recover between challenging duty-related events and wellness is the continuing benefit of being able to do so as [workers] reap the ongoing benefits of self-care. Coping is the long-term outcome of resilience and wellness. (p. 83)

Coping and resilience may result from consciously applying the abovementioned strategies, working in a trauma-informed workplace, or subconsciously leveraging a person's internal and external supports to manage work-related stressors. People in the justice system work in a range of roles with varying degrees of contact with (people with) trauma. Some people can experience post-traumatic growth—even when it relates to secondary trauma (Paterson, 2021). Post-traumatic growth is more than being resilient; it is about becoming a stronger person by dealing with trauma through the application of personal and organisational strategies (James, 2022).

Indeed, post-traumatic growth can be associated with compassion satisfaction, which centres around a worker's pleasure from doing their work well (Stamm, 2010, p. 12). This sense of purpose at work helps workers to cope with secondary traumatisation. For example, research with 21 mental health professionals in Scotland found that clinicians who work with people with trauma often felt that they had a calling or vocation to do that work (Coleman et al., 2021). They "spoke of how they felt that they had expanded, grown, and developed through this work. Some described this work as giving their own life meaning and of developing a sense of fulfilment as a result" (Coleman et al., 2021, p. 2802). Similarly, research with 50 South Australia Police officers found that, despite the lack of "significant" organisational support, many officers' "sense of duty encourages them to adopt measures that contribute to their long-term well-being, personal and professional growth" (Paterson, 2021, p. 12).

7.7 Conclusion

Working in the criminal justice sector can be stressful, as illustrated in this chapter, which focuses on police, correctional service officers, and legal practitioners. Work-related distress is due to both direct adverse experiences and exposure to the distress and trauma of others. The potential manifestations of direct and secondary trauma are likely to undermine a professional's ability to do their job well. However, early recognition and intervention are likely to help limit the impact of work-related adversity. Various strategies exist which can be implemented both by workers and their employers. However, employers must also work to ensure organisational cultures that support help-seeking behaviours and prevent organisational distress due to harassment, bullying, or unsupportive leadership. If the criminal justice sector applied a trauma-informed response framework, this would promote practices which ensure workers' safety, trust, and empowerment to cope, and build resilience effectively.

Key Points

- Working in the criminal justice system can be stressful due to both direct adverse experiences and exposure to the distress and trauma of others.
- Research indicates that police officers, correctional workers, and legal practitioners are often diagnosed as having higher levels of anxiety, depression, and PTSD than the general population, as well as alcohol use disorders.
- Surprisingly, evidence indicates that work-related distress in the criminal justice sector is often not caused by critical incidents or the nature of the job per se but by an employer or leadership team perceived as unsupportive and uncaring.
- A trauma-informed response can help promote a healthy workplace for workers, clients, and others. A trauma-informed organisational response does not require that everyone has experienced trauma to be helpful in reducing risk of psychosocial harms.

References

American Psychological Association (APA). (2018). *APA Dictionary of Psychology.* https://dictionary.apa.org/mindfulness

Bercier, M. L., & Maynard, B. R. (2015). Interventions for Secondary Traumatic Stress with Mental Health Workers: A Systematic Review. *Research on Social Work Practice, 25*(1), 81–89. https://doi.org/10.1177/1049731513517142

Birze, A., Regehr, K., & Regehr, C. (2023). Workplace Trauma in a Digital Age: The Impact of Video Evidence of Violent Crime on Criminal Justice Professionals. *Journal of Interpersonal Violence, 38*(1–2), 1654–1689. https://doi.org/10.1177/08862605221090571

Burton, K., & Paton, A. (2021). Vicarious trauma: Strategies for legal practice and law schools. *Alternative Law Journal, 46*(2), 94–99. https://doi.org/10.1177/1037969X21999850

Chan, J., Poynton, S., & Bruce, J. (2014). Lawyering stress and work culture: An Australian study. *UNSW Law Journal, 37*, 1062–1102.

Coleman, A. M., Chouliara, Z., & Currie, K. (2021). Working in the Field of Complex Psychological Trauma: A Framework for Personal and Professional Growth, Training, and Supervision. *Journal of Interpersonal Violence, 36*(5–6), 2791–2815. https://doi.org/10.1177/0886260518759062

Collier, R. (2016). Wellbeing in the Legal Profession: Reflections on Recent Developments (Or, what do we Talk About, When We Talk About Wellbeing?). *International Journal of the Legal Profession, 23*(1), 41–60. https://doi.org/10.1080/09695958.2015.1113970

Conn, S. M., & Butterfield, L. D. (2013). Coping with Secondary Traumatic Stress by General Duty Police Officers: Practical Implications. *Canadian Journal of Counselling and Psychotherapy, 47*(2), 272–298.

Devilly, J., & Varker, T., (2013). *The Prevention of Trauma Reactions in Police Officers: Decreasing Reliance on Drugs and Alcohol.* National Drug Law Enforcement Research Fund.

Doyle, R. (2021). *Power and Consent.* Monash University Publishing.

Duran, F., & Woodhams, J. (2022). Impact of Traumatic Material on Professionals in Analytical and Secondary Investigative Roles Working in Criminal Justice Settings: A Qualitative Approach. *Journal of Police and Criminal Psychology, 37*, 904–917. https://doi.org/10.1007/s11896-022-09532-8

Edwards, G. (2024, February 13). *The Dualism of Fostering Trauma-informed Approaches in Policing: Nurturing Healing and Empathy*. [Conference Presentation] 2024 Trauma Informed Policing and Law Enforcement Conference, Melbourne.

Equal Opportunity Commission (EOC). (2016). *Sex Discrimination, Sexual Harassment and Predatory Behaviour in South Australia Police: Independent Review.* State of South Australia.

Fallot, R. D., & Harris, M. (2011). *Creating Cultures of Trauma-Informed Care (CCTIC): A Self-Assessment and Planning Protocol*. Community Connections.

Fenton, J., & Kelly, T. B. (2017). 'Risk is King and Needs to take a Backseat!' Can Social Workers' Experiences of Moral Injury Strengthen Practice? *Journal of Social Work Practice, 31*(4), 461–475. https://doi.org/10.1080/02650533.2017.1394827

Figley, C. R. (Ed.). (1995). *Compassion Fatigue: Coping with Secondary Traumatic Stress Disorder in Those Who Treat the Traumatized.* Brunner-Routledge.

Figley, C. R. (2002). Compassion Fatigue: Psychotherapists' Chronic Lack of Self Care: Chronic illness. *Journal of Clinical Psychology, 58*(11), 1433–1441. https://doi.org/10.1002/jclp.10090

Foley, J., Hassett, A., & Williams, E. (2022). 'Getting on with the Job': A Systematised Literature Review of Secondary Trauma and Post-Traumatic Stress Disorder (PTSD) in Policing Within the United Kingdom (UK). *The Police Journal: Theory, Practice and Principles, 95*(1), 224–252. https://doi.org/10.1177/0032258X21990412

Gilmour, S. (2024, February 12). *Beyond the Bars: Neurodisability, Trauma, and the Criminal Justice System.* [Conference Presentation]. 2024 Trauma Informed Policing and Law Enforcement Conference, Melbourne.

Grupe, D. W., Stoller, J. L., Alonso, C., McGehee, C., Smith, C., Mumford, J. A., Rosenkranz, M. A., & Davidson, R. J. (2021). The Impact of Mindfulness Training on Police Officer Stress, Mental Health, and Salivary Cortisol Levels. *Frontiers in Psychology, 12*, 1–13. https://doi.org/10.3389/fpsyg.2021.720753

Iversen, S., & Robertson, N. (2021). Prevalence and Predictors of Secondary Trauma in the Legal Profession: A Systematic Review. *Psychiatry Psychology and Law, 28*(6), 802–822. https://doi.org/10.1080/13218719.2020.1855270

James, C. (2020). Towards Trauma-informed Legal Practice: A Review. *Psychiatry, Psychology and Law, 27*(2), 275–299. https://doi.org/10.1080/13218719.2020.1719377

Kezelman, C., & Stavropoulos, P. (2012). *"The Last Frontier": Practice Guidelines for Treatment of Complex Trauma and Trauma Informed Care and Service Delivery*. Adults Surviving Child Abuse.

Kezelman, C., & Stavropoulos, P. (2016). *Trauma and the Law: Applying Trauma-informed Practice to Legal and Judicial Contexts*. Blue Knot Foundation.

Ko, H., & Memon, A. (2023). Secondary Traumatization in Criminal Justice Professions: A Literature Review. *Psychology, Crime & Law, 29*(4), 361–385. https://doi.org/10.1080/1068316X.2021.2018444

Maguire, G., & Byrne, M. K. (2017). The Law is Not as Blind as it Seems: Relative Rates of Vicarious Trauma Among Lawyers and Mental Health Professionals. *Psychiatry, Psychology and Law, 24*(2), 233–243. https://doi.org/10.1080/13218719.2016.1220037

Martínez, N., Connelly, C. D., Pérez, A., & Calero, P. (2021). Self-care: A Concept Analysis. *International Journal of Nursing Sciences, 8*, 418–425. https://doi.org/10.1016/j.ijnss.2021.08.007

McKendy, L., Ricciardelli, R., & Konyk, K. (2021). Trauma in the Correctional Field and the Correctional Worker Habitus. *Incarceration, 2*(2), 1–18. https://doi.org/10.1177/26326663211021727

O'Sullivan, K., Hunter, J., Kemp, R. I., & Vines, P. (2022). Judicial Work and Traumatic Stress: Vilification, Threats, and Secondary Trauma on the Bench. *Psychology, Public Policy, and Law, 28*(4), 532–545. https://doi.org/10.1037/law0000363

Page, J., & Robertson, N. (2022). Extent and Predictors of Work-Related Distress in Community Correction Officers: A Systematic Review. *Psychiatry, Psychology and Law, 29*(2), 155–182. https://doi.org/10.1080/13218719.2021.1894259

Paterson, A. (2021). *Trauma and Resilience in Contemporary Australian Policing: Is PTS Inevitable for First Responders?* Springer.

Perez, L. M., Jones, J., Englert, D. R., & Sachau, D. (2010). Secondary Traumatic Stress and Burnout Among Law Enforcement Investigators Exposed to Disturbing Media Images. *Journal of Police and Criminal Psychology, 25*(2), 113–124. https://doi.org/10.1007/s11896-010-9066-7

Petrie, K., Spittal, M., Zeritis, S., Phillips, M., Deady, M., Forbes, D., Bryant, R., Shand, F., & Harvey, S. B. (2023). Suicide Among Emergency Service Workers: A Retrospective Mortality Study of National Coronial Data, 2001–2017. *Psychological Medicine, 53*, 5470–5477. https://doi.org/10.1017/S0033291722002653

Polak, S., Bailey, R., & Bailey, E. (2019). Secondary Traumatic Stress in the Courtroom: Suggestions for Preventing Vicarious Trauma Resulting from Child Sexual Abuse Imagery. *Juvenile and Family Court Journal, 70*(2), 69–75.

Porter, C. N., & Lee, R. (2024). The Policing Culture: An Exploration into the Mental Health of Former British Police Officers. *Current Psychology, 43*, 2214–2228. https://doi.org/10.1007/s12144-023-04365-y

Rauvola, R. S., Vega, D. M., & Lavigne, K. N. (2019). Compassion Fatigue, Secondary Traumatic Stress, and Vicarious Traumatization: A Qualitative Review and Research Agenda. *Occupational Health Science, 3*, 297–336. https://doi.org/10.1007/s41542-019-00045-1

Regehr, C., Carey, M., Wagner, S., Alden, L. E., Buys, N., Corneil, W., Fyfe, T., Fraess-Phillips, A., Krutop, E., Matthews, L., Randall, C., White, M., & White, N. (2021). Prevalence of PTSD, Depression and Anxiety Disorders in Correctional Officers: A Systematic Review. *Corrections, 6*(3), 229–241. https://doi.org/10.1080/23774657.2019.1641765

Schrever, C. (2019). Australia's First Research Measuring Judicial Stress: What Does It Mean for Judicial Officers and the Courts? *Judicial Officers' Bulletin, 31*(5), 41–43.

Schrever, C., Hulbert, C., & Sourdin, T. (2019). The Psychological Impact of Judicial Work: Australia's First Empirical Research Measuring Judicial Stress and Wellbeing. *Journal of Judicial Administration, 28*(3), 141–168.

Skilnick, K. D. (2017). Judicial Wellness: Vicarious Trauma and Secondary Traumatic Stress in Judges. *PCJ News, 19*(2), 35–46.

Stamm, B. H. (2010). *The Concise ProQOL Manual* (2nd ed.). ProQOL.org.

Substance Abuse and Mental Health Services Administration (SAMHSA). (2014). *SAMHSA's Concept of Trauma and Guidance for a Trauma-Informed Approach*. US Department of Health and Human Services.

Thomas, C. (2021a). *2020 UK Judicial Attitude Survey: Report of findings covering salaried judges in England & Wales Courts and UK Tribunals*. UCL Judicial Institute.

Thomas, C. (2021b). *2020 UK Judicial Attitude Survey: Report of findings covering salaried judges in Scotland*. UCL Judicial Institute.

Turgoose, D., Glover, N., & Maddox, L. (2022). Burnout and the Psychological Impact of Policing: Trends and Coping Strategies. In P. Barbosa Marques & M. Paulino (Eds.), *Police Psychology: New Trends in Forensic Psychological Science* (pp. 63–86). Academic Press. https://doi.org/10.1016/C2018-0-00608-8

WA Police Union (WAPU). (2023). *Police Officer Suicides in Australia*. WAPU.

Part III

Part III: Responding to Traumatised Defendants: Trauma-Informed Sentencing

8

Trauma-Informed Sentencing

8.1 Introduction

The sentencing calculus comprises sentencing purposes, principles, factors, and non-legal considerations. Judicial decisions are made by balancing relevant elements of the sentencing calculus in each case. Elements of the sentencing calculus may be partially informed by trauma or explicitly trauma-informed. There is a difference between sentencing where trauma has been acknowledged compared to "trauma-informed sentencing" as a conscious, evidence-informed strategy that acknowledges trauma-crime relationships. Trauma-informed sentencing involves more than just the acknowledgement of a defendant's (or victim's) trauma. A trauma-informed approach acknowledges and strives to minimise everyone's trauma. By addressing criminogenic risks associated with unresolved trauma, sentencing sanctions may reduce individual recidivism and future intergenerational criminality. Trauma-informed sentencing helps achieve sentencing purposes, notably community safety. Given that individualised sentencing is a fundamental precept in Australia, the US, the UK, Canada, and Aotearoa New Zealand, if judges focus on sentencing goals or outcomes (e.g., increasing community safety by reducing risks associated with offending), trauma evidence

K. J. McLachlan, *Trauma-informed Criminal Justice*,
https://doi.org/10.1007/978-3-031-59290-4_8

could inform strategies to achieve rehabilitation and recidivism. Such approaches would also better reflect public expectations than relying on purposes such as deterrence that neither resonate with the public nor result in effective sentencing.

8.2 The Sentencing Process and Sentencing Remarks

Before examining whether trauma-informed practice exists in sentencing, it is essential to understand what sentencing is and how it works. ***Sentencing*** is the process of determining an appropriate sanction in response to proven criminal behaviour based on the law, the context, and the surrounding circumstances of the offence. State, territory, and Commonwealth legislation guides the sentencing process in Australia. The sentencing process usually involves a hearing for sentencing submissions and a second hearing for the judge to deliver the sentence in the form of sentencing remarks. Sentencing submissions include pre-sentence reports and victim impact statements. Pre-sentence reports in South Australia (SA) are typically provided by the Department for Correctional Services (most often social workers), a psychologist or psychiatrist, or someone with specialist knowledge. The defence, prosecution, or court may also seek expert advice. Victim impact statements (VIS) were introduced into SA in 1989 (Erez & Rogers, 1999) to inform the court about the impact of the crime on the victim, their family, and, in some cases, the broader community.

Judges use their discretion when giving regard to sentencing submissions. In doing so, they must "act reasonably and justly, in accordance with legal principle, relevant statutory and common law, in the public interest, and not arbitrarily, capriciously, or by giving effect to the judicial officer's private opinion" (JCV, 2020, p. 21f). The judge then delivers the sentencing decision, in the form of sentencing remarks. ***Sentencing remarks*** summarise the context of the offending behaviour, various aspects of the sentencing calculus upon which the judicial officer has relied, and the sanction itself. Sentencing remarks are key in communicating the sentencing outcome to various audiences. Martin (2013) highlights the importance of "structured, clear and concise" (p. 85) sentencing remarks, given that judicial decision-making may be scrutinised by defendants, victims, lawyers, and any potential appeal court, as well as the community and media. However, there is a need for greater transparency and clarity in the sentencing process. Sentencing remarks are designed to serve an educative purpose. However, if they are not readily availableor are not a holistic representation of the sentencing logic, they do not achieve that purpose. Australian research by Lorana Bartels et al. (2018) and Caroline Spiranovic and colleagues (2012) found that when sentencing remarks are sufficiently detailed, members of the public agree with sentencing judges' decisions and support alternative sentences for vulnerable and low-risk defendants (e.g., where mental illness, youth, non-violent offending are factors).

8.3 The Sentencing Calculus

The ***sentencing calculus*** is the "system of... reasoning by which a sentence is devised" (Bagaric et al., 2021, p. 5) and includes sentencing purposes, principles, factors, and non-legal considerations, all of which are inter-related (Ashworth & Kelly, 2021). In Australia, the sentencing calculus is applied through "***instinctive synthesis***", an unstructured and individualised approach to sentencing. As explained by the High Court in Wong v The Queen (2001) 207 CLR 584:

> ... the task of the sentencer is to take account of all of the relevant factors and to arrive at a single result which takes due account of them all. That is what is meant by saying that the task is to arrive at an "instinctive synthesis". This expression is used, not as might be supposed, to cloak the task of the sentencer in some mystery, but to make plain that the sentencer is called on to reach a single sentence which, in the case of an offence like the one now under discussion, balances many different and conflicting features. (p. 611, para 75, per Gaudron, Gummow and Hayne JJ; footnote omitted)

Instinctive synthesis promotes individualised sentencing, for it is "a subjective judgment largely intuitively reached" (*R v Williscroft* [1975] VR 292, p. 300). Thus, sentencing is not simply formulaic nor a science; instead, it is the considered application of the sentencing calculus (Bagaric et al., 2021). This approach, involving judicial discretion, is similar in the US, Canada (Berger, 2020), England and Wales (Sentencing Council, 2024), and Scotland (SSC, 2021). However, England and Wales also have sentencing guidelines to promote consistency for specific offences (Sentencing Council, 2024).

In Australia—like the UK, Canada, and Aotearoa New Zealand—sentencing exists on a continuum underpinned by both utilitarian and retributivist theories and based on individual justice and consistency (Bagaric, 2014; Krasnostein & Freiberg, 2013; Warner et al., 2017). Consistency may relate to approach or sanction, with the consistency of sanction tending to be more closely equated with sanction severity than fairness (Krasnostein & Freiberg, 2013). This chapter is based on the proposition that fair and just sentencing requires effectiveness (i.e., reducing future offending) and consistency of approach.

8.3.1 Sentencing Purposes

Eight sentencing purposes (or objectives) are common to sentencing legislation across Australian jurisdictions, namely:

1. accountability,
2. community protection,
3. denunciation,
4. general deterrence
5. personal/specific deterrence,
6. harm recognition,
7. punishment, and
8. rehabilitation.

Sentencing purposes are both backward-looking (e.g., punishment, accountability, denunciation) and future-focused (e.g., community safety, deterrence, rehabilitation; Warner et al., 2017). Sentencing purposes are not necessarily complementary. Despite this tension, the High Court has emphasised that sentencing "purposes overlap and none of them can be considered in isolation from the others when determining what is an appropriate sentence in a particular case" (*Veen v The Queen (No 2)* (1988) 164 CLR 465, pp. 476–477, para 13 per Mason CJ, Brennan, Dawson, and Toohey JJ).

Tasmania and SA specify community protection as the principal purpose of sentencing without clarifying how to achieve this. Community protection is often equated with reducing recidivism through either rehabilitation or deterrence. The sentencing purpose of rehabilitation is premised on the idea that:

> the causes of criminality [exist] in individual pathology or individual maladjustment, whether psychiatric, psychological or social. Whereas deterrence theory regards offenders as rational and calculating, rehabilitative theory is aimed at those who are regarded as being in need of help and support. (Ashworth, 2015, p. 91)

As highlighted by the Victorian Court of Appeal, "... the protection of the community... requires that offenders... be given access to the support services and specialised treatment on which their rehabilitation depends" (*DPP v Herrmann* [2021] VSCA 160, para 112, per Maxwell, Kaye, Niall, Forrest and Emerton JJA). Community safety is most often equated with rehabilitation for young people and individuals with limited criminal histories. Judges are less forgiving of people with serious offending histories, whose criminal behaviour is considered more entrenched (Bagaric & Alexander, 2012). In those cases, protecting the safety of the community is more often equated with deterrence, punishment, retribution, and incapacitation (Warner et al., 2017; *Veen v The Queen (No 2)*), highlighting the subjective discretion influencing judges' interpretation and application of sentencing legislation.

Despite its popularity in justifying judges' sentencing decisions, deterrence has been criticised by legal scholars as lacking an empirical foundation and community support, as well as undermining principles of justice (Ashworth & Kelly, 2021; Warner et al., 2017). Judges often refer to deterrence as a strategy to discourage the defendant or others from intentionally committing similar future crimes. Nevertheless, judges also recognise the limitations of deterrence. Recent Australian research involving interviews with 12 judicial officers from SA, NSW, Victoria, and Queensland found that judges' views regarding deterrence were mixed (Bull et al., 2021). Thus, deterrence may prevail as an oft-cited purpose, not necessarily because judges believe it will achieve a reduction in crime but as a symbolic gesture of denunciation of the offending behaviour.

8.3.2 Sentencing Principles

The sentencing principles of parity, parsimony, totality, and proportionality are based on common law. They may be embedded in legislation and, like sentencing purposes, guide sentencing judges' decision-making. ***Parity*** or consistency requires that people who offend who are similarly situated should be treated similarly. Parity may refer to the process of sentencing and the sanction (Krasnostein & Freiberg, 2013). Most often, parity is applied narrowly to ensure comparable sentencing of co-offenders. Parity is difficult to reconcile with utilitarian purposes of rehabilitation and personal deterrence as these depend on a defendant's circumstances and degree of criminality. The most efficacious interpretation of parity is the recognition that as no two defendants or offences are entirely alike, to "stand equally before the law" should not be regarded as the need to punish equally but rather to have the same opportunities for all relevant factors, including individual factors such as general background, to be taken into consideration in sentencing (JCV, 2020). ***Parsimony*** aims to ensure "that a term of imprisonment should only be imposed when there is no other less onerous sanction appropriate in all circumstances of the offence and the offender" (Bagaric et al., 2021, p. 639).

Totality is related to proportionality and the defendant's overall criminality (JCV, 2020, p. 65). The High Court in Mill v The Queen (1988) 166 CLR 59 quoted the definition of "totality" from DA Thomas's *Principles of Sentencing, 2nd ed.* (1979). Thomas wrote:

> The effect of the totality principle is to require a sentencer who has passed a series of sentences, each properly calculated in relation to the offence for which it is imposed and each properly made consecutive in accordance with the principles governing consecutive sentences, to review the aggregate sentence and consider whether the aggregate is 'just and appropriate'. (cited in *Mill v The Queen*, p. 63 per Wilson, Deane, Dawson, Toohey and Gaudron JJ)

In considering totality, judges often work to ensure that the sentence imposed is not so severe as to be regarded as "crushing", such that the defendant gives up all hope of a life beyond prison (JCV, 2020).

Proportionality requires the imposition of sanctions that reflect the seriousness of the offence without being too harsh or lenient (JCNSW, 2006, s. 2–230). The principle of proportionality effectively sets the upper limit of an appropriate sentence that may be imposed based on the objective seriousness of criminal behaviour. Proportionality has been described as "the central doctrine of sentencing" (Kirchengast, 2010, p. 1), championed by the High Court as well as legal scholars Andrew von Hirsch, Andrew Ashworth, and Julian Roberts, as foundational to just and fair sentencing outcomes and promoting equity in sentencing (Bagaric et al., 2021; von Hirsch, 1998). However, proportionality has also been described as "devoid of clear criteria" and "a meaningless, abstract aspiration" (Bagaric et al., 2017, pp. 790f). The most common grounds for appeal are legal errors or arguments based on (dis)proportionality: the sentences are manifestly excessive or inadequate.

Moral culpability relates to intent, motive, and the offending circumstances (Bagaric et al., 2019) and may reduce what would otherwise be a proportionate sentence but cannot increase the sentence beyond what would be proportionate (Bagaric et al., 2021). Moral culpability is influenced by sentencing factors (as detailed below), which may indicate a higher or lower culpability (Ashworth, 2011). There is a logical alliance between the principle of proportionality and the purposes of general and personal deterrence (Ashworth, 2011). Nevertheless, proportionality does not preclude sentencing decisions from being influenced by other sentencing principles, except by setting a limiting maximum term and preventing excessively long sentences solely to protect the community's safety. Ashworth (2011) argues that, depending on the prevailing sentencing purposes, the courts may give more or less weight to sentencing factors that impact on culpability (e.g., reducing culpability may assist in the application of community-based sanctions that more effectively promote rehabilitation).

8.3.3 Sentencing Factors and Individualised Justice

The High Court emphasised in Elias v The Queen (2013) 248 CLR 483 at 494f, para 27 per French CJ, Hayne, Kiefel, Bell and Keane JJ that "[t]he administration of the criminal law involves individualised justice". ***Individualised justice*** is partly achieved by considering factors specific to the defendant and the offending behaviour, such as the nature, circumstances, and impact of the offending, as well as the characteristics of the person who has offended and the person who has been victimised. A court may only consider factors "known to the court", for example, submissions by the parties, expert reports, pre-sentence reports, and victim impact statements.

In addition to sentencing factors set out in legislation, the common law elaborates on the relevance of those factors while also making many other factors relevant in sentencing. Research shows courts rely on hundreds of factors that "can exert a powerful influence over sentence outcomes; they may well determine whether custody is justified and necessary or may mean a significant difference in the duration of any custodial term imposed" (Roberts, 2011, p. 3; see also Ashworth & Kelly, 2021; Bagaric, 2014). While individualised sentencing and judicial discretion are intended to promote fair and just sentences, judges are not required to disclose how they have weighted sentencing considerations when making sentencing decisions (except in so far as discounts may be available; Bagaric et al., 2021). The sheer volume of sentencing factors makes it difficult to predict the likely sentencing outcome for each defendant (Bagaric, 2014). Thus, it is sometimes prudent for judges to articulate all the relevant aspects and individual factors relied upon in their decision-making in sentencing remarks to avoid any grounds for appeal.

8.3.4 Non-legal Considerations

The sentencing calculus also includes non-legal factors, such as defendant characteristics (e.g., gender, race, social class, and physical attractiveness; Casey & Wilson, 1998) and judges' characteristics (such as age, experience, religious, and political beliefs; Barry, 2021). Brian Barry (2021) found that judges are influenced by heuristics, cognitive biases, personal emotions, and specialised legal practice knowledge. Judicial assumptions about public confidence also influence sentencing (Mack et al., 2018). There is a widely accepted belief that public confidence in the judiciary's ability to make good sentencing decisions is low and can be bolstered by punitive approaches. When judges believe that the general public is punitive and expects harsh court responses, this may influence judges' decisions about sanctions and which sentencing purposes on which to rely.

8.4 The 4Rs of Trauma-Informed Sentencing

As demonstrated in Chapter 4, the Substance Abuse and Mental Health Services Administration (SAMHSA, 2014) 4Rs trauma-informed practice framework can be used to examine the degree to which criminal justice practices are trauma-informed. A small body of literature has examined how judges may be trauma-informed in the courtroom (Griffin & Sallen, 2013; Jackson et al., 2021; McKenna & Holtfreter, 2021; McLachlan, 2022; SAMHSA, 2013). Using the SAMHSA (2014) model, as illustrated in Fig. 8.1, trauma-informed sentencing involves a judge:

- **realising** trauma may be present, based on a general understanding of trauma, e.g., acknowledging the prevalence of adversity in defendants' lives and how adversity may result in trauma (e.g., impacting brain function, emotional regulation, and social ability),
- **recognising** specific adversity in a defendant's life and how the resulting trauma has impacted the defendant's social and emotional wellbeing and their (criminal) behaviour,

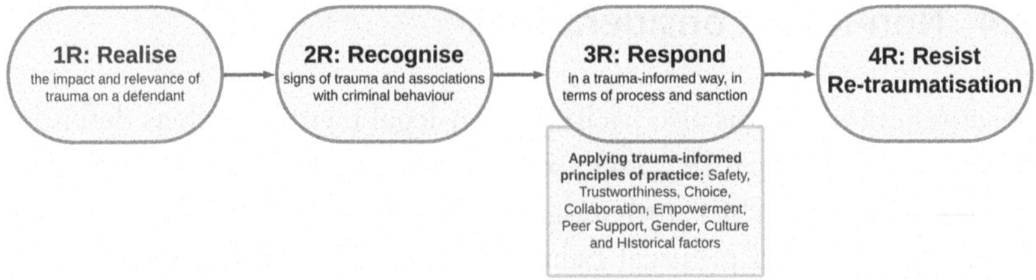

Fig. 8.1 The SAMHSA (2014) 4Rs trauma-informed practice framework, as applied to sentencing

- **responding** by applying the trauma-informed practice principles (Kezelman & Stathopoulos, 2012; SAMHSA, 2014) to the sentencing process and imposing sanctions likely to promote recovery and community safety, and
- **resisting re-traumatisation** for the defendant and other court participants by avoiding traumatic triggers throughout the process and when imposing the sanction.

8.4.1 Realising and Recognising Trauma

Courts may realise and recognise the relevance of trauma as a sentencing factor to be given weight in the sentencing calculus. Trauma may be either—or both—an aggravating and mitigating sentencing factor. An ***aggravating factor*** "makes the offense worse or otherwise justifies a heavier penalty", whereas a ***mitigating factor*** "is a consideration that justifies a more lenient penalty" (Bagaric, 2014, p. 1160). Mitigating factors are not excuses for criminal behaviour but rather put the behaviour into context (Gohara, 2018). Trauma may be regarded as an "ambiguous sentencing factor" in that it may be perceived as an aggravating or mitigating factor and may manifest as cognitive impairments, remorse, and the impact of substance misuse (Warner et al., 2018).

For most defendants, mental health issues associated with trauma are sentencing factors rather than the basis of a mental impairment defence. The Victorian Court of Appeal in *R v Verdins* [2007] VSCA 102., cited by Australian courts thousands of times, states that the diagnostic label is less significant than the impact of a "mental disorder or abnormality" on the defendant's mental functioning at the time of offending and post-offending (para 13, per Maxwell P, Buchanan JA, Vincent JA). The court outlined at least six ways that mental impairment can be relevant to sentencing, including:

- reducing the defendant's moral culpability,
- influencing the sanction,
- "moderating or eliminating" general and personal deterrence, and
- influencing a lesser sanction where it might otherwise "weigh more heavily" on them than a person in good mental health, including diversion from prison, where imprisonment might present a serious risk to the defendant's mental health (para 32, per Maxwell P, Buchanan JA, Vincent JA).

The relationships between trauma, mental health, and criminality were explored in detail in Chapter 3.

8.4.2 Responding to Trauma

Sentencing responses include both the sentencing process and the sentencing outcome.

8.4.2.1 Responding to Trauma: The Court Process

A trauma-informed sentencing court process reflects ***procedural fairness,*** which relates to the fairness of the administration of justice, the process by which a legal decision is made (Aronson & Groves, 2013). Procedural fairness "recognizes that affording voice, respect, trustworthiness, and neutrality are essential" in achieving justice (Heuston, 2021, p. 104). Both trauma-informed sentencing and procedural fairness are based on practices that demonstrate respect for participants' dignity. Procedural fairness is reflected in the trauma-informed practice principles. For example, safety in sentencing requires that defendants feel included and respected, participate, and are heard, and their privacy is respected wherever possible. Identifying ways for judges to ensure defendant safety in court is challenging. This is partly because:

> [s]afety is more than physical safety; it is also emotional safety. It is more than feeling protected from external danger; it is also feeling protected from internal danger… Traumatic experiences that are interpersonal as well as chronic or life threatening are especially pernicious in their effect on an individual's sense of safety. An impaired sense of safety can have varied and long-lasting effects. The survivor might not know how to feel safe in his or her body or even what it means to feel safe. (Classen & Clark, 2017, p. 515)

Not all defendants have experienced significant adversity resulting in trauma, but a significant proportion have. All defendants would benefit from a trauma-informed sentencing process characterised by trauma-informed practice principles (see Fig. 8.1). These principles align with desistance research. ***Desistance*** from crime is "the long-term abstinence from criminal behaviour among those for whom offending had become a pattern of behaviour" (McNeill et al., 2012, p. 3). Shadd Maruna and Ruth Mann (2019) have emphasised that "people are more likely to desist when they… [receive] recognition of their worth from others, feelings of hope and self-efficacy, and a sense of meaning and purpose in their lives" (p. 7). Desistance may be supported through trauma-informed sentencing processes that emphasise the importance of defendants being perceived as agents of change, not just "offenders".

So, how might the trauma-informed principles of practice be incorporated into the sentencing process?

Safety and empowerment may be promoted by ensuring the defendant understands the court process and the sanction. In addition, by directly conversing with defendants to ensure they understand what is happening, judicial officers show concern, use less punitive language and personalise the message, reinforcing that they are "a person worthy of direct communication, regardless of legal representation. This judicial behaviour may display or communicate values of procedural justice that could facilitate the defendant's acceptance of this news" (Roach Anleu & Mack, 2015, p. 1060; see also SAMHSA, 2013).

Empowerment by the courts is best demonstrated by "expressing concern and using less negative, punitive, or judgmental language" (SAMHSA, 2013, p. 5), with reference to rehabilitation and statements made by the courts that recognise the importance of individual strengths and characteristics, such as culture, history, and gender. Empowerment depends on how judges "convey empathy, understanding, cultural sensitivity, motivation, genuine interest in the parties to promote dialogue, rehabilitation and resolution" (Hueston, 2021, p. 6). In addition, empowerment is also achieved when judges directly address and account for factors that may prevent the defendant from fully understanding the implications of the court process and sanction (e.g., due to a defendant's cognitive function, oral language skills, or literacy), ensuring that the defendant understands the sentencing decision (Hueston, 2021).

Trustworthiness and transparency are evidenced when judges ensure defendants understand the process (and any delays) and the implications of the sentencing decision while validating defendants' concerns or fears. **Choice** requires that courts recognise defendants' rights, such as participation in the court process. Defendants have few opportunities to choose how they might influence court processes to increase their sense of personal safety. Further, safety in sentencing is undermined by the possibility that the defendant will be incarcerated. **Collaboration** with defendants and service providers is overt in problem-solving courts, where "the sentencing process is shared, but power is not" (Bennett, 2016, p. 53) but difficult to demonstrate in sentencing in mainstream courts. Arguably, shared decision-making is impossible, although the defence counsel can provide the court with individual factors the defendant believes are relevant to sentencing and propose the defendant's preferred sanction. Nicole McKenna and Kristy Holtfreter (2021) argued that collaboration is also demonstrated when support agencies work together to provide defendants with multiagency case management and services.

While Blue Knot practice principles incorporate **gender, historical, and cultural factors** into the principle of empowerment (Kezelman & Stavropoulos, 2012), SAMHSA (2014) proposed a separate trauma-informed practice principle, as discussed in Chapter 7. Chapter 10 considers the sentencing of Australian First Nations peoples in greater detail.

8.4.2.2 Responding to Trauma: The Sentencing Outcome

Trauma-informed sanctions are designed to assist in the resolution of criminogenic factors or risks. Trauma-informed sanctions may include strategies to rehabilitate the defendant through extended supervision in the community to achieve public safety both in the short and long term. In some cases, trauma-informed sentencing may result in sentences of imprisonment where the manifestations of trauma present too significant a risk to the community, particularly in the immediate future. Prison may be perceived to be necessary to incapacitate an individual, but sentencing should not inherently re-traumatise. Ideally, services and treatment would be available in both custody and the community to help resolve trauma symptoms and reduce future risk of criminal justice system engagement.

While prison accomplishes the sentencing purpose of punishment (and community protection while the individual is incarcerated), there is limited evidence that imprisonment (especially short sentences) results in deterrence, rehabilitation, or enduring community safety. Imprisonment is an ineffective approach to long-term community safety, with more than a 40-percent reincarceration rate in Australia, within two years (SCRGSP, 2023). Lawrence Jones has highlighted that prison may result in a "deprivation of opportunity", preventing people from developing a sense of mastery, competence, or positive identity (Jones, 2018, p. 106). Desistance from crime might be better achieved through trauma-informed court responses designed to maximise trauma-focused rehabilitative strategies and resist re-traumatisation. This way of working is not new or unique: emerging strategies to improve the efficacy of the criminal justice system also focus on compassionate and scientifically based sentencing responses and investment in "smart" sanctions that draw from research evidence.

8.4.3 Resisting Re-traumatisation when Sentencing

Judges may resist re-traumatisation through the sentencing process (by applying the trauma-informed practice principles) and the sentencing sanction. In some cases, where the defendant may be vulnerable due to their age, physical or mental health, or disability, the courts have recognised that imprisonment or harsh sanctions may be exceptionally or additionally burdensome for that defendant. Hardship is a mitigating factor both in terms of the defendant but also for their dependents (Walsh & Douglas, 2016). The concept of "***exceptional circumstances***" relates to "special or uncommon" mitigating factors (*R v Constant* [2016] SASCFC 87, para 67 per Nicholson, Lovell & Hinton JJ), including family hardship (at common law) and legislated factors. In SA, judges are only able to suspend a sentence of imprisonment for specified serious offences (e.g., firearm offences, serious repeat offending) where "the person's personal circumstances are so exceptional as to outweigh the paramount consideration of protecting the safety of the community (whether as individuals or in general) and personal and general deterrence" (*Sentencing Act 2017* (SA), e.g., s 51).

8.5 Trauma-Informed Sentencing is 'Smart' Justice

Smart justice focuses on evidence-informed sentencing rather than hollow, punitive approaches. As highlighted by Samantha Battams and colleagues (2021):

> An alternative to the public and political discourse on the need to be "tough on crime" would be the adoption of a more compassionate, human rights based discourse on imprisonment and recidivism, particularly when it comes to Aboriginal and Torres Strait Islanders who have the worst incarcerations rates in the world, and for people with mental health conditions and disabilities who are over-represented in our prison system. (p. 637)

Smart justice may be perceived as the antithesis of tough justice.

Since the late twentieth century, "smart justice" initiatives have emerged, including restorative justice, problem-solving courts, neighbourhood justice centres, and therapeutic jurisprudence (TJ). As most traumatised defendants are sentenced in mainstream courts, this chapter has focused on sentencing within mainstream rather than problem-solving courts. Specialist problem-solving courts include Drug Courts, Mental Health Courts, Aboriginal Sentencing Courts (Freiberg et al., 2016), and the Neighbourhood Justice Centre in Melbourne, as discussed in Chapter 5. Smart justice approaches are designed to be cost-effective, take a more person-centric approach, address the underlying causes of crime, and reduce recidivism and future offending (Bowen & Whitehead, 2013; Hora, 2010). Each of these elements will be discussed in turn.

8.5.1 Trauma-Informed Sentencing is Cost-Effective

Trauma-informed sentencing enables ***justice reinvestment*** (JR), diverting money from ineffective criminal justice strategies to those resulting in a better investment return. While there is no single definition, JR promotes the diversion of funds from ineffective interventions, such as over-incarceration, to strategies that reduce the risk of future offending and promote desistance from crime, such as intensive community-based sanctions (McLachlan, 2023a). Indeed, in some cases, home detention is more effective than prison in reducing recidivism (Cale et al., 2019, 2023). Intensive community-based supervision with an individualised case plan (which might include substance misuse counselling, mental health support, financial counselling, and supported accommodation) could be used for a broad cohort of justice-involved people who have trauma histories. There is promising evidence from a six-year trial in SA of the Home Detention Integrated Support Services Program (HISSP), run by a not-for-profit organisation, Community Transitions, and funded by the Department for Correctional Services (DCS). The "program is resulting in significant positive benefits and system cost offsets. These benefits... [are] potentially offsetting the cost of HD investment many times over" (Cale et al., 2023, p. 78). In 2022, 19.6 percent of people engaged with HISSP were returned to custody within two years, compared with 39.3 percent released from prison (DCS, 2022).

Trauma-informed sentencing is a form of JR that addresses the underlying causes of crime through individualised sentencing and focuses on sentencing purposes such as rehabilitation and community safety (rather than punishment and deterrence). This JR "proportionate" approach, based on longer terms of supervision in the community, would divert spending from prison to stable accommodation and evidence-informed, long-term therapeutic interventions. In addition, it would have the additional benefit of avoiding prison's criminogenic and re-traumatising impacts.

8.5.2 Trauma-Informed Sentencing is Person-Centred

Hopkins et al. (2022) focus not on "tough on crime" responses but on humanising the people who offend "to understand the individual and systemic causes of their criminality…" (p. 2). Thus, a compassionate approach is evidence-informed, focusing on addressing the drivers of crime, ultimately improving community safety. Correctional service agencies assess individuals' risks of re-offending and criminogenic needs that influence future offending, as per Chapter 3. Given that trauma is associated with significant criminogenic needs and responsivity to intervention programs, a person-centred sentencing approach is imperative to maximising the success of imposed sentencing sanctions. As stated by the American criminologist Francis Cullen (2012):

> [I]t would be foolish to argue that criminals are the 'other' – super predators beyond redemption. This objectification of offenders as a different species – as having a different essence – is a prelude to repressive, incapacitation oriented policies; it also is scientifically indefensible. But [nor should you] make the opposite mistake of implying that there is homogeneity in criminal propensity. Vast amounts of criminological knowledge

> now show that this benign view of law-breakers is incorrect: There is substantial heterogeneity in criminality. (p. 102)

Considering a defendant's mental health and wellbeing in sentencing is not new. In addition to the courts recognising cognitive impairments, which affect how people think, feel, and act, trauma-informed sentencing may be a form of ***therapeutic jurisprudence*** (TJ; McLachlan, 2021). TJ was introduced by David Wexler in the late 1980s, who recognised that justice processes, including sentencing, can exacerbate or lead to psychological trauma (Backhouse, 2016). Wexler and his colleague, Bruce Winnick, in developing TJ, suggested that the law should be as therapeutic as possible within legal rules and precedent (Wexler, 2000). TJ may influence sentencing across a continuum: from court processes to sanction and incidental and inadvertent applications by judicial officers to intentional recognition of TJ principles in practice. However, trauma-informed approaches are more likely to see the law as part of the problem rather than part of the solution, to be improved through legislative reforms and practice change. Unlike TJ, which has law as its focus, trauma-informed approaches are person-centric, advocating for positive outcomes for the individual, which can also lead to the best outcomes for the community by reducing crime and promoting desistance.

8.5.3 Trauma-Informed Sentencing is "Evidence-Based"

"Evidence-based sentencing" in the US focuses on the Risk-Need-Responsivity (RNR) Model, discussed in Chapter 3 (NCSC, 2018). In Australia, the concept of evidence-based (or evidence-informed) sentencing is broader, drawing from empirical evidence relating to risk, desistance research, strengths-based practice, and research indicating the likely effectiveness of different sanctions. As stated above, judges should acknowledge criminogenic needs when designing a sanction to achieve the sentencing purposes of rehabilitation and community safety. Mirko Bagaric and colleagues (2017) have argued, "[t]he most pressing and important issue relating to sentencing law and practice is its continued disregard of expert knowledge and empirical evidence" (p. 786).

Both evidence- and trauma-informed sentencing strive to prioritise early intervention strategies that aim to resolve complex trauma before the effects become entrenched and compounded by additional re-traumatising experiences. True evidence-informed sentencing requires a shift from legal precedent and the excessive use of incarceration, which has been found to increase recidivism, towards sentencing policy and practice driven by empirical evidence. Such an approach would truly reserve incarceration for the most serious offending, where individuals' risks and needs cannot be managed in the community (Bagaric et al., 2017). Other defendants might receive intensive community-based sanctions that include conditions designed to promote community safety through risk management and mitigation strategies and desistance-based strategies that assist in reintegrating individuals.

For many adults who have offended, the opportunity for early intervention has been lost. However, courts do recognise and work to resist re-traumatisation by diverting children and young people away from formal justice processes and custodial sanctions. Youth Courts and Children's Courts often impose sanctions that promote treatment and other evidence-informed interventions, hoping that young people will desist from crime. In other situations, young people are diverted from the system before reaching the courts. Not surprisingly, once young people continue their criminal behaviour into adulthood, court sympathy for developmental trauma may begin to wane. Later in a defendant's life, personal trauma histories may increase the severity of sentences if judges perceive trauma to be an aggravating factor, associated with a poor likelihood of rehabilitation and increased risk to community safety. When sentencing children or adults, therapeutic, community-based, trauma-informed approaches may offer more effective sanctions to promote positive behaviour change and prevent entrenched trauma and criminalisation (McLachlan, 2023b).

8.6 Barriers to Trauma-Informed Sentencing

There are currently pragmatic limitations to trauma-informed sentencing. The barriers to trauma-informed sentencing are not based on a poor judicial appetite for trauma-informed sentencing for, as demonstrated in Chapter 9, judges often strive to be compassionate. Rather, there is a need for broader awareness and education of the general public to demand a political will for primary crime prevention strategies rather than reactive strategies reliant on incarceration. As outlined in Chapter 1, parliaments often amend legislation to curtail judicial discretion due to the false argument that judges are out of touch with the general public's wishes (Freiberg, 2017; SACV, 2019). The "tough on crime" rhetoric has also influenced government investment in prisons and tertiary crime prevention rather than primary and secondary crime prevention strategies. Funding JR strategies requires a political appetite to facilitate legislative reform and reallocating funding. Furthermore, even when sanctions are informed by defendant trauma, sentencing judges have limited control over how imposed sanctions "work" in practice, relying on correctional service and health agencies (particularly drug and alcohol and mental health services) to support and implement sentencing recommendations. For example, a judge may impose a sanction, presuming the defendant will participate in a relapse-prevention program for substance abuse issues or mental health treatment. The judge will probably know that barriers may delay or prevent engagement with rehabilitation programs: waiting lists are long, services are limited, and defendants may only be compelled to engage during their sentence.

8.7 Conclusion

This chapter provided an overview of trauma-informed sentencing. As a form of "smart justice", trauma-informed sentencing may be a cost-effective and evidence-informed approach to promote community safety. Evidence-informed sentencing is challenging for judges, given that they must also apply sentencing principles and purposes refined through decades of legal practice within and across common law jurisdictions. The emergence of trauma-informed practice in other justice system areas (as per Chapter 5) provides the impetus for sentencing judges to embed trauma-informed practice in their work. As Corrections' sentence management evolves, sentencing must reflect the range and nature of sanctions available. The next chapter explores a specific case study in SA, which examined the degree to which trauma-informed sentencing currently exists in practice.

Key Points

- Sentencing involves determining an appropriate sanction in response to proven criminal behaviour based on the law, the context, and the surrounding circumstances of the offence.
- Judges must articulate how they reach their sentencing decision in sentencing remarks. These remarks can inform defendants, victims, lawyers, and any potential appeal court, as well as the community and media, what the judge referred to and relied on in making their decision.
- The sentencing calculus includes sentencing purposes, principles, factors, and non-legal considerations, which aid the judge in deciding on an appropriate sanction.
- Sentencing purposes include accountability, community protection, denunciation, general deterrence, personal/specific deterrence, harm recognition, punishment, and rehabilitation. Judges need not give regard to all sentencing purposes but must demonstrate how they weighted relevant sentencing purposes.
- The sentencing principles of parity, parsimony, totality, and proportionality are based on common law, may be embedded in legislation, and, like sentencing purposes, guide sentencing judges' decision-making.
- Individualised justice is partly achieved by considering factors specific to the defendant and the offending behaviour, such as the nature, circumstances, and impact of the offending, as well as the characteristics of the person who has offended and the person who has been victimised.
- Trauma-informed sentencing is "smart justice", but it requires a political will that currently does not exist. Punitive populism and "tough on crime" approaches, rather than evidence-based strategies, continue to inform the reform of legislative frameworks that inform the parameters of sentencing judges' work.

References

Aronson, M & Groves, M. (2013). *Judicial Review of Administrative Action.* Thomson Reuters Australia.

Ashworth, A. (2011). Re-evaluating the Justifications for Aggravation and Mitigation at Sentencing. In J. V. Roberts (Ed.), *Mitigation and Aggravation at Sentencing* (pp. 21–39). Cambridge University Press.

Ashworth, A. (2015). *Sentencing and Criminal Justice* (6th ed.). Cambridge University Press.

Ashworth, A., & Kelly, R. (2021). *Sentencing and Criminal Justice* (7th ed.). Hart.

Backhouse, C. B. (2016). An Introduction to David Wexler, the Person Behind Therapeutic Jurisprudence. *University of Ottawa Working Paper Series, 13*(May), 1–20.

Bagaric, M. (2014). A Rational Theory of Mitigation and Aggravation in Sentencing: Why Less is More When it Comes to Punishing Criminals. *Buffalo Law Review, 62*, 1159–1239.

Bagaric, M., & Alexander, T. (2012). The Capacity of Criminal Sanctions to Shape the Behaviour of Offenders: Specific Deterrence Doesn't Work, Rehabilitation Might and the Implications for Sentencing. *Criminal Law Journal, 36*(3), 159–172.

Bagaric, M., Edney, R., & Alexander, T. (2021). *Sentencing in Australia* (8th ed.). Thomson Reuters.

Bagaric, M., Fischer, N., & Wolf, G. (2017). Bringing Sentencing into the 21st Century: Closing the Gap Between Practice and Knowledge by Introducing Expertise into Sentencing Law. *Hofstra Law Review, 45*, 785–850.

Bagaric, M., Wolf, G., & Isham, P. (2019). Trauma and Sentencing: The Case for Mitigating Penalty for Childhood Physical and Sexual Abuse. *Stanford Law and Policy Review, 30*, 1–59.

Barry, B. M. (2021). *How Judges Judge: Empirical Insights into Judicial Decision-Making.* Routledge.

Bartels, L., Fitzgerald, R., & Freiberg, A. (2018). Public Opinion on Sentencing and Parole in Australia. *Probation Journal, 65*(3), 269–284.

Battams, S., Delany-Crowe, T., Fisher, M., Wright, L., McGreevy, M., McDermott, D., & Baum, F. (2021). Reducing Incarceration Rates in Australia Through Primary, Secondary, and Tertiary Crime Prevention. *Criminal Justice Policy Review, 32*(6), 618–645. https://doi.org/10.1177/0887403420979178

Berger, B. (2020). Judicial Discretion and the Rise of Individualization: The Canadian Sentencing Approach. In K. Ambos (Ed.), *Sentencing: Anglo-American and German Insights* (pp. 249–278). Göttingen University Press.

Bennett, P. (2016). *Specialist Courts for Sentencing Aboriginal Offenders: Aboriginal Courts in Australia.* Federation Press.

Bowen, P., & Whitehead, S. (2013). *Better Courts: Cutting Crime Through Court Innovation.* Centre for Justice Innovation.

Bull, M., Coomber, R., Moyle, L., Durnian, L., & O'Brien, W. (2021). Sentencing for Social Supply of Illicit Drugs in Australia. *Trends & Issues in Crime and Criminal Justice, 638*, 1–15.

Cale, J., Zmudzki, F., Hilferty, F., Lafferty, L., Whitten, T., Doyle, M., & Valentine, K. (2019). *Evaluation of Home Detention in South Australia: Final Report. SPRC Report/18.* Social Policy Research Centre, UNSW.

Cale, J., Zmudzki, F., & Whitten, T. (2023). *Evaluation of Home Detention in South Australia: Final Report*. UNSW Social Policy Research Centre.

Casey, S. N., & Wilson, J. C. (1998). Discretion, Disparity or Discrepancy? A Review of Sentencing Consistency. *Psychiatry, Psychology and Law, 5*(2), 237–247. https://doi.org/10.1080/13218719809524937

Classen, C. C., & Clark, C. S. (2017). Trauma-informed Care. In *APA Handbook of Trauma Psychology: Trauma Practice* (pp. 515–541). American Psychological Association. https://doi.org/10.1037/0000020-025

Cullen, F. T. (2012). Taking Rehabilitation Seriously: Creativity, Science, and the Challenge of Offender Change. *Punishment & Society, 14*(1), 94–114. https://doi.org/10.1177/1462474510385973

Department for Correctional Services. (DCS). (2022). *Partners Forum 2022. 10by20 Highlights.* Government of South Australia.

Erez, E., & Rogers, L. (1999). Victim Impact Statements and Sentencing Outcomes and Processes. The Perspectives of Legal Professionals. *British Journal of Criminology, 39*(2), 216–239. https://doi.org/10.1093/bjc/39.2.216

Freiberg, A. (2017). Parole, Populism and Penal policy. *Alternative Law Journal, 42*(4), 247. https://doi.org/10.1 177/1037969XI7733160

Freiberg, A., Payne, J., Gelb, K., Morgan, A., & Makkai, T. (2016). *Drug and Specialist Courts Review.* Department of Justice and Attorney General (Qld).

Gohara, M. S. (2018). In Defense of the Injured: How Trauma-informed Criminal Defense Can Reform Sentencing. *American Journal of Criminal Law, 45*(1), 1–53.

Griffin, G., & Sallen, S. (2013). Considering Child Trauma Issues in Juvenile Court Sentencing. *Children's Legal Rights Journal, 34*(1), 1–22.

Hopkins, A., Dodd, S., Nolan, M., & Bartels, L. (2022). At the Heart of Sentencing: Exploring Whether More Compassionate Delivery of Sentencing Remarks Increases Public Concern for People Who Offend. *Psychiatry, Psychology and Law, 30*(4), 459–485. https://doi.org/10.1080/13218719.2022.2040398

Hora, P. F. (2010). *Smart Justice: Building Safer Communities, Increasing Access to the Courts, and Elevating Trust and Confidence in the Justice System.* Government of South Australia.

Hueston, J. (2021). The Compassionate Court: Reforming the Justice System Inside and Outside. *Court Review, 57*(2), 100–118.

Jackson, V., Sullivan, D. H., Mawren, D., Freiberg, A., Kulkarni, J., & Darjee, R. (2021). Trauma-informed Sentencing of Serious Violent Offenders: An Exploration of Judicial Dispositions with a Gendered Perspective. *Psychiatry, Psychology and Law, 28*(5), 748–773. https://doi.org/10.1080/13218719.2020.1855267

Jones, L. (2018). Trauma-Informed Care And 'Good Lives' In Confinement: Acknowledging and Offsetting Adverse Impacts of Chronic Trauma And Loss Of Liberty. In G. Akerman, A. Needs, & C. Bainbridge (Eds.), *Transforming Environments and Rehabilitation: A Guide for Practitioners in Forensic Settings and Criminal Justice* (pp. 92–114). Routledge.

Judicial College of Victoria. (JCV). (2020). *Victorian Sentencing Manual* (4th ed.). JCV.

Judicial Commission of New South Wales (JCNSW). (2006). *Sentencing Bench Book*. JCNSW.

Kezelman, C., & Stavropoulos, P. (2012). *'The Last Frontier': Practice Guidelines for Treatment of Complex Trauma and Trauma Informed Care and Service Delivery.* Adults Surviving Child Abuse (ASCA).

Kirchengast, T. (2010). Proportionality in Sentencing and the Restorative Justice Paradigm: 'Just Deserts' for Victims and Defendants Alike? *Criminal Law and Philosophy, 4*(2), 197–213. https://doi.org/10.1007/s11572-010-9088-3

Krasnostein, S., & Freiberg, A. (2013). Pursuing Consistency in an Individualistic Sentencing Framework: If you Know Where You're Going, how do you Know When You've Got There? *Law and Contemporary Problems, 76*(1), 265–288.

Mack, K., Anleu, S. R., & Tutton, J. (2018). The Judicial and the Public: Judicial Perceptions. *Adelaide Law Review, 39*, 1–35.

Martin, W. (2013). Judicial Education. In Australasian Institute of Judicial Administration (AIJA; Ed.) *Australian Courts: Serving Democracy and its Publics* (pp. 81–92). AIJA.

Maruna, S., & Mann, R. (2019). *Reconciling 'Desistance' and 'What Works'*. HM Inspectorate of Probation.

McKenna, N. C., & Holtfreter, K. (2021). Trauma-Informed Courts: A Review and Integration of Justice Perspectives and Gender Responsiveness. *Journal of Aggression, Maltreatment & Trauma, 30*(4), 450–470. https://doi.org/10.1080/10926771.2020.1747128

McLachlan, K. J. (2023a). Trauma-Informed Sentencing: How South Australian Sentencing Judges Use Information About Defendants' Child Sexual Abuse Victimization and Subsequent Trauma. *Journal of Child Sexual Abuse*. https://doi.org/10.1080/10538712.2023.2219674

McLachlan, K. J. (2023b). Using a Trauma-informed Practice Framework to Operationalise the #raisetheage Campaign. *Current Issues in Criminal Justice*. https://doi.org/10.1080/10345329.2023.2196099

McLachlan, K. J. (2022). Trauma-informed Sentencing in South Australian Courts. *Journal of Criminology, 55*(4), 495–513. https://doi.org/10.1177/26338076221113073

McLachlan, K. J. (2021). Same, Same or Different? Is Trauma-informed Sentencing a Form of Therapeutic Jurisprudence? *European Journal of Current Legal Issues, 25*(1), 1–20.

McNeill, F., Farrall, S., Lightowler, C., & Maruna, S. (2012). How and why people stop offending: Discovering desistance. *IRISS Insights, 15*, 1–12.

National Center for State Courts (NCSC). (2018). *Introduction to the Evidence-Based Judicial Decision Making Curriculum.* NCSC.

Roach Anleu, S., & Mack, K. (2015). Performing Authority: Communicating Judicial Decisions in Lower Criminal Courts. *Journal of Sociology, 51*(4), 1052–1069. https://doi.org/10.1177/1440783313495765

Roberts, J. V. (2011). Punishing, More or Less: Exploring Aggravation and Mitigation at Sentencing. In J. V. Roberts (Ed.), *Mitigation and Aggravation at Sentencing* (pp. 1–20). Cambridge University Press.

Scottish Sentencing Council (SSC). (2021). *The Sentencing Process: Sentencing Guideline.* Crown.

Sentencing Advisory Council of Victoria (SACV). (2019). *Rethinking Sentencing for Young Adult Offenders.* State of Victoria.

Sentencing Council. (2024). *Sentencing guidelines for use in Crown Court.* Crown.

Spiranovic, C. A., Roberts, L. D., Indermaur, D., Warner, K., Gelb, K., & Mackenzie, G. (2012). Public Preferences for Sentencing Purposes: What Difference Does Offender Age, Criminal History and Offence Type Make? *Criminology & Criminal Justice, 12*(3), 289–306. https://doi.org/10.1177/1748895811431847

Steering Committee for the Review of Government Service Provision (SCRGSP). (2023). *Report on Government Services 2023. Part C: Justice.* Productivity Commission.

Substance Abuse and Mental Health Services Administration (SAMHSA). (2013). *Essential Components of Trauma-informed Judicial Practice.* SAMHSA.

Substance Abuse and Mental Health Services Administration (SAMHSA). (2014). *SAMHSA's Concept of Trauma and Guidance for a Trauma-Informed Approach.* US Department of Health and Human Services.

von Hirsch, A. (1998). Proportionate Sentences: A Desert Perspective. In A. von Hirsch & A. Ashworth (Eds.), *Principled Sentencing: Readings on Theory and Policy* (2nd ed., pp. 168–179). Hart Publishing.

Walsh, T., & Douglas, H. (2016). Sentencing Parents: The Consideration of Dependent Children. *Adelaide Law Review, 37*, 135–161.

Warner, K., Davis, J., & Cockburn, H. (2017). The Purposes of Punishment: How Do Judges Apply a Legislative Statement of Sentencing Purposes? *Criminal Law Journal, 41*, 69–85.

Warner, K., Spiranovic, C., Freiberg, A., Davis, J., & Bartels, L. (2018). Aggravating or Mitigating? Comparing Judges' and Jurors' Views on Four Ambiguous Sentencing Factors. *Journal of Judicial Administration, 28*, 51–66.

Wexler, D. B. (2000). Therapeutic Jurisprudence: An Overview. *Thomas m. Cooley Law Review, 17*(1), 125–134.

Case Law

DPP v Herrmann [2021] VSCA 160

Elias v The Queen (2013) 248 CLR 483

Mill v The Queen (1988) 166 CLR 59

R v Constant [2016] SASCFC 87

R v Verdins [2007] VSCA 102

R v Williscroft [1975] VR 292

Veen v The Queen (No 2) (1988) 164 CLR 465

Wong v The Queen (2001) 207 CLR 584.

Legislation

Sentencing Act 2017 (SA)

9

Trauma-Informed Sentencing in South Australia (A Case Study)

9.1 Introduction

With eight years of experience as a member of the Parole Board of SA, I have participated in face-to-face interviews with more than 1000 adults, many with chronic offending histories. There is a large cohort of chronic offenders who tend to be convicted of drug offences, property offences, driving offences, and violent offences. Women often have a history of childhood sexual abuse and abuse within domestic/intimate relationships. Men are often raised in households without father figures; their childhoods are characterised by abuse, neglect, drug use, and domestic abuse perpetrated by a series of 'stepfathers'. Many of these individuals used drugs as children and disengaged from school. They came to the attention of the child protection and youth justice systems and many are Aboriginal. I learned that people who continue to offend into adulthood regularly exhibit manifestations of complex trauma: they find it challenging to regulate their emotions, make rational decisions, or deal with the adversity plaguing their lives.

A parole board's primary concern is to protect community safety. In deciding whether someone should be released into the community and under what conditions, it is necessary to understand research

K. J. McLachlan, *Trauma-informed Criminal Justice*,
https://doi.org/10.1007/978-3-031-59290-4_9

relating to criminogenic risks and needs, recidivism, behaviour change, and desistance from crime. To develop my knowledge, I began to read about neuroplasticity, epigenetics, and the limitations of the DSM (APA, 2022). I spoke with forensic psychologists who believed that anyone can be "rehabilitated" with enough of the right supports in place. I also recognised that some people had never been "habilitated", with lives blighted by high levels of adverse childhood experiences (ACEs), exceptional circumstances, and adversity in adulthood. I wondered: What if we focused on "What has happened to you?" rather than "What is wrong with you?". Would we better identify strategies to divert adults from prison and the criminal justice system? Despite the emerging research that now exists on trauma-informed practice across various sectors, when I began my Ph.D. in October 2018, I could not find any peer-reviewed publications on trauma-informed sentencing. One article was published during my tenure (Jackson et al., 2021). I wanted to add to this body of research evidence.

9.2 The Case Study Sample

To explore the degree to which sentencing in SA may be regarded as trauma-informed, I relied on publicly available sentencing remarks. As highlighted in Chapter 8, ***Sentencing remarks*** summarise the information upon which the judicial officer has relied in making their decision (e.g., context of the offending behaviour, background information of the person who has offended and the victim, sentencing purposes, principles, and factors). Despite the purpose of sentencing remarks to bring transparency to the sentencing process, in SA, sentencing remarks are only published online for four weeks. Then, they are no longer available to the general public (without a hefty fee involved).

South Australia has three courts: Magistrates, District, and Supreme, with only remarks from the two higher courts available for inclusion in this study. The sample consisted of 448 sentencing remarks from 1 May 2019 to 30 November 2019. The sample was based on the number of defendants rather than files (as multiple files were dealt with together) or hearings (as some hearings had multiple defendants) and captured most matters within the time frame. Some sentencing remarks were "not for publication on the Internet", such as some child sex offences, and were excluded. To identify which sentencing remarks included content relating to adversity or trauma, manifest content (i.e., the overt, "visible, surface content"; Maxfield & Babbie, 2015, p. 348f) was used rather than inferring judges' intentions. Both the defendants and the judicial officers have been de-identified.

Arguably, the most trauma-informed remarks articulated little detail of the defendants' lives, protecting the privacy and safety of the defendants. For example, within the sample, judges made statements such as you "had a very troubled childhood, which I will not detail in open court" (*R v JSW*). However, these types of remarks allow for little analysis and were extraordinary; judges more often provided detailed accounts of defendants' backgrounds to help demonstrate to the defendant and "the public... the basis of fact and the reasons why a sentencing option has been chosen" (JCV, 2020, para 2.49).

9.3 1R: Realising when Adversity was Present

Within the sample of 448 sentencing remarks, judges explicitly realised adversity in 233 defendants' lives (52.0% of the total). As can be seen from Fig. 9.1, and as expected, most defendants were non-Aboriginal men (n = 336).

- For most non-Aboriginal men (n = 187, 55.7%), judges did not realise traumatic stressors were present.
- For most Aboriginal and female defendants (and all female Aboriginal defendants), judges realised that adversity was present in their lives.

Some judges made no mention of defendant trauma in their remarks. This may have been because judges were unaware of adversity and trauma or perceived it as irrelevant. However, a lack of reference to defendant trauma did not necessarily mean that defendants had not experienced trauma or that judges had not accounted for defendant trauma in the

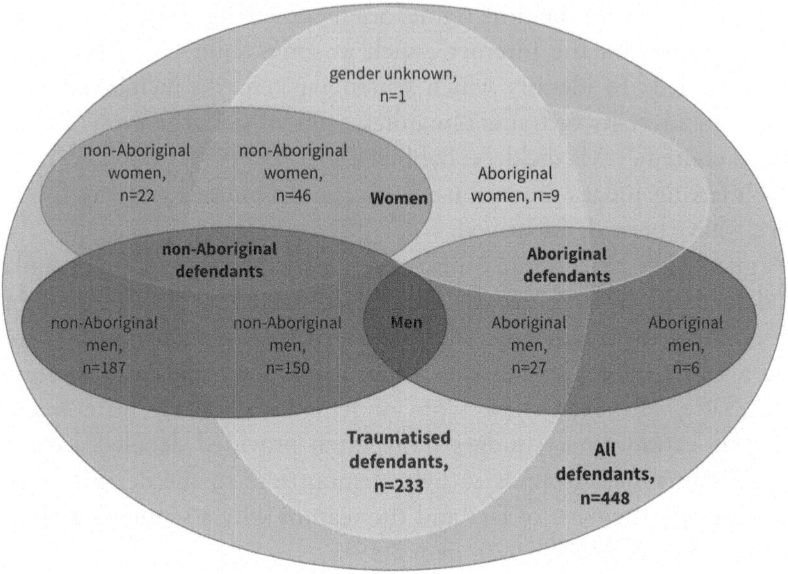

Fig. 9.1 The sample of defendants, where judges realised adversity was present by gender and Aboriginality

sentencing calculus. Judges may have chosen not to highlight identified defendant trauma in sentencing remarks. Adverse events were so commonplace in the defendant population as to be unremarkable. Thus, some judges may have been less inclined to mention "minor" adversity, given that other defendants' trauma was complex and extreme. All that can be deduced from the data was that in 52 percent of the original sample of sentencing remarks, judges realised that defendants were often exposed to adversity and experienced resulting trauma.

9.3.1 Realising when Adversity was Present in Defendants' Lives

Judges realised the presence of acute traumatic events, chronic trauma experiences, and accumulated exposure to adversity. Judges used both specific (as per Table 9.1) and general terms to refer to adversity, the latter including:

- "sad history" (*R v AML*),
- "tragic background" (*R v ABT*),
- "past difficulties" (*R v BTS*),
- "troubled childhood" (*R v JSW*), and
- 'traumatic life" (*R v SAM*).

In addition to the individual adverse experiences set out in Table 9.1, judges realised that some defendants had experienced complex and layered exposure to multiple adverse experiences. The relative prevalence of ACEs (refer to Chapter 4) across the sample meant that judges did not identify the presence of one or more of Felitti et al.'s (1998) ACEs as necessarily traumatic. Judges realised extreme examples of dysfunction and hardship were potentially traumatic, such that the original ACEs could be refined as follows:

- chronic and repeated child abuse and neglect, *often resulting in homelessness and/or out-of-home care*,
- household substance abuse, *often compounded by other dysfunction such as domestic abuse and family hardships*,
- household mental illness, *including parental and sibling suicidality*,
- domestic abuse, *which often involved serial exposure to personal and maternal victimisation, violence, and abuse perpetrated by birth fathers, stepfathers and mothers' boyfriends*, and
- incarcerated household members and parental separation/divorce were less commonly referred to than *parental absence due to abandonment or death*.

In many cases, judges noted the presence of multiple ACEs in defendants' lives. While most defendants had trauma histories from childhood, judges also cited adulthood adversity, including acute events and chronic experiences. Acute events included the deaths of loved ones, car accidents, and an assault. Chronic experiences included domestic abuse.

Table 9.1 Types of adverse events and experiences judges identified when sentencing defendants

	Acute adversity	Chronic adversity
Across the life-course or any time during life-course	• Death/suicide of a significant other (parent, grandparent, child, partner) and associated grief and loss • Vehicle accident or workplace accident resulting in physical injuries, an acquired brain injury, or chronic pain • One-off assault or sexual assault	• Exposure to domestic abuse • Exposure to war and displacement
Childhood		• Child abuse (emotional, physical, sexual) • Neglect • Bullying at school • Parental absence or incarceration • Parental dysfunction (e.g., mental health or substance abuse issues) • Family dysfunction/ hardships • Removal from birth family
Late childhood/ Adulthood	• Breakdown and/or end of an intimate partner relationship • Loss of contact with children	• Workplace bullying

As expected, exposure to ongoing adversity was frequent in defendants' lives. Many judges realised that defendants experienced adversity throughout their life-course, such as the judge when sentencing BSC, who said:

> Your biological father died in a car accident when you were nine months old… Your childhood was not easy. Your mother and her new partner

> were both alcoholics and would regularly get into alcohol-fuelled arguments. Their relationship was often violent and you can remember your mother suffering serious injuries at the hand of her partner. They were both neglectful of and violent towards you and your siblings and, as a result, your youngest brother and sister were taken into care... Your counsel submitted that the most significant and traumatic event was the death of your son... from SIDS when he was four months old. (*R v BSC*)

Mr BSC's life was notable but not remarkable within the sample. The sample of 233 sentencing remarks included almost 1000 references to various adverse events and experiences. The ***trauma load*** (i.e., how severe it was, how often it happened) varied considerably for each defendant, as each identified traumatic stressor may have represented a single acute event or prolonged, chronic experience in a defendant's life.

9.3.2 Realising when Adversity led to Defendant Trauma

Judges' acknowledgement of adversity in defendants' lives is not the same as judges realising trauma was present (although it implies this was the case). Even when judges identified the presence of adversity in defendants' lives, they were less likely to articulate explicitly how adversity led to psychological, social, or physiological trauma. Judges are likely aware that exposure to adversity does not mean trauma is inevitable. Nevertheless, when judges detailed specific adverse life experiences (refer to Table 9.1), it is implicit that they believed these experiences were relevant to the criminal behaviour that followed, or they would not have been included in the sentencing remarks.

When judges explicitly identified trauma, they most often acknowledged psychological trauma, using terms such as 'distress'. For example, in sentencing BH, Judge #14 quoted an expert report that stated that "the distress caused by these traumas, as well as your emotional lability, a symptom of your borderline personality disorder, often leads to maladaptive coping strategies of self-harming and substance abuse" (*R v BH*). The sentencing remarks of BA cite a forensic psychologist's report that acknowledges "...years of psychological distress caused by your childhood sexual abuse..." (*R v BA*).

In addition, where ***complex trauma*** was identified (i.e., the compounded impact of multiple or prolonged traumatic stressors leading to chronic dysfunction; Higgins & McCabe, 2001; Kezelman & Stravropoulos, 2019), this was based on evidence from expert reports of psychologists and psychiatrists. These reports often explicitly linked exposure to traumatic stressors with complex trauma in terms of mental health diagnoses, e.g., post-traumatic stress disorder (PTSD), complex post-traumatic stress disorder (cPTSD), personality disorders, depression and suicidality, bipolar disorder, attention deficit disorder (ADD) or attention deficit hyperactivity disorder (ADHD), behavioural and cognitive impairments or "personality traits" (refer *R v JM*) such as poor coping skills, low tolerance for stress and frustration resulting in aggression (i.e., anger management issues), poor impulse control and impaired judgment, learned helplessness, poor emotional reasoning and social skills, and a "corrupted... identity formation" (*R v SEW*).

9.4 2R: Recognising Associations Between Trauma and Crime

I reviewed the sample of 233 sentencing remarks where adversity was realised to identify when and in what circumstances judges recognised an association between adversity, trauma, and offending behaviour. Judges recognised that trauma influenced criminal behaviour in 111 of the 233 sentencing remarks (47.6%). Judges most often recognised that the offending behaviour of female (n = 26) and Aboriginal defendants (n = 13) was influenced by trauma. Overall, while criminal convictions related to diverse offending behaviour, where a trauma-crime association was recognised, a significant proportion of offences were drug-related (e.g., drug trafficking, drug possession, or drug use while on bail or parole; n = 42; 37.8% of the sample).

9.4.1 Recognising Associations Between an Adverse Event and Crime

Judges most often identified an association between crime and the impact of a discrete adverse event in adulthood despite adult-onset adversity being less common than childhood adversity. Trauma was articulated as an emotional or psychological reaction to adversity. Judges' language indicated acceptance of an association between single incident adversity, resulting trauma, and criminal behaviour, e.g., "led to" (*R v NW*), "caused" (*R v JRV*), "had its origins" (*R v TH*), "began after" (*R v HPD*). For example, in the case of SKM, the judge said:

> Your father's sudden death in December 2014 [when the defendant was about 29 years old] had a significant impact on you. You say **you started to use methamphetamine around that time in order to deal with your depression.** (*R v SKM*, emphasis added)

Thus, analysis of the sentencing remarks indicated that judges recognised the trauma-crime relationship as existing on a continuum from adversity being present at or around the same time as the criminal conduct ("began after") to trauma being associated with crime ("led to"), to trauma being perceived as criminogenic ("caused").

9.4.2 Recognising Associations Between the Impact of Chronic Adversity (Complex Trauma) and Crime

Judges often received expert reports that articulated pre-existing adversity, resultant trauma symptoms (e.g., distress, poor emotional regulation, aggression, and impulsivity), and an association with the criminal behaviour. For example, in the case of MYS, Judge #28 cited the opinion of a forensic psychologist to explain how others led the defendant to offend.

> Dr [Forensic psychologist] is also of the opinion that you suffer chronic mental health difficulties, including social anxiety, depressed mood and

> stress and that these are an extension of your poor self-esteem and low confidence. They arise from your dysfunctional childhood...
>
> Dr [Forensic psychologist] expressed the view that you would have presented as a very attractive target for exploitation and manipulation by your peers...
>
> She believes that you will benefit from individual psychotherapy to resolve your mental health issues, improve your low self-assertive skills and develop a wider range of problem-solving strategies.... (*R v MYS*)

Trauma information was not always included in sentencing remarks in chronological order (e.g., from realising trauma was present to recognising its significance). A lack of chronology is unsurprising, given that sentencing remarks begin by acknowledging that the defendant has been found guilty of (or pleaded guilty to) an offence. So, in the case of MYS, the remarks linked trauma and crime before acknowledging the cause of the trauma and how it led to MYS offending with antisocial peers.

MB pleaded guilty to assisting her ex-partner to avoid apprehension or prosecution after he had assaulted her child (*R v B, M*). While MB had tried to protect her child from the assault, the judge noted:

> I am told that your former partner was also physically violent to you and that he threatened your life and those of your children should you report his assaults on your children to the authorities. I am told that it was out of fear for your safety and that of your children that you assisted him to escape apprehension.

The judge continued:

> Dr [Forensic psychologist] considers that you meet the diagnostic criteria for chronic PTSD arising from a violent incident you experienced at the age of 13, as well as from the domestic violence you experienced at the hands of your former partners. Dr [Forensic psychologist] says you suffer from an attitude of learned helplessness and disempowerment, often adopted by victims of longstanding emotional, psychological and physical violence. (*R v B, M*)

The forensic psychologist found MB lacked both the internal and external supports required to keep her children and herself safe because of the trauma she had experienced. Interestingly, Judge #9 did not comment on the veracity of the information provided, referring to what they "had been told" and what the forensic psychologist "considers" to be true. In other cases, judges were more overt in accepting expert evidence (e.g., *R v SSB*), independently outlining an association between trauma and crime in their remarks.

9.4.3 Recognising the Association Between Trauma, Substance Abuse and Crime

Judges recognised an indirect relationship between trauma and criminal behaviour mediated by drug use. Judges applied multiple theoretical pathways between unresolved trauma, substance abuse, and criminal behaviour, similar to those outlined in Chapter 3. Some judges accepted that trauma influenced drug use, which was either a criminal act or led to criminal behaviour. Judges recognised that substance abuse (which had often begun in response to previous unresolved trauma) became the solution for defendants who lacked the capacity or support to deal with adversity. More specifically, substance abuse precipitated:

- the selling or trafficking of illicit drugs to assist in accessing drugs for personal use,
- weapons offences (to protect themselves or their drugs),
- violence and driving offences committed under the influence of substances, or
- property-related crimes to finance the acquisition of drugs or necessities.

For example, in the remarks of PAW, the judge said, "because you spent all your money funding your drug habit, you never had any money left over for food which caused you to turn to theft and deception" (*R v PAW*).

Judges commonly recognised poly-drug use as a precursor to offending behaviour. In sentencing TAW, the judge said, "Your use of alcohol, marijuana and methamphetamine has been a significant factor in your offending" (*R v TAW*). BJG was sentenced for murder after stabbing a man in a road rage incident. His poly-drug use was extraordinary:

> using four points of methamphetamine a day, an ounce and a half of cannabis a week, a 50 shot of heroin each morning as well as snorting 80 mg of Oxycontin two or three times per day when available. You would also take morphine or methadone when you could... in addition to your prescription medication. On the morning of the murder you had a shot of heroin. At that time you had been on a methamphetamine binge and had not slept for days. (*R v BJG*)

Most often, judges cited the use of methamphetamine, alcohol, and cannabis. It was less common to refer to cocaine and opiates (such as heroin or the prescription drugs oxycontin and buprenorphine) as a precursor to criminal behaviour. Defendants with a cited history of heroin use often moved onto or between other drugs, including cannabis, alcohol, and methamphetamine. Common elements existed regarding specific drug-related offending behaviour. For example:

- alcohol was often associated with angry outbursts and violent offending.
- cannabis use in childhood often pre-dated both adult offending and the use of other illicit drugs, such as methamphetamines and opiates.
- methamphetamines were commonly used to self-medicate, particularly in response to symptoms of depression.[1] Ongoing methamphetamine use is associated with "psychopharmacologically induced violence" (White & Gorman, 2000, p. 200), and any sense of well-being initially achieved through methamphetamine use is lost with ongoing, chronic abuse (Barr et al., 2006).

[1] It is perhaps not surprising that individuals self-medicated with methamphetamine to address depression and grief, for it may be successful in the short term. Methamphetamine was previously used post-WWII as an anti-depressant due to its mood-enhancing benefits; it stimulates the release of neurotransmitters such as dopamine, noradrenaline, and serotonin that promote a sense of euphoria (Parsons, 2013).

Judges noted that the advance from cannabis use to methamphetamine abuse (and other drugs) was not so much a foregone progression as the result of re-traumatisation causing or exacerbating further substance abuse. MWP, for example, had been "a regular recreational user of cannabis from [his] mid-teens" but had not used methamphetamines until after his brother's death when MWP was 40 years old" (*R v MWP*). Judges recognised that people returned to or increased their reliance on substances when faced with the compounding impact of new, re-traumatising adversity in adulthood. Compounding or secondary stressors often included experiences such as death, the breakdown of intimate partner relationships, the removal of children, and (for women) being exposed to violence and abuse in intimate partner relationships. Less often, judges acknowledged drug offences were partially driven by illicit drug use to help resolve chronic pain issues. However, drug dependency was more often cited in the context of self-medication.

Caroline Atkinson (2008) explains that:

> [i]n order to cope with the intense feelings associated with traumatic experiences, some people self-medicate with alcohol and other drugs as a form of emotional avoidance, in an attempt to anesthetise the negative effects associated with traumatic experiences or subsequent trauma memories. (p. 41)

The term "self-medicate" was used by seven District Court judges in sentencing eight defendants and indicated judicial recognition of unresolved trauma. Judges also recognised that substance abuse was used to manage or forget unresolved grief and loss issues.

Judges did not identify substance dependence as a mental illness (or DSM-5-TR diagnosis, APA, 2022) but instead treated it as a lifestyle choice and indicator of criminality. Few judges referred to "suffering from addiction" in the same way that they referred to "suffering from PTSD" (e.g., *R v DLH*). Judges instead referred to substance dependence as "a failure of morals, personality, or willpower" (Broyles et al., 2014, p. 218). This is demonstrated in the following examples:

- "I note your ***candid admission*** of addiction" (*R v WTJ*, emphasis added) implies shame associated with substance dependency.
- Judge #7 stated CC made "a number of ***bad decisions*** in the context of your drug addiction, whilst struggling to deal with your own diminishing mental health" (*R v CC*, emphasis added), suggesting CC could choose to make better decisions.
- KMS was described as "***falling heavily*** into drug addiction" (*R v KMS*, emphasis added).
- Judge #8 described how SDL was able to "***break*** his addiction" to methamphetamine (*R v SDL,* emphasis added)
- JLH was "able to ***free yourself*** from an addiction" (*R v JLH*, emphasis added).

It is difficult to imagine a judge saying someone could "break away" from depression or "free themselves" from PTSD. Judges' strange combination of medical and emotive language to describe substance dependence is both uncomfortable and familiar. In some sentencing remarks, particularly for drug offences and breaches of justice orders, judges perceived substance use as a risk to be managed through strategies such as deterrence and rehabilitation rather than acknowledging that substance use was perhaps a (re)lapse in response to compounding adversity.

9.4.4 Recognising the Associations Between Trauma, Mental Illness, and Crime

In some remarks, judges relied on psychologists' and psychiatrists' diagnoses to support a trauma-crime link. In the sentencing remarks of at least 80 defendants with trauma histories (34.3%), judges recognised that defendants had been diagnosed with psychological conditions, including schizophrenia, mood disorders (e.g., bipolar disorder and depression), anxiety disorders (including PTSD), various personality disorders (most often borderline personality disorder, BPD), and substance use disorders.

Often, these diagnoses were directly attributed to the unresolved trauma of the defendant, particularly BPD, PTSD, depression, anxiety, and substance abuse disorders. In sentencing KRB, Judge #22 accepted expert evidence recognising that childhood trauma had a long-lasting effect on Mr B's functioning. The judge stated:

> At age nine you witnessed your father's suicide. It was particularly gruesome, occurring directly in front of you. He had been violent to your mother in the past. Unsurprisingly, you suffer from post-traumatic stress symptoms. They include vivid images of your father's death. You became withdrawn and reported hearing voices.
>
> ... Dr [Forensic psychiatrist] diagnosis is one of a chronic post-traumatic stress disorder arising from the childhood experiences to which I have referred, and this has led to an enduring personality change. It involves chronic depression alternating with rage, disturbance of self-image and poor decision making. You are familiar with that diagnosis. (*R v KRB*)

KRB's sentencing remarks reflect the decision in *R v Monks [2019] SASCFC 47*, which emphasised that it was not the diagnosis per se but its impact on the defendant's "mental functioning at the time of the offending" that was most relevant.

Judges often relied on the insight of expert witnesses to understand trauma and its enduring or resolved symptoms. For example:

- *"In her report, Dr [Forensic psychiatrist] acknowledges that the death of your niece and her children in 2016 led to an understandable grief reaction and an increase in your dependence on substances. That was, no doubt, a contributing factor to the breaching offences as well, which occurred only a week or so after the suspended sentence was imposed, as I have already said. Your* ***grief had obviously not resolved*** *by then."* (*R v REK*, emphasis added)
- *"[Forensic psychologist]... noted that you were not currently suffering depression, anxiety or stress. She noted that you had used drugs as a coping mechanism and of the relationship between that drug use and the development by you of paranoia of delusional intensity. Those* ***symptoms have largely resolved*** *with sustained drug abstinence while you have been in custody."* (R v KMS, emphasis added)

- *"[Forensic psychologist] found that in addition to the problems with your physical health, you also exhibit* ***fluctuating symptoms of post-traumatic stress disorder*** *and chronic depression."* (*R v DR*, emphasis added)

Judges also recognised that trauma could manifest as impulsivity, aggression, and an impaired ability to regulate emotions. For example, in sentencing KJB for drug trafficking, Judge #4 stated, "[o]wing to your traumatic upbringing, you find it difficult to maintain calm when triggered, especially about your past life" (*R v KJB*). Judge #10, in sentencing ATA for child exploitation offences, noted a psychologist had assessed Mr A's:

> psychological health... as being quite fragile and reactive across your adolescent and adult years, with you struggling to deal with emotional pain and suffering, such that you have never developed appropriate coping mechanisms to help you assuage your emotional trauma. (*R v ATA*)

In sentencing JDG, a financial advisor who stole millions of dollars from 30 clients, Judge #4 recognised that Mr G's depression was relevant to his offending (which itself was influenced by his violent childhood). Judge #4 said:

> You suffered from depression as a result of the global financial crisis. That depression led to the deterioration of your marriage. **I accept that your depression**, coupled with your longstanding low self-esteem and lack of confidence, **was part of the motivation for your offending**. Your clients lost a lot of money in the global financial crisis and, instead of facing up to that fact and telling them the truth about it, you offended to save face. You could not admit to them that you had failed them. (*R v JDG*, emphasis added)

Judges sometimes accepted mental health diagnoses without looking behind the evidence to reflect on the ways mental health conditions may impact social and emotional wellbeing and behaviour. For example, at least 15 sentencing remarks referred to defendants having an adjustment disorder. Judges did not recognise that, by definition, an adjustment disorder is a short-term mental health issue which "[o]nce the stressor or its consequences have terminated, the symptoms do not persist for more than an additional 6 months" (APA, 2022). For some defendants, the adjustment disorder may have resolved before the offending behaviour occurred. This means that either the defendant's mental health diagnosis was not relevant in sentencing or other cognitive impairments present at the time of the offending may have been more relevant.

Thus, in linking trauma, mental health, and criminal behaviour, judges relied on expert evidence, personal interpretations of that evidence and what can be described as a "common sense" understanding of the traumatic impact of adversity in terms of mental health, wellbeing, and functioning.

9.4.5 Rejecting the Trauma 'Excuse'

Some sentencing judges explicitly recognised that trauma explained criminal behaviour but regarded trauma as no "excuse" for the crime. The potential motivations for such an approach are discussed later in this chapter. Often, judges treated trauma, substance abuse, and mental illness as stable long-term conditions that explained (but did not excuse) defendants' behaviour. An alternative approach would be for judges to accept these criminogenic risk factors/needs as dynamic and changeable, as explanations "to be given due weight" in a way that enables trauma-informed sentencing.

> I accept the offending arose out of your all-consuming drug addiction, in the context of your ongoing grief at the loss of your brother. However, **this explains, but does not excuse the offending.** (*R v SWT*, emphasis added)

In the Victorian Court of Appeal, Redlich and Tate JJA explained in *Marrah v The Queen* [2014] VSCA 119, para 16:

> Circumstances of deprivation, abuse and other social disadvantage occurring during an offender's formative years are more than matters of historical significance to the administration of justice. The effects of such social disadvantage do not generally diminish with the passage of time, and are likely to have profound and lasting consequences. The common experience of the law is that very frequently such disadvantage precedes the commission of crime, and often explains and contributes to an offender's criminal behaviour. The frequency with which criminal conduct can be explained by such disadvantage does not relieve each sentencing judge of the obligation to take such matters into account. Though they do not provide an excuse for offending behaviour, they must be **given due weight** in the sentencing calculus. (para 16, citations omitted, emphasis added)

Their point differs from that of the SA judges: trauma may explain crime, not as an excuse but as a factor to be "given due weight in the sentencing calculus".

The Victorian approach reflects the position of Jill Levenson and Gwenda Willis (2019), who stated:

> Viewing criminal behavior through the lens of early trauma does not excuse crime or victimization; rather, it enriches our understanding of how criminal behavior develops and informs intervention strategies. In this way, we can improve desired outcomes such as reduced recidivism and successful reintegration. (p. 481f)

Judges in the sample were not necessarily aware that people with neurophysiological trauma may have an impaired ability to make a rational and conscious choice to act in a pro-social manner. Rather than using language such as "explains but does not excuse", a more helpful response would have been for judges to ensure their remarks included an evidence-informed justification for referring to trauma as a risk and sentencing factor. Judges could articulate how trauma explained the criminal behaviour and why, as a criminogenic risk factor, it needed to be addressed in the sentencing response.

9.5 3R: Trauma-Informed Response (Sentencing Process)

A trauma-informed response includes both the sentencing process and the sanction imposed. A trauma-informed sentencing process was characterised by the "five foundational principles" of trauma-informed care: safety, trustworthiness, choice, collaboration, and empowerment (Fallot & Harris, 2011; Kezelman & Stavropoulos, 2019).[2] The manifest content of sentencing remarks was used as a proxy measure of each practice principle, as per Table 9.2. At least one of the four proxy measures of a trauma-informed process was present in the sentencing remarks of 157 of the 233 defendants.

The following section explores how each trauma-informed practice principle was demonstrated in sentencing remarks before identifying,

Table 9.2 The proxy measures and presence of trauma-informed practice principles in the sentencing process of 233 defendants

Trauma-informed principle of practice	Proxy measures of trauma-informed practice principles	Sentencing Remarks where proxy measure was present (Total = 233)
Safety	Judges referred to defendants directly and by name in the sentencing remarks beyond the opening acknowledgement	n = 133. For 15 individuals, this was the sole example of trauma-informed practice
Trustworthiness and transparency	Judges explained an element of the sentencing process to the defendant	n = 120
Empowerment and safety	Judges asked the defendant whether they understood the sentencing sanction	n = 70
Choice, collaboration, and empowerment	Judges asked the defendant whether they accepted and would abide by the sentencing decision	n = 74

[2] SAMHSA (2014) additional principle of "peer support" was unable to be identified from sentencing remarks, and the consideration of "historical, cultural and gender issues" are discussed later in this chapter and in Chapter 10.

later in this chapter, sentencing responses characterised by all four principles.

9.5.1 Safety

Safety was demonstrated when a judge recognised a defendant as more than "an offender"; as an individual with specific experiences, needs, and strengths. For example, Judge #14 discussed BSC's ongoing medical issues and his need to attend medical appointments. The judge then prioritised BSC's health, emphasising to the Department for Correctional Services (DCS) the importance of supporting Mr C in recovering and rehabilitating while on home detention (*R v BSC*). Safety was lacking when judges referred to defendants indirectly (i.e., in the third person), even when defendants were in court. Judge #6 consistently referred to defendants as "the offender" in sentencing remarks. Sometimes Judge #6 switched from the third person ("the offender") to the second person ("you"). Interestingly, Judge #6 rarely referred to "the victim", more often using victims' names. This "othering" language excluded the defendant from the community of the judge and victim. Such dehumanising, labelling language entrenches the self-identity as "offender" and is the opposite of what is required to achieve desistance from crime (Anderson, 2016; Richards & Jones, 2004). A more helpful judicial response would treat the defendant "… as a citizen who will ultimately regain a valued place in the society from which they have been temporarily excluded, the twin objectives of hope and normality will be fostered" (Samuels, 2020, p. 82).

9.5.2 Collaboration

Collaboration was demonstrated, alongside choice and empowerment, when judges asked defendants if they would abide by sentencing decisions (involving community-based sanctions in all but one case). Judges also recognised pro-social progress made by some defendants post-arrest. For example, in sentencing WTJ, the judge said:

> ... no-one should underestimate how difficult it is to rehabilitate themselves from a terrible drug like methylamphetamine. You should be commended for the work that you have put in to date. I will, therefore, suspend your sentence upon you entering into a bond... (*R v WTJ*)

Rather than collaborate, judges often directed defendants to change their behaviour with statements such as:

- *"Don't get back with that man again. And find a better one next time, okay" (R v JMT)*
- *"[T]ry not to take drugs... [and] don't get in fights... try and walk away..." (R v CJK)*
- *"... get your act together... Don't go back into gaol" (R v MWAC).*

In sentencing SAM for drug trafficking, Judge #8 requested that she "please take up the offer of assistance that will be available to you from your Community Corrections Officer" (*R v SAM*). In this case, the judge acknowledged that SAM had a choice whether to engage with the justice system and requested that she make the most of community-based opportunities, influencing the judge's decision to suspend a prison sentence.

9.5.3 Trustworthiness and Transparency

Trustworthiness and transparency were present when judges explained the sentencing process to ensure "fairness and equity" (McKenna & Holtfreter, 2021, p. 461). Judges sometimes spoke directly to defendants to ensure they understood the implications of the sentencing decision.For example, Judge #11 regularly advised defendants that, while they would not be further punished for past criminal behaviour, the court would treat them with less leniency than if it had been their first offence. In sentencing DAJB, Judge #11 discussed a technical discussion with counsel about judicial powers to set a non-parole period. Once the issue was resolved, the judge explained the implications to Mr B and ensured the defendant understood his obligations to "be of good behaviour" (*R v DAJB*). Some judges spoke with defendants to ensure they understood that a breach of their community-based order would result in incarceration.

9.5.4 Choice

Choice was difficult to identify from sentencing remarks alone and was most often apparent when non-custodial sanctions were imposed. In such cases, judges stated that defendants had a choice (sometimes a difficult choice but a choice nonetheless) to remain in the community by being drug-free, offence-free and "of good behaviour". Indeed, to desist from crime, the criminal justice system must respect and foster self-determination (Graham, 2016). Some judges wished defendants "good luck", "best of luck", or "all the best" in the future. By wishing a defendant good luck, the judge (often Judge #11) indicated the power to desist from crime sat with defendants. Defendants did not have a choice as to the sanction imposed. However, judges' comments sometimes indicated a belief that defendants could choose to engage with service providers post-sentencing and be honest about their progress and challenges (e.g., drug use) to work to establish a new, pro-social self-identity.

Judges often saw engagement with rehabilitation services and supports as a choice. Judges referred to defendants "rehabilitating themselves" (e.g., *R v NDK*; *R v TLK, R v TS*), implying that defendants had the internal and external resources necessary to resolve trauma and overcome other criminogenic risk factors. In sentencing JJL, Judge #3 said:

> People are happy to help you now but support will not be there if you do not help yourself… Hopefully… you will take up the offer… to participate in supported rehabilitation and can this time make something of your time on parole. Otherwise, all you can expect is more time wasted in custody. (*R v JJL*)

Given the dearth of specialised services to assist people in developing strategies to manage behaviour and regulate emotions, statements of self-rehabilitation may indicate judges' lack of understanding of the entrenched impact of unresolved and unaddressed trauma on social and emotional functioning.

References to "self-rehabilitation" also highlighted judges' potential ignorance of evidence-informed behaviour change and community safety strategies. In their Queensland study, Bronwyn Honorato and colleagues (2016) found that "while participants [in prison] may have had considerable insight into their problems and what had brought them about, they did not have access, or the knowledge or services available, to enable them to receive adequate treatment for their psychological issues" (p. 6). Psychologists and psychiatrists did not refer to defendants "rehabilitating themselves" in expert evidence. Thus, at best, when judges offered defendants the choice to rehabilitate, it was a Hobson's choice; an apparently free choice, but dependent on the individual being able to access effective and appropriate services at the time and in the location required (e.g., based on culture, gender, age, wealth, capacity).

9.5.5 Empowerment

Empowerment may occur when judges give defendants a sense of autonomy and control by engaging with them directly and sentencing them to develop personal skills (Harris & Fallot, 2001). Empowerment was demonstrated when judges asked defendants if they understood and accepted the sentencing decisions. After delivering the sentence, judges often spoke directly with defendants to ensure that the defendant understood and agreed to the sanction conditions (e.g., "Are you prepared to enter that bond?"). In some cases, judges explained sanctions to defendants and then asked defendants to explain in their own words what was required of them under the terms of the sentencing decision.

Like collaboration, empowerment occurred when judges acknowledged and commended defendants for rehabilitating themselves. For example, in sentencing SJB for a historical breach of bond (by committing further offences), Judge #11 identified that Mr B, an Aboriginal man, had genuinely believed he had no outstanding matters. In the ten years since the breach, he stopped using alcohol and illicit drugs, obtained full-time employment, and "substantially rehabilitated" himself. Judge #11 imposed a suspended sentence with a bond, noting that, "[f]rom what I've said in my sentencing remarks and what I've seen on paper I'm confident that you won't [breach the bond]" (*R v B, SJ*). Empowerment of defendants was often demonstrated through statements made by judges indicating trust that the individuals would not offend in the future.

9.6 3R: Trauma-Informed Response (Sanction)

Sanctions were classified as trauma-informed when judges explicitly adjusted them in response to the defendant's trauma history, not because they were necessarily evidence-informed. In SA, judges may impose various sanctions, including custodial sentences (in prison or at home) and community-based sentences, including suspended sentences and good behaviour bonds. Sometimes, judges are restricted from using certain sanctions, for example, where defendants are deemed "serious repeat offenders". Despite this, judges retain wide discretionary powers determining defendants' trajectories through the criminal justice system. Trauma-informed sanctions were based on judges' overt statements of intention rather than whether the imposed sanction was likely to reduce re-traumatisation based on empirical evidence.

In 82 sentencing remarks, judges made overt statements that indicated an adjustment of sanction in response to defendants' trauma histories. Despite this, the most common sanction was imprisonment (n = 36), with 30 suspended sentences with bonds, five sentences of home detention, and 11 bonds or no further penalties. Imprisonment and suspended sentences were often imposed for offences against the person (n = 26) and drug offences (n = 25). While trauma-informed sanctions could be longer than usual (e.g., *R v LAM*), judges often reduced the overall period of imprisonment, reduced the non-parole period, or downgraded the sentence from incarceration to a community-based sanction. For example, in sentencing LSJ, Judge #24 said:

> … I consider that a short prison sentence is justified. It will be much shorter than would normally be the case because of your chaotic and unstable childhood, disrupted education and all the mental health aspects

> which [your lawyer] has gone through, which I do not need to repeat... (*R v LSJ*)

Such sentences were well-intentioned but not necessarily evidence-informed (Samuels, 2020). Short non-parole periods were common (n = 18 or 50% of people imprisoned) despite evidence indicating the detrimental effects of short sentences on accommodation, employment, and stable relationships (O'Donnell, 2020). Prison sentencesshorter than 12 months do not "allow for therapeutic interventions or a meaningful incapacitative effect while disrupting employment, family and community ties and exposing offenders to criminal peers" (O'Donnell, 2020, p. 38). Thus, trauma-informed sanctions were indicative of judges' intentions to be merciful. However, those sanctions were rarely informed by evidence-informed strategies that might best achieve community safety (i.e., by resolving trauma and reducing recidivism).

New sanctions (or different ways of using current sanctions) are required to achieve trauma-informed sentencing. I suggest:

> For a traumatised defendant, an effective sanction might be an extended period of intensive community-based supervision, treatment and intervention requirements and stepped-down freedom of movement restrictions. The defendant would need to commit to engage in counselling ... to learn affect-regulation skills ... This "proportionate" approach, based on longer terms of supervision in the community, would also allow for cost savings and justice-reinvestment, diverting spending from prison to stable accommodation, and evidence-informed, long-term therapeutic interventions. (McLachlan, 2021, p. 227)

Such an approach is still punishment, for "surveys of offenders reveal that they are more likely to dread intensive and lengthy community-based punishments than shorter prison terms" (Cullen et al., 2011, p. 52S). Certainly, it has been argued that drug courts are successful because the defendant is effectively serving a prison sentence in the community, and the defendant chooses to commit to an intensive reporting and engagement regime throughout that sanction. While engaging with community supervision, they also have the benefit of formal and informal supports in the community which would not be available in custody (Parsons, 2024).

9.7 4R: Resisting Re-traumatisation

Judges acknowledged that a lengthy prison sentence would lead to traumatic impacts on the defendant or defendants' dependents in 74 sentencing remarks. Vincent Felitti and colleagues (1998) identified parental incarceration as a significant ACE. Parental absence can lead to additional adversity, including contact with the child protection system and the youth justice system and increasing a child's risk of abuse and neglect (Millar & Dandurand, 2018). In the sentencing remarks of 32 defendants (17 women and 15 men), judges focused on how incarceration would traumatise defendants' children or family members. While the judges realised that all the defendants had trauma histories within this sample, they only recognised a trauma-crime association in 16 sentencing remarks. Twenty-one received suspended sentences, five were sentenced to home detention, and two received a bond. Four defendants (two men and two women) received prison sentences, three with shorter than usual non-parole periods.

The judges were required to apply the common law and show that family hardship was likely to be exceptional in order to mitigate the sanction. Tamara Walsh and Heather Douglas (2016) examined Australian sentencing appeals heard between January 2000 and June 2014 in which the defendant appealed their sentence, arguing family hardship. From 85 cases across all Australian jurisdictions where family hardship was considered, they concluded that their review indicated that defendants:

> who have children with serious disabilities or medical conditions may be more likely to be understood as presenting a case of exceptional circumstances. However, and perhaps surprisingly, it suggests that pregnancy and breastfeeding is not generally considered exceptional. Finally our review of the cases shows that the human rights of children are rarely (explicitly) considered by judicial officers. We suggest that the consideration of the human rights of the child and, relatedly, the family should play a more

important role in consideration of the appropriate sentence in Australian jurisdictions. (Walsh & Douglas, 2016, p. 160)

This was reflected in the findings of my study. Judges recognised that families relied on defendants to provide emotional and financial support and parental care. Family hardship was recognised as a mitigating factor for other defendants (or their partners) who were pregnant or defendants who were the sole carers for their children.

Sometimes, judges actively imposed sanctions to avoid incarceration. Some judges recognised that incarcerated people might experience re-traumatisation both in custody and upon release back into the community (Pettus-Davis et al., 2020). The adversity that occurs post-release may be both chronic (e.g., unemployment, unstable housing, and a lack of transportation due to no licence or no car) and acute (e.g., death of a relative or friend, witnessing or experiencing violence, the breakdown of a relationship, loss of access to children or life-threatening injury or illness; Pettus-Davis et al., 2020). For example, Judge #10, in sentencing ATA for child exploitation offences, noted that a psychological report indicated the defendant "would not be able to cope with imprisonment" (*R v ATA*). The judge imposed a sentence of home detention.

While judges acknowledged the relevance of defendant trauma when imposing a sanction and seeking to avoid re-traumatisation, this was sometimes in the absence of a trauma-informed sentencing process.

9.8 Individual Defendants' Experiences of a Trauma-Informed Response

The 233 remarks (where trauma was realised) were reviewed to identify how many individual defendants received a trauma-informed sentencing process characterised by all five practice principles. This was illustrated by depicting a defendant's sentencing experience as a horizontal row, per Table 9.2.

- Column 1 represents the presence of 1R, where judges realise adversity and trauma were relevant.

- Column 2 represents 2R (Recognise) and was shaded when the judge recognised an association between trauma and crime, for the defendant.
- Column 3 represents 3R (Respond). This is broken down into the court process (four columns reflecting the operationalisation of the trauma-informed practice principles) and a trauma-informed sanction. A trauma-informed court response was present when the following boxes were shaded:
  - Column 3.1 (S = Safety), 3.2 (T = Trustworthiness) and 3.4 (Ch = Choice, C = Collaboration, E = Empowerment), or
  - Column 3.2 (T = Trustworthiness), 3.3 (S = Safety, E = Empowerment) and 3.4 (Ch = Choice, C = Collaboration, E = Empowerment), were shaded.
- Column 4 represents 4R and is shaded when judges actively resisted re-traumatisation.

Sixty-four defendants (27.5%) received a trauma-informed sentencing response (3R) in terms of process. However, this did not mean that the overall experience for every defendant was trauma-informed, as seen in Table 9.3. Only the first nine defendants (from the sample of 233) experienced all 4Rs, with a further three defendants' experiences lacking evidence of 'choice' and 'collaboration' but otherwise reflected the 4Rs. For many of these defendants, judges realised that their exposure to adversity was chronic and lifelong throughout childhood and adulthood (e.g., *R v GLD, R v AML, R v SAM*). Their offending was diverse, including drug offences (the most common), violent offences, a sex offence, a deception offence, and breaches of justice conditions. None were incarcerated.

Table 9.3 Individual sentencing experiences, highlighting where the court process was characterised by all five trauma-informed practice principles (Safety, Trustworthiness, Empowerment, Choice, Collaboration)

	1R	2R	3R					4R
#	Realise	Recognise	Respond (Process)				Respond (Sanction)	Resist re-trauma
			3.1 S	3.2 T	3.3 S,E	3.4 Ch,C,E		
1								
2								
3								
4								
5								
6								
7								
8								
9								
10								
11								
12								
13								
14								
15								
16								
17								
18								
19								
20								
21								
22								
23								
24								
25								
26								
27								
28								
29								
30								
31								
32								
33								
34								
35								
36								
37								
38								
39								
40								
41								
42								
43								
44								
45								
46								
47								
48								
49								
50								
51								
52								

(continued)

Table 9.3 (continued)

	1R	2R	3R					4R
#	Realise	Recognise	Respond (Process)				Respond (Sanction)	Resist re-trauma
			3.1 S	3.2 T	3.3 S,E	3.4 Ch,C,E		
53								
54								
55								
56								
57								
58								
59								
60								
61								
62								
63								
64								

9.8.1 How Did Aboriginality and Gender Influence Trauma-Informed Practices in Sentencing?

Defendants identified as Aboriginal and/or women experienced different levels of trauma-informed sentencing. None of the Aboriginal defendants received a sentencing response characterised by the 4Rs.

1R: Realise adversity and trauma were present

- Overall, judges realised trauma was present in 52 percent of the original sample (n = 448).
- For Aboriginal men and Aboriginal women, judges realised trauma was present in 81.2 percent and 100 percent, respectively.

2R: Recognise a trauma-crime association

- Judges were unlikely to make a statement that overtly recognised the trauma-crime association for any defendant; however, Aboriginal defendants were less likely than non-Aboriginal defendants to have any trauma-crime association recognised.

3R: Response

- Aboriginal men were the least likely to experience a trauma-informed sentencing process.

- Non-Aboriginal women were most likely to experience a trauma-informed response, with a sentencing process characterised by all the trauma-informed principles of practice and a trauma-informed sanction.

4R: Resist Re-traumatisation

- Judges rarely sentenced to resist re-traumatisation, with Aboriginal defendants the least likely to receive a sentence that resisted re-traumatisation.
- Judges were more likely to resist re-traumatisation for non-Aboriginal women in two-thirds of cases (65%) because they had dependent children.

The trauma-crime association may have been overlooked for Aboriginal defendants due to judges' over-reliance on the medicalised model of mental health, given that DSM-5-TR diagnoses have limited cultural appropriateness. In her research regarding the trauma histories of 58 Aboriginal men convicted of violent crimes, Atkinson (2008) highlighted that many of the traumatic stressors experienced by the Aboriginal men did not reflect PTSD diagnostic criteria. Indeed, she found:

> PTSD symptomatology was not significantly associated with any of the traumatic stressors most commonly endorsed by over 80% of the research participants, such as constant sorry business, family violence, and drug and alcohol misuse. All of these events were viewed by some of the research participants as both a symptom and a cause of distress and, in some cases, as a catalyst to violent behaviours. (p. 232)

By relying on diagnostic labels, judges often overlooked cultural conceptualisations of trauma and the presence of intergenerational trauma and its association with crime.

In the sentencing remarks where judges recognised trauma as relevant, they were more likely to have been provided with psychiatrists' and psychologists' reports that explained how trauma was relevant both in terms of criminality and rehabilitative strategies. Judges also indicated that information from sources such as Aboriginal sentencing conferences, pre-sentencing reports, and reports provided by the Parole Board helped them to understand the significance of trauma for Aboriginal defendants. Judges could have also sought cultural reports or detailed trauma reports to help devise an evidence-informed sanction most likely to achieve community safety. Cultural reports are examined in more detail in Chapter 10.

Judges were more inclined to realise the presence of trauma and recognise its impact on (Aboriginal and non-Aboriginal) women than Aboriginal men. In terms of sanctions, women are more burdened by prison than men, with long sentences eroding family and community ties (Day et al., 2021). While seven custodial sentences were imposed for violent offences (i.e., manslaughter, assault, sexual assault, robbery), 16 women were incarcerated for non-violent offences, including two women who received short non-parole periods (for a breach of bond due to drug use and serious criminal trespass respectively). Instead of prison, trauma-informed community-based are more likely to reduce future offending, particularly for women who offend (Pemberton et al., 2019). Judicial education would assist in highlighting the merits of trauma-informed sentencing as a mechanism to promote community safety through rehabilitation.

As highlighted in his work on women's desistance from crime, Robin Gålnander (2020) found that: "victimisation and condemnation complicate desistance even further, and the barriers commonly faced by people with convictions are even tougher to overcome when struggling with trauma and internalised stigma" (p. 76). In SA, DCS released a strategy in 2017 that focused on the implementation of "holistic therapeutic approaches". The strategy states:

> Women's known offence profile and life characteristics reinforces that it is important to ensure safe and supportive correction environments in which women can experience and respond to their emotions and gain insight into issues relating to problem behaviours and the potential for impact on their children. We know that as many as 80% of women have experienced trauma in their lives and that their life trajectory has

frequently involved poverty, negative peer, family and interpersonal relationships. The prevalence rate of substance dependency is high as is the number of women with impulsive personality traits. (DCS, 2017, p. 13)

Thus, the need for gender-specific trauma-informed approaches has been recognised by DCS. There is a clear appetite by the SA judiciary to use trauma-informed sentencing approaches with women who offend, but perhaps a lack of recognition that such an approach would work best if applied systemically across all justice agencies and incorporating health, housing, social welfare, and agencies that support children.

9.9 Conclusion

This chapter examined whether trauma-informed practice exists in sentencing, using an SA case study. In most cases, where adversity was acknowledged, sentencing was only partially trauma-informed. Within the sample of 233 sentencing remarks where judges realised that adversity was present, they also recognised the trauma-crime association in only about half the cases. Trauma-informed sentencing experiences were not linear. Even when judges realised defendant trauma was present and recognised the trauma-crime link, this did not guarantee a trauma-informed response or that the judge would resist re-traumatisation. The opposite was also true: it was possible to receive a trauma-informed sentencing response or for a judge to resist re-traumatisation without overtly recognising an association between defendant trauma and crime.

In Australia, the *Guide to Judicial Conduct* (AIJA, 2017) requires that judicial officers act with integrity and be independent and impartial. Arguably, applying trauma-informed practice principles in sentencing is impartial—aiming "to be fair and even-handed, to be patient and attentive, and to avoid stepping into the arena or appearing to take sides" (AIJA, 2017, p. 5). How judges recognised trauma-crime associations highlight the apparent need to educate judges on the differences between adversity and trauma, how trauma manifests as symptoms of mental illness, and the limitations and significance of different diagnoses. Judges in mainstream courts could learn from judicial officers in specialised courts, such as the Aboriginal sentencing courts. The latter overtly apply trauma-informed practice principles in sentencing, ensuring defendants understand the sentencing process and sanction. Judges in mainstream courts seemed particularly reticent to use trauma-informed principles of practice when imposing a sanction of imprisonment, where arguably it was even more critical to ensure that defendants understood why the sanction had been imposed.

Key Points

- In the SA case study, very few defendants experienced trauma-informed sentencing, characterised by the SAMHSA (2014) 4Rs: Realise, Recognise, Respond, and Resist Re-traumatisation.
- In about half of the sentencing remarks, defendant trauma was acknowledged by judges to be present. Judges realised adversity included adverse childhood experiences (ACEs) as well as adult-onset adversity.
- Judges recognised that a trauma-crime relationship existed most often when the trauma was recent, adversity led to drug and alcohol abuse, and the defendant had been diagnosed with a DSM mental health diagnosis.
- Elements of safety, trustworthiness, transparency, choice, and collaboration characterised a trauma-informed sentencing response. This was present in about one-quarter of cases.
- When judges actively decide to impose a trauma-informed sanction, this most often involves a short non-parole period with a longer period of supervision in the community.
- Judges sought to resist re-traumatisation in cases where exceptional circumstances were identified, such as when the defendant was the sole carer of a child with special needs.

References

American Psychiatric Association (APA). (2022). *Diagnostic and Statistical Manual of Mental Disorders, Fifth Edition – Text Revised (DSM-5-TR®)*. American Psychiatric Publishing.

Anderson, S. E. (2016). The Value of 'Bearing Witness' to Desistance. *Probation Journal, 63*(4), 408–424. https://doi.org/10.1177/0264550516664146

Atkinson, C. L. (2008). *The Violence Continuum: Australian Aboriginal Male Violence and Generational Post-traumatic Stress* [PhD thesis], Charles Darwin University.

Australian Institute of Judicial Administration. (AIJA). (2017). *Guide to Judicial Conduct* (3rd ed.). AIJA.

Barr, A. M., Panenka, W. J., MacEwan, G. W., Thornton, A. E., Lang, D. J., Honer, W. G., & Lecomte, T. (2006). The Need for Speed: An Update on Methamphetamine Addiction. *Journal of Psychiatry & Neuroscience, 31*(5), 301–313.

Broyles, L. M., Binswanger, I. A., Jenkins, J. A., Finnell, D. S., Faseru, B., Cavaiola, A., Pugatch, M., & Gordon, A. J. (2014). Confronting Inadvertent Stigma and Pejorative Language in Addiction Scholarship: A Recognition and Response. *Substance Abuse, 35*(3), 217–221. https://doi.org/10.1080/08897077.2014.930372

Cullen, F. T., Jonson, C. L., & Nagin, D. S. (2011). Prisons Do Not Reduce Recidivism: The High Cost of Ignoring Science. *The Prison Journal, 91*(3_suppl), 48S–65S. https://doi.org/10.1177/0032885511415224

Day, A., Ross, S., & McLachlan, K. (2021). *The Effectiveness of Minimum Non-parole Period Schemes for Serious Violent, Sexual and Drug Offenders and Evidence-based Approaches to Community Protection, Deterrence, and Rehabilitation.* Queensland Sentencing Advisory Council.

Department for Correctional Services. (DCS). (2017). *Stronger Together: Safe Children & Strong Families.* Government of South Australia.

Fallot, R. D., & Harris, M. (2011). *Creating Cultures of Trauma-Informed Care (CCTIC): A Self-Assessment and Planning Protocol.* Community Connections.

Felitti, V. J., Anda, R. F., Nordenberg, D., Williamson, D. F., Spitz, A. M., Edwards, V., Koss, M. P., & Marks, J. S. (1998). Relationship of Childhood Abuse and Household Dysfunction to Many of the Leading Causes of Death in Adults: The Adverse Childhood Experiences (ACE) Study. *American Journal of Preventative Medicine, 14*(4), 245–258. https://doi.org/10.1016/s0749-3797(98)00017-8

Gålnander, R. (2020). *Maintaining Desistance: Barriers and Expectations in Women's Desistance from Crime* [PhD thesis]. Stockholm University.

Graham, H. (2016). *Rehabilitation Work: Supporting Desistance and Recovery.* Routledge.

Harris, M., & Fallot, R. D. (2001). Envisioning a Trauma-informed Service System: A Vital Paradigm Shift. *New Directions for Mental Health Services, 2001*(89), 3–22. https://doi.org/10.1002/yd.23320018903

Higgins, D. J., & McCabe, M. P. (2001). Multiple Forms of Child Abuse and Neglect: Adult Retrospective Reports. *Aggression and Violent Behavior, 6*, 547–578. https://doi.org/10.1016/s1359-1789(00)00030-6

Honorato, B., Caltabiano, N., & Clough, A. R. (2016). From Trauma to Incarceration: Exploring the Trajectory in a Qualitative Study in Male Prison Inmates from North Queensland, Australia. *Health and Justice, 4*(3), 1–10. https://doi.org/10.1186/s40352-016-0034-x

Jackson, V., Sullivan, D. H., Mawren, D., Freiberg, A., Kulkarni, J., & Darjee, R. (2021). Trauma-informed Sentencing of Serious Violent Offenders: An Exploration of Judicial Dispositions with a Gendered Perspective. *Psychiatry, Psychology and Law, 28*(5), 748–773. https://doi.org/10.1080/13218719.2020.1855267

Judicial College of Victoria (JCV). (2020). *Victorian Sentencing Manual* (4th ed.). JCV.

Kezelman, C., & Stavropoulos, P. (2019). *Practice Guidelines for Clinical Treatment of Complex Trauma.* Blue Knot Foundation.

Levenson, J. S., & Willis, G. M. (2019). Implementing Trauma-informed Care in Correctional Treatment and Supervision. *Journal of Aggression, Maltreatment & Trauma, 28*(4), 481–501. https://doi.org/10.1080/10926771.2018.1531959

Maxfield, M. G., & Babbie, E. R. (2015). *Research Methods for Criminal Justice and Criminology* (7th ed.). Cengage Learning.

McKenna, N. C., & Holtfreter, K. (2021). Trauma-Informed Courts: A Review and Integration of Justice Perspectives and Gender Responsiveness. *Journal of Aggression, Maltreatment & Trauma, 30*(4), 450–470. https://doi.org/10.1080/10926771.2020.1747128

McLachlan, K. J. (2022). Trauma-informed sentencing in South Australian courts. *Journal of Criminology, 55*(4), 495–513. https://doi.org/10.1177/26338076221113073

McLachlan, K. (2021). *'I Cannot Dismiss from My Mind Your Traumatic and Tragic Upbringing': Judges' Use of Defendant Trauma in Sentencing.* [PhD thesis], University of South Australia.

Millar, H., & Dandurand, Y. (2018). The Best Interests of the Child and the Sentencing of Offenders with Parental Responsibilities. *Criminal Law Forum, 29*, 227–277. https://doi.org/10.1007/s10609-017-9340-9

O'Donnell, I. (2020). *An Evidence Review of Recidivism and Policy Responses.* Department of Justice and Equality.

Parsons, N. L. (2013). *Meth Mania.* Lynne Rienner.

Parsons, T. (2024, February 12). *Thinking about Trauma across the Justice Process* [Conference Presentation]. 2024 Trauma Informed Policing and Law Enforcement Conference, Melbourne.

Pemberton, S., Balderston, S., & Long, J. (2019). *Trauma, Harm and Offending Behaviour: What Works to Address Social Injury and Criminogenic Need with Criminal Justice Involved Women?* University of Birmingham.

Pettus-Davis, C., Renn, T., & Kennedy, S. (2020). *Trauma and Loss During Reentry: Early Findings from a multi-state trial.* Florida State University.

Richards, S. C., & Jones, R. S. (2004). Beating the Perpetual Incarceration Machine: Overcoming Structural Impediments to Re-entry. In S. Maruna & R. Immarigeon (Eds.), *After Crime and Punishment: Pathways to Offender Reintegration* (pp. 201–232). Willan.

Samuels, J. (2020). Casting off the Gilded Blindfold: The Role of Judges in Creating a Fairer, More Rehabilitative, Justice System. In L. Rowles & I. Haji (Eds.), *Humane Justice: What role do kindness, hope and compassion play in the criminal justice system?* (pp. 75–82). Monument Fellowship.

Substance Abuse and Mental Health Services Administration. (SAMHSA). (2014). *SAMHSA's Concept of Trauma and Guidance for a Trauma-Informed Approach.* US Department of Health and Human Services.

Walsh, T., & Douglas, H. (2016). Sentencing Parents: The Consideration of Dependent Children. *Adelaide Law Review, 37*, 135–161.

White, H. R., & Gorman, D. M. (2000). Dynamics of the drug crime relationship. In G. Lafree (Ed.), *Criminal Justice 2000: Volume 1: The nature of crime: Continuity and change* (pp. 151–218). National Institute of Justice.

Case Law

Marrah v The Queen [2014] VSCA 119

R v Monks [2019] SASCFC 47

Sentencing remarks

R v ABT, Supreme Court of SA, #1 J, 25 September 2019

R v AML, District Court of SA, Judge #18, 17 September 2019

R v ATA, District Court of SA, Judge #10, 6 June 2019
R v B, SJ, District Court of SA, Judge #11, 22 May 2019
R v BA, District Court of SA, Judge #18, 19 November 2019
R v BH, District Court of SA, Judge #14, 4 June 2019
R v BJG, Supreme Court of SA, #19 J, 8 November 2019
R v B, M, District Court of SA, Judge #9, 4 June 2019
R v BSC, District Court of SA, Judge #14, 22 August 2019
R v BTS, District Court of SA, Judge #10, 1 May 2019
R v CC, District Court of SA, Judge #7, 25 June 2019
R v CJK, District Court of SA, Judge #17, 4 June 2019
R v DAJB, District Court of SA, Judge #11, 2 May 2019
R v DLH, District Court of SA, Judge #5, 6 September 2019
R v DR, District Court of SA, Judge #3, 17 October 2019
R v GLD, District Court of SA, Judge #18
R v HPD, District Court of SA, Judge #5, 23 August 2019
R v JDG, District Court of SA, Judge #4, 10 July 2019
R v JJL, District Court of SA, Judge #3, 4 July 2019
R v JLH, District Court of SA, Judge #25, 7 November 2019
R v JM, District Court of SA, Judge #8, 23 May 2019
R v JMT, District Court of SA, Judge #11, 14 August 2019
R v JRV, District Court of SA, Judge #5, 23 August 2019
R v JSW, District Court of SA, Judge #2, 11 June 2019
R v KJB, District Court of SA, Judge #4, 14 August 2019
R v KMS, District Court of SA, Judge #7, 3 September 2019
R v KRB, District Court of SA, Judge #22, 2 October 2019
R v LAM, District Court of SA, Judge #9, 21 May 2019
R v LSJ, District Court of SA, Judge #24, 24 September 2019
R v MWAC, District Court of SA, Judge #11, 28 August 2019
R v MWP, District Court of SA, Judge #15, 25 September 2019
R v MYS, District Court of SA, Judge #28, 19 August 2019
R v NDK, District Court of SA, Judge #14, 7 May 2019
R v NW, District Court of SA, Judge #22, 17 June 2019
R v PAW, District Court of SA, Judge #7, 12 June 2019
R v REK, District Court of SA, Judge #2, 9 August 2019
R v SAM, District Court of SA, Judge #8, 25 June 2019
R v SDL, District Court of SA, Judge #8, 19 August 2019
R v SEW, District Court of SA, Judge #3, 25 June 2019
R v SKM, District Court of SA, Judge #3, 7 August 2019
R v SSB, District Court of SA, Judge #23, 2 May 2019

R v SWT, District Court of SA, Judge #7, 28 August 2019
R v TAW, District Court of SA, Judge #17, 7 August 2019
R v TH, District Court of SA, Judge #18, 10 July 2019
R v TLK, Supreme Court of SA, #30 J, 4 June 2019
R v TS, Supreme Court of SA, #19 J, 15 October 2019
R v WTJ, District Court of SA, Judge #31, 13 August 2019

10

Sentencing First Nations Defendants: Resisting Re-traumatisation

10.1 Introduction

First Nations peoples are over-represented in the criminal justice system in Australia (ABS, 2023), Canada (Robinson et al., 2023), and Aotearoa New Zealand (DOC, 2023). This is part of the ongoing legacy of colonisation. First Nations communities have consistently demonstrated significant resilience in the face of compounded adversity, with community resilience potentially strengthened through collective responses to this shared history (Usher et al., 2021). For a significant minority of First Nations people, prisons and the criminal justice system have extended the impact of past adverse government practices, continuing to destroy connections to family, country, community, spirituality, and cultural identity. These connections are a source of strength and protection (Zubrick et al., 2014). Imprisonment breaks these ties and increases criminogenic risks. The criminal justice system's current policies and punitive strategies will continue to fail to break the cycle of offending within First Nations populations or promote safer communities, while First Nations sources of resilience and wellbeing are overlooked.

K. J. McLachlan, *Trauma-informed Criminal Justice*,
https://doi.org/10.1007/978-3-031-59290-4_10

Given this history, to reduce recidivism and promote community safety, courts, and the criminal justice system need to recognise the relevance of current individual and collective trauma as well as intergenerational trauma in influencing the wellbeing and behaviour of First Nations peoples. Most Indigenous[1] people in prison have past convictions for criminal behaviour and have been previously imprisoned (SCRGSP, 2016). High levels of entrenched trauma are associated with Indigeneity, including intergenerational trauma, over-representation in the justice and child protection systems, poverty and homelessness, racism, and substance abuse (Atkinson et al., 2014). The criminal justice system must respond with evidence-informed strategies. The Australian Law Reform Commission (ALRC, 2017) recommended "[s]entencing legislation should provide that, when sentencing Aboriginal and Torres Strait Islander offenders, judges take into account unique systemic and background factors affecting Aboriginal and Torres Strait Islander peoples" (p. 204). This chapter uses the Substance Abuse and Mental Health Services Administration's (SAMHSA, 2014) 4Rs model of trauma-informed practice to explore current practices and future opportunities to provide First Nations defendants with trauma-informed sentencing experiences.

10.2 1R: Realising the Significance of Trauma

10.2.1 Realising the Relevance of Chronic and Compounded Trauma

First Nations peoples who have contact with the criminal justice system have often experienced both direct and intergenerational trauma, as discussed in Chapter 4. First Nations peoples often have a history of adversity in childhood, including for some people, forceable removal from family by the State. In Australia, Aboriginal children are almost

[1] For consistency and simplicity, the broad terms "First Nations peoples", "Indigenous", and "Aboriginal peoples" are most often used when discussing the experiences of First Nations peoples and communities across Australia, Canada, and Aotearoa New Zealand. No offence is intended to Māori or Torres Strait Islanders or other specific First Nations populations.

eight times more likely to be removed from their families and live in out-of-home care than non-Aboriginal children (AIHW, 2020). Childhood adversity may be exacerbated by additional adversity across the life-course. As noted by Ed Heffernan et al. (2014):

> This nexus between social adversity, poor health and incarceration for Aboriginal people can at least in part be understood in terms of the impact of historical factors such as the colonisation of lands and the forced removal of children, discrimination, and associated experiences of unemployment, poverty, poor education and a lack of social capital. (p. 167)

The lack of social capital leads to risk and adversity. People are not inherently vulnerable if they have the right supports around them (Gilmour, 2024). However, chronic, ongoing adversity results in significant "changes in mind, emotions, body, and relationships... including severe problems with dissociation, emotional dysregulation, somatic distress [and] relational or spiritual alienation" (Ford & Courtois, 2014, p. 13). The chronic and compounded nature of trauma in the lives of First Nations defendants may impact all human domains, including psychological, emotional, physical, and social wellbeing, as discussed in Chapter 3.

First Nations peoples are disproportionately more likely to be victims of crime than non-Indigenous people. Australian First Nations communities experience significantly higher interpersonal violence, including domestic abuse and family violence, than non-Indigenous families and communities in Australia (SCRGSP, 2016). Indigenous women are 27 times more likely than non-Indigenous women in Australia to be hospitalised due to assault, and 51 times more likely if they come from remote areas of Australia (AIHW, 2024). Crime victimisation for Indigenous women in remote communities is likely to be entrenched by additional adversity such as poverty, inadequate housing, and poorer access to health services (AIHW, 2024) compared to First Nations peoples who live in urban areas. In a Western Australia (WA) study of 54 incarcerated Aboriginal and Torres Strait Islander mothers, Mandy Wilson and colleagues (2017) found that women who had been incarcerated for violent offences had themselves experienced multiple traumas and been victims of violence. They found that:

> many women used violence, primarily, but not exclusively, in response to their own victimization. [They argued] that eclipsing women's own violence from discussions of Aboriginal violence is doing these women a disservice and may be placing them at greater risk of future harm. (Wilson et al., 2017, p. 11)

Their research supports the claim that violence often becomes "normalised" in the lives of Aboriginal people, such that assaults are under-reported and little support is available to mitigate the impact of trauma.

An additional form of normalised violence (and a manifestation of intergenerational trauma) in First Nations communities is lateral violence, which is often described as "internalised colonialism" (Frankland & Lewis, 2011, cited in Gooda, 2011, p. 52). ***Lateral violence*** has been defined as "negative behaviours of oppressed groups towards each other as a result of internalising oppression" (Lewis & Frankland, 2019, p. 5). Lateral violence may be overt (e.g., physical) but is more commonly covert (e.g., emotional, psychological, social; Clark, 2017; Clark et al., 2016; Gooda, 2011), and includes bullying, harassment, intimidation, gossiping, and shaming others (Gooda, 2011; Lewis & Frankland, 2019). Lateral violence occurs in communities that have been oppressed, discriminated against, and experience significant disadvantage, and is associated with feelings of powerlessness and a loss of identity (Gooda, 2011; Lewis & Frankland, 2019). It is both associated with intergenerational trauma, and the cause of direct trauma experiences (Lewis & Frankland, 2019).

10.2.2 Judges Tend to Realise That Trauma is Present: Is that Enough?

The study outlined in Chapter 9 included a sample of sentencing remarks of 42 South Australian defendants identified as Aboriginal (McLachlan, 2022; refer to Chapter 9). Judges **realised** that most Aboriginal defendants' lives were characterised by adverse events (n = 36/42, 85.7%).

This was significantly higher than for non-Indigenous defendants (n = 196/405, 48.4%; McLachlan, 2022). Examples of identified adversity included:

> ... you yourself had a terrible background. I will not set out in detail the disadvantages that you have suffered but they are considerable... your mother and stepfather abused you in just about every way imaginable. They neglected you, they both abused you physically and sexually. (R v DLH)

> You had a rough childhood marked by chronic instability, neglect and dysfunction... You were exposed to alcohol abuse and illicit drug use from an early age. There was always domestic violence in the home. Not surprisingly, your education was very disrupted and you are illiterate. (R v DH)

> You... left school in about year 9... your schooling life was characterised by being bullied and your home life was plagued with alcohol and violence. From a relationship that began when you were very young, you have four children who range in ages from nine through to 19. You say your relationship was characterised by domestic violence and alcohol abuse, which led to [Child Protection authorities] ordering your two eldest daughters to live with your parents... you returned to using alcohol and illicit drugs... you were heavily pregnant and granted home detention bail... You were eventually rushed to the hospital for an emergency caesarean, however your child was stillborn. You were then returned to custody where you have remained. (R v KK)

> You grew up in a household marred by excessive alcohol use and violence. Your parents separated when you were five years of age. Your mother struggled to raise your family by herself and she relied on the help of relatives. Your older brother passed away when you were 10 years of age... Your mother passed away when you were 17; her passing devastated you... (R v CLS)

> You are the product of a devastating long-term effect of serial childhood abuse of one sort or another. There is no doubt you have been

> a victim of abuse and neglect since a very young age. Yours is a very tragic background. (R v ABT)

Despite judges identifying adversity in Aboriginal defendants' lives, they:

- rarely **recognised** an association between Aboriginal defendants' trauma and the defendant's offending behaviour (n = 13/42),
- sometimes **responded** in a way that was trauma-informed (in terms of either sanction or process), and
- seldom sought to **resist re-traumatisation** of the defendants or their children (n = 9/42).

A reasonable question to ask is why judges overwhelmingly acknowledged adversity in the lives of Aboriginal defendants when they rarely used that information to inform their sentencing decision or response. Judges may consider various factors without mentioning them in their sentencing remarks. A lack of acknowledgement of individual factors in remarks does not mean that specific factors were not considered.

While sentencing judges appear to accept that Aboriginal peoples are more likely than non-Aboriginal people to have experienced adversity, the SA judges were also quick to focus on direct experiences of adversity rather than intergenerational trauma. Such an approach may be based on erroneous beliefs, such as a reticence to homogenise all Aboriginal peoples or, as Thalia Anthony (2013) argues, a reimagining of "Indigenous offenders and communities as dysfunctional or so entrenched in postcolonial society that they are no longer Indigenous" (p. 15). This is somewhat surprising given that higher Australian courts have previously acknowledged Aboriginality as relevant in sentencing, as outlined below.

10.3 2R: Recognising Trauma or Responding to Aboriginality in Sentencing?

In 1988, the ALRC, in their *Sentencing Inquiry*, recommended: "[t]he fact that an offender is Aboriginal should not be a matter relevant to sentence but special factors arising from disadvantages suffered by Aboriginals (sic), or Aboriginal customary practices, should be considered" (p. xlv). At the time, the concept of intergenerational trauma was not even in the minds of the judiciary. However, since then there has been increased recognition of the over-representation of Aboriginal people in custody and the compounded challenges faced by Aboriginal people who offend. The High Court decisions of Munda v WA (2013) 302 ALR 207 and *Bugmy v The Queen* (2013) 249 CLR 571 have raised the issue of Aboriginality as a sentencing consideration. These decisions demonstrate how the judiciary is moving to recognise the impacts of adverse childhood experiences and direct adversity in adulthood on criminal behaviour but remain reticent in acknowledging intergenerational trauma associated with Aboriginality.

10.3.1 *Munda v WA* (2013) 302 ALR 207: Aboriginal People are no "Less Capable Than Others of Decent Behaviour"

In the case of Munda v WA (2013) 302 ALR 207 ("*Munda*"), Ernest Munda assaulted his de facto spouse in 2010, fracturing her jaw, breaking her ribs, and ultimately causing her death from a traumatic brain injury. They had been in a relationship for 16 years and had four children. Mr Munda had a limited but significant history of violently assaulting the victim, breaking bones, and using weapons (*Munda,* para 9). Mr Munda pleaded guilty and was sentenced in the Supreme Court of WA to imprisonment for five years and three months, with a non-parole period of three years and three months. The WA Director of Public Prosecutions (DPP) appealed, arguing the sentence was manifestly inadequate. On appeal, his sentence was increased to seven years and nine months. Mr Munda appealed. One of his grounds was that the Court of Appeal:

> failed to have proper regard to the appellant's personal circumstances as an Aboriginal man. In particular, it is said that systemic deprivation and disadvantage, including an environment in which the abuse of alcohol is endemic in indigenous communities, should have been, but was not, taken into account by the Court of Appeal. (*Munda*, para 3)

The majority of the High Court dismissed his appeal. They cited Brennan J in Neal v The Queen (1982) 149 CLR 305, who stated:

> The same sentencing principles are to be applied … in every case, irrespective of the identity of a particular offender or his membership of an ethnic or other group. But in imposing sentences courts are bound to take into account, in accordance with those principles, all material facts including those facts which exist only by reason of the offender's membership of an ethnic or other group… (p. 326)

The majority in *Munda* held:

> It would be contrary to the principle stated by Brennan J in Neal to accept that Aboriginal offending is to be viewed systemically as less serious than offending by persons of other ethnicities. To accept that Aboriginal offenders are in general less responsible for their actions than other persons would be to deny Aboriginal people their full measure of human dignity. It would be quite inconsistent with the statement of principle in Neal to act upon a kind of racial stereotyping which diminishes the dignity of individual offenders by consigning them, by reason of their race and place of residence, to a category of persons who are less capable than others of decent behaviour. Further, it would be wrong to accept that a victim of violence by an Aboriginal offender is somehow less in need, or deserving, of such protection and vindication as the criminal law can provide. (para 53, per French CJ, Hayne, Crennan, Kiefel, Gageler and Keane JJ, citations removed)

In some ways, the High Court has misunderstood how Aboriginality should be relevant in sentencing. The issue is not that Aboriginal offending should be viewed as less serious or that Aboriginal victims of crime should be treated with less respect than non-Indigenous victims. Nor is the issue that Aboriginal people deserve less human dignity. Most

First Nations people do not offend. When they do, the issue is that trauma and culture both help to contextualise the criminal behaviour, inform the risk of future offending, and presence of protective factors, and should therefore be considered by the judge when determining and imposing a sanction to better promote future community safety.

10.3.2 *Bugmy v The Queen* (2013) 249 CLR 571: Aboriginality is not Specifically Relevant in Individualised Justice

In the same year as *Munda*, the High Court also handed down their decision in the case of *Bugmy v The Queen* (2013) 249 CLR 571 ("Bugmy"). William Bugmy had experienced chronic adversity in childhood and adulthood. In this case, Mr. Bugmy pleaded guilty to assaulting two prison officers and blinding a prison officer, Jason Gould, by throwing pool balls at him. The court heard that Mr. Bugmy had been exposed to parental alcohol abuse and violence as a child; he had an extensive substance abuse history, child protection and youth justice contact, and adult offending history; with suicide attempts, grief and loss issues, head injuries and psychosis (para 12–13). The majority in *Bugmy* stated:

> [a]n Aboriginal offender's deprived background may mitigate the sentence that would otherwise be appropriate for the offence in the same way that the deprived background of a non-Aboriginal offender may mitigate that offender's sentence. (p. 592-4, para 37, per French CJ, Hayne, Crennan, Kiefel, Bell, Keane JJ)

The decision in *Bugmy* highlighted the High Court's resistance to acknowledge Aboriginality per se as a factor likely to mitigate sentencing. However, Sarah Krasnostein has argued Aboriginality is relevant in sentencing, for:

> Only by reason of his Aboriginality, does Mr Bugmy come from a place where life expectancy—and expectations from life—are less than half that for White Australians. Only by reason of his Aboriginality, was he always

> more likely than his White counterparts to be exposed to violence, addiction, unemployment, policing and imprisonment. Only by reason of his Aboriginality, was he less likely to have housing, and more likely to be disadvantaged with respect to education, employment and health care.
>
> These matters, on their own, do not automatically justify a "race discount" for Aboriginal offenders and their consequence is not absolution from punishment. Rather, where they are relevant, they provide the "necessary context" for fairly evaluating case facts and deciding on an appropriate sentence. (Krasnostein, 2014, p. 13)

Krasnostein (2014) concluded: "[b]y virtue of what went unsaid, as much as by what was, this decision represents a lost chance to strike an effective balance between the concepts of individual justice and equality" (p. 14). Acknowledging trauma rather than the cultural context of that trauma for First Nations peoples is to pretend to be blind to the shared history that helps to understand the over-representation of First Nations peoples in the justice system.

Aboriginal defendants have relied on the decision of *Bugmy* to argue that personal circumstances (such as exposure to childhood adversity and alcohol abuse) are relevant and should result in more lenient sanctions. This strategy is sometimes, but not consistently, successful. Additionally, the NSW Public Defenders (2023) has created *The Bugmy Bar Book* to aid legal practitioners and the judiciary in understanding the impacts of disadvantage and adversity (i.e., realising and recognising trauma) and strengths-based rehabilitation. While the judiciary is moving to recognise the impacts of chronic deprivation and developmental trauma on criminal behaviour, they remain slow to acknowledge intergenerational trauma associated with Aboriginality. In the SA case of *R v Grose* [2014] SASCFC 42, while Aboriginality per se was not always seen to be relevant to sentencing, Gray J made the uncommon step of acknowledging the intergenerational impact of Aboriginal people being removed from their families and communities (p. 14, para 51). Such decisions also highlight that the courts often devise a sanction in the absence of community consultation, disregarding the importance of self-determination for First Nations communities and instead assessing risk and best solutions through White-men's eyes.

10.3.3 *R v Gladue* [1999] 1 SCR 688

Unlike Australia, Canada has national legislation that specifically refers to Aboriginality as a sentencing factor. Section 718.2(e) of the Canadian *Criminal Code* states:

> all available sanctions, other than imprisonment, that are reasonable in the circumstances and consistent with the harm done to victims or to the community should be considered for all offenders, with particular attention to the circumstances of Aboriginal offenders.

In practice:

> [t]he provision is not simply a codification of existing jurisprudence. It is remedial in nature and is designed to ameliorate the serious problem of overrepresentation of aboriginal people in prisons, and to encourage sentencing judges to have recourse to a restorative approach to sentencing. There is a judicial duty to give the provision's remedial purpose real force. (*R v Gladue* [1999] 1 SCR 688 ("*Gladue*"), p. 690)

In the case of *Gladue*, the interpretation and application of s 718.2(e) were reviewed by the Canadian Supreme Court. The defendant was a 19-year-old Cree and Metis woman, Jamie Tanis Gladue, who fatally stabbed her de facto husband, Reuben Beaver, while under the influence of alcohol. She pleaded guilty to manslaughter. While the sentencing judge took several individual factors into account, he found that Aboriginality was not relevant as the defendant lived "off-reserve" and "not within the Aboriginal community" (*Gladue,* p. 701). The Supreme Court in *Gladue* disagreed with the trial judge; stating that the legislation applied to all Aboriginal defendants. The Court argued that "[t]here is no discretion as to whether to consider the unique situation of the aboriginal (sic) offender; the only discretion concerns the determination of a just and appropriate sentence" (*Gladue*, p. 731, para 82).

The Canadian Supreme Court suggested that courts should consider:

> How has the offender who is being sentenced been affected by, for example, substance abuse in the community, or poverty, or overt racism,

> or family or community breakdown? Would imprisonment effectively serve to deter or denounce crime in a sense that would be significant to the offender and community, or are crime prevention and other goals better achieved through healing? What sentencing options present themselves in these circumstances? (*Gladue*, p. 730, para 80)

The Court reiterated that while individual factors must be considered in sentencing, s 718.2(e) changed the weighting, such that Aboriginality was to be regarded as a key consideration when determining the most appropriate sanction "because those circumstances are unique" and may make imprisonment "a less appropriate or less useful sanction" (*Gladue*, p. 708, para 37). Aboriginality, in *Gladue*, effectively referred to:

> (A) The unique systemic or background factors which may have played a part in bringing the particular aboriginal (sic) offender before the courts; and
>
> (B) The types of sentencing procedures and sanctions which may be appropriate in the circumstances for the offender because of his or her particular aboriginal heritage or connection. (Gladue, p. 724, para 66)

Relevant background information was provided by the defence counsel and through pre-sentence reports. The decision of Gladue was upheld in R *v Ipeelee* [2012] 1 SCR 433 ("*Ipeelee*").

10.3.4 *R v Ipeelee* [2012] 1 SCR 433

Manasie Ipeelee was a 39-year-old Inuk man whose mother died when he was five years old. He was abusing alcohol from the age of 11 years. He had an extensive youth justice history from the age of 12. As an adult, he was convicted of multiple offences, including assaults, sexual assaults, and public intoxication offences. He was placed on a 10-year Long-Term Supervision Order (LTSO), which came into effect on 14 March 2007 (*Ipeelee,* p. 447). In 2009, he was sentenced for breaches of the LTSO, which he appealed.

The key issue for the Canadian Supreme Court was how to determine an appropriate sanction under s. 718.2(e). The Court held:

> courts must take judicial notice of such matters as the history of colonialism, displacement, and residential schools and how that history continues to translate into lower educational attainment, lower incomes, higher unemployment, higher rates of substance abuse and suicide, and of course higher levels of incarceration for Aboriginal peoples. These matters, on their own, do not necessarily justify a different sentence for Aboriginal offenders. Rather, they provide the necessary **context** for understanding and evaluating the case-specific information… (p. 469, para 60, emphasis in original)

Notably, the defendant did not need to show an association between their cultural heritage and criminal behaviour (Clark, 2014).

10.3.5 Individualised Justice and Substantive Equity

While Canada has recognised systemic discrimination resulting in the over-incarceration of First Nations people with intergenerational trauma (LSS, 2022), Australian research has argued that the over-representation of Indigenous people in prison is more likely to be attributed to extensive criminal histories (associated with social exclusion and trauma) rather than any inherent racism in judicial decision-making (Bond & Jeffries, 2012; Jeffries & Bond, 2009). This view has been challenged by Rothman J of the Supreme Court of NSW, who has argued that the Australian criminal justice system currently overlooks (racial and cultural) discrimination, to the detriment of equal justice (see also Warner, 2011). He proposed that equal justice (or ***parity***), requires that:

> Every individual before the courts for sentencing must be treated equally—as that notion is described above—and as an individual. Any non-Aboriginal who has suffered as a part of a 200 year history of dispossession from their own land; exclusion from society; discrimination; and disempowerment is entitled to have such circumstances considered. In Australia, such persons are confined to the Indigenous population. To treat Aboriginal persons differently in Australia by taking account of such factors is an application of equal justice; not a denial of it. Of course, even within the totality of Aboriginal offenders, individuals will differ.

> Some will suffer the consequences of such conduct more than others. Some may not have suffered any such consequences. (2018, p. 7)

As explained in Chapter 8, ***Individualised justice*** is partly achieved by considering factors specific to the defendant and the offending behaviour, such as the nature, circumstances, and impact of the offending, as well as the characteristics of the person who has offended and the person who has been victimised.

Paul Bennett, a Magistrate in the Nunga Aboriginal Court in SA, is also an advocate for "'***substantive equality***', that is treating people, whether an individual or a group differently according to their specific circumstances to reduce disadvantage" (Bennett, 2016, p. 94; see also Clark, 2014). There is increasing recognition of the importance of "substantive equality". In *DPP v Herrmann* [2019] VSC 694, Maxwell J of Victoria's Court of Appeal requested a pre-sentence report on "[I]ndigenous disadvantage… a matter which white middle-aged judges don't know" (Cooper, 2020, p. 2). As highlighted by Edwige and Gray (2021), "Culture is not merely 'important' in the provision of rehabilitation, treatment and other healing or wellbeing services, but is a fundamental element of the concept of wellbeing for Aboriginal and Torres Strait Islander people" (p. 12). Therefore, sentencing responses—in terms of process and sanction should be culturally informed to ensure their relevance and appropriateness.

10.4 3R: Culturally Informed Sentencing Responses

Elliott Johnston AO QC's brilliance was lost on me when he taught me first-year law. But as the Commissioner and author of the 387-page, the second volume of the *Final Report for the Royal Commission into Aboriginal Deaths in Custody* (RCIADIC, 1991), he clearly articulates the devastating impacts of colonisation on Australia's First Nations communities. He states:

> One of the deepest legacies of history for Aboriginal people, and one that has contributed to deaths in custody, is that their lives have been controlled, and in many cases still are controlled, by people who share neither their culture nor their perspectives, because they have not shared their history. **Self-determination** the gaining by Aboriginal people of control over the decision-making processes affecting themselves, and gaining the power to make the ultimate decisions wherever possible. (p. 340, emphasis added)

Self-determination for First Nations peoples does not require a sovereign state or the application of pre-colonial community sanctions (Clark, 2014). Self-determination would be achieved if the justice system worked with community to develop evidence- and culturally informed strategies to keep the community safe (while including the defendant as a community member). This is particularly true for the minority of First Nations peoples who live in rural and remote communities.

10.4.1 The Importance of a Culturally Safe Response

To help address chronic and compounded trauma requires culturally safe responses (Lewis & Frankland, 2019). There are other similar terms used across various sectors, such as "culturally informed" or "culturally appropriate", with cultural safety emerging from nursing practices in Aotearoa New Zealand (Williams, 2012). ***Cultural safety*** refers to the provision of services in an environment which is physically, emotionally, and spiritually safe and respectful of a person's identity and their needs (Edwige & Gray, 2021; Workman et al., 2023). It is about "shared meaning, shared knowledge and experience, of learning together with dignity, and truly listening" (Williams, 2012, p. 2). It is not enough to merely understand trauma is associated with the over-representation of First Nations peoples in the criminal justice system. Responses must be culturally informed and culturally safe. There has been little work in criminal justice to examine how to be culturally safe, with most work in this area emerging from healthcare, particularly midwifery and nursing (Workman et al., 2023).

Cultural safety is aligned with the concept of self-determination, and is best determined by First Nations peoples, families, and communities; indeed, it can only truly be shown to exist if the service recipient feels culturally safe. Due to the diversity of First Nations cultures, there is no single way of responding that is culturally safe. Cultural safety requires acknowledgement from the criminal justice system that cultural identity influences social and emotional wellbeing, and thus behaviour. As outlined in Chapter 2, ***social and emotional wellbeing*** (SEWB) may be regarded as incorporating social, political, and historical factors and includes connection to body and mind, family and community, culture, land, and spirituality (Lewis & Frankland, 2019; Newton et al., 2015).

To be culturally safe, practitioners must recognise the justice system traditionally exacerbates disadvantage for First Nations peoples. Current justice responses to First Nations peoples are not reducing rates of incarceration. As highlighted by Vanessa Edwige and Paul Gray (2021):

> Numerous, repeated reviews have hardened the well-worn ground of the social determinants of incarceration, the over-incarceration of Aboriginal and Torres Strait Islander people in Australia, and the characteristics of services of supports which promote wellbeing and healing, and reduce recidivism… (p. 4)

Nevertheless, the lack of meaningful action taken to acknowledge and address these social determinants means that current justice practices are not culturally safe.

Drawing from a health model (AHPRA, 2020, p. 9), culturally safe sentencing requires that judges:

1. Acknowledge adversity in the form of "colonisation and systemic racism, social, cultural, behavioural and economic factors" which impact an individual's SEWB and result in intergenerational trauma and an increased risk of criminality;
2. Acknowledge and address individual racism, "their own biases, assumptions, stereotypes and prejudices" and provide court responses that are holistic, free of bias and racism;

3. Understand "the importance of self-determined decision-making, partnership and collaboration" driven by the individual, family, and community; and
4. Advance "a safe working environment through leadership to support the rights and dignity of Aboriginal and Torres Strait Islander people and colleagues".

Culturally safe ways of working clearly align with trauma-informed practice. The first point above (i.e., acknowledging adversity and its impacts) aligns with realising the presence of intergenerational trauma and recognising the existence of a trauma-crime association. The third point and fourth points (i.e., understanding the importance of self-determination, collaboration, and safety) reflect trauma-informed responses. Safety, empowerment, choice, trust and transparency, and self-determination are all trauma-informed principles that are also core to cultural safety (Williams, 2012; Workman et al., 2023).

There are currently three broad practice examples that aim to promote the consideration of culture in the sentencing process and sanction: Aboriginal Community Courts, Sentencing Conferences, and Cultural Reports. Each is outlined below.

10.4.2 Specialist Courts and Sentencing Conferences

Aboriginal community courts (e.g., Koori Courts in Vic, circle sentencing in NSW, Murri Court in Qld, Nunga Court in SA, Aboriginal Community Courts in WA) are used for low-level offences. The Nunga Court in SA has existed since 1999 but was only embedded in legislation in March 2023. The court's purpose is to provide First Nations peoples an opportunity to participate in and discuss the sentencing process and increase Aboriginal and Torres Strait Islander communities' confidence in the criminal justice system (s 9AA, *Magistrates Court Act 1991* (SA)). The Nunga Court helps to determine culturally appropriate sanctions for First Nations peoples who have pleaded guilty. In NSW, sentencing conferences or circle sentencing have been found to be more effective than traditional sentencing approaches in reducing incarceration and the associated criminogenic impacts (Yeong & Moore, 2020).

Aboriginal courts tend to be less formal than mainstream courts, allowing for a more conversational approach between all parties (e.g., the Magistrate, the defendant, the Elders, community members, victim, police, etc.). A significant benefit of Aboriginal courts, in terms of trauma-informed culturally safe practice is that criminal behaviour should be understood:

> … not only as a consequence of the offender's individual characteristics, but also in the context of the prevailing social conditions and cultural mores in defendant's community… the institutional guarantees of Aboriginal participation in the Aboriginal Couret ensures a greater emphasis and appreciation of Aboriginality in sentencing. (Bennett, 2016, p. 57)

In the Higher Courts in SA, before sentencing a First Nations defendant, a judge may seek agreement from the defendant to hold a sentencing conference (per *Sentencing Act 2017* (SA) s 22). Aboriginal sentencing conferences are designed to provide:

> a culturally responsive restorative justice forum in which the defendant has an opportunity to better understand the gravity of their offending, including the impact on the victim, families and the community…
>
> Defendants are encouraged to explain the background to their offending. Aboriginal Elders and Respected Persons assist the judicial officer by providing cultural and community advice to the Court and the defendant. Victims, the defendant's family and support services are invited to attend and contribute to the conference. Aboriginal Justice Officers support Aboriginal sentencing conferences across all jurisdictions. (CAA, 2023, p. 20)

Such a conference typically occurs in a courtroom and involves the judicial officer, the defendant, their family member(s), their lawyer, the prosecutor, and the victim. It may also involve an Aboriginal Elder, a cultural advisor, the defendant's counsellor, and any other person. The defendant can talk directly with the judge, and matters raised at the conference may be taken into consideration by the judge in sentencing.

10.4.3 Cultural Reports

Courts can receive information about Indigenous cultures in Canada, Aotearoa New Zealand, and Australia. In Canada, a *Gladue* Report is a pre-sentence report that contains two key types of information: information about an Indigenous person's unique systemic or background factors (historical and personal) relevant to the case, and proposed appropriate sanction options e.g., alternatives to incarceration or restorative justice options (Barkaskas et al., 2019; LSS, 2022). Even if the defendant waives their right to have their personal circumstances considered and no report is prepared, the court must apply the Gladue factors and principles when sentencing a First Nations defendant (*Ipeelee,* LSS, 2022). Submissions may be made in writing in a report prepared by a cultural expert or orally in court, by the defence, prosecution (Crown), or the individual (Barkaskas et al., 2019; LSS, 2022). Most *Gladue* submissions are made orally by defence counsel (42.6%), followed by full *Gladue* reports (38.9%), the latter being perceived to be the most satisfactory. Defence counsel submissions were considered variable: "from borderline incompetent to excellent" (Dickson & Smith, 2021, p. 31). Judges also preferred Gladue reports to standard pre-sentence reports because they were more often written by an Aboriginal person and were the product of multiple interviews with family and community members (Dickson & Smith, 2021). Limitations to accessing *Gladue* reports were often due to the resourcing of the author organisations (such as Aboriginal Legal Services), rather than a lack of court interest (Dickson & Smith, 2021).

Similarly, in Aotearoa New Zealand, s 27 of the *Sentencing Act 2002* (NZ), allows a defendant to request a witness be called to discuss the relevance of their cultural background including their personal whānau (i.e., extended family group), community, or cultural background (and how these may be protective), how their background may have influenced the offending behaviour, cultural processes previously tried to address the offending, and culturally informed sanction options.

In Australia, culture is legislated as a sentencing factor in the Australian Capital Territory (*Crimes (Sentencing) Act 2005* (ACT), s 33) and Queensland (*Penalties and Sentences Act 1992* (Qld), s 9). In the Northern Territory (NT), the court must request an Aboriginal Experience Report (*Sentencing Act 1995* (NT), Div 3A), and a party may present information about punishment under customary law or a cultural practice (*Sentencing Act 1995* (NT), s. 104A). The Acts in other jurisdictions do not preclude culture from being considered. Aboriginal Community Justice Reports (ACJR) have been trialled in Victoria for women defendants (VALS, 2021). These reports have been compiled by Indigenous women and tend to include information about the historical and personal circumstances of the defendant, connection to community and culture, and cultural identity and culturally informed sanctions.

A cultural guide has also been developed for SA for expert witnesses (i.e., psychologists and psychiatrists) preparing pre-sentence reports for Aboriginal defendants (The Magnolia Project & ALRM, 2023) to promote the inclusion of relevant cultural information. As explained in Chapter 8, pre-sentence reports are intended to inform the sentencing judge of relevant sentencing factors, such as a defendant's "character, general background and criminal history" (*Sentencing Act 2017* (SA), s 11(1)(d)), risk of recidivism, physical and mental health, and remorse. Pre-sentence reports may also:

> provide information to the courts about a person's engagement with programs and rehabilitative services, their family and housing arrangements, and their social, educational, health and employment history, and link this information to past offending, predictors of future offending and prospects for rehabilitation in the community. (Coulter et al., 2022, p. 1)

They assist judges in developing their awareness of relevant sentencing factors that promote individualised justice. Pre-sentence reports can help determine how best to achieve community safety (e.g., through strategies that promote rehabilitation or incapacitation; Ashworth & Kelly, 2021).

10.4.4 Culturally Appropriate Trauma-Informed Correctional Care

The second element of a trauma-informed sentencing response relates to the sanction imposed. First Nations peoples are often re-traumatised by imprisonment within a small cell, far from their country and family (Atkinson et al., 2014). There has been very little written about culturally appropriate trauma-informed correctional care (TICC) and how to implement trauma-informed principles of practice in custody. Perhaps this is because it is an oxymoron: removing someone from their community and country and locking them up—compounding direct and intergenerational traumas—can rarely be culturally appropriate. However, the reality is that First Nations people are over-incarcerated, and far more thought should be given to how corrections are and should be responding. Despite the limited progress in this area, the Healing Foundation (2021), the Australian Law Reform Commission (2017), and the Law Council of Australia (2018) highlight the importance of embedding culturally appropriate and trauma-informed practice across the criminal justice system.

Working therapeutically with First Nations peoples requires recognition of a broader understanding of wellbeing and healing than mainstream mental health models currently use, including "reconnecting with culture, strengthening identity, restoring safe and enduring relationships, and supporting communities to understand the impact that their experiences have had on their behaviour and create change" (Carlson et al., 2021, p. 9). As explained by the Healing Foundation (2021):

> Culture is the gateway to healing. For Aboriginal and Torres Strait Islander peoples, culture comprises four elements – lore, country, family, and spirit. Culture gives purpose, identity and connection, acting as a compass, and guiding people through challenges. Stronger connections to culture and country build stronger individual and collective identities, a sense of self-esteem, resilience and improved outcomes. (p. 46)

Culture is protective and the key to promoting resilience. From an Aboriginal perspective, the concept of ***resilience*** may be defined as:

> The ability to have a connection and belonging to one's land, family and culture, therefore an identity. Allowing pain and suffering caused from adversities to heal. Having a dreaming, where the past is brought to the present and the present and the past are taken into the future. A strong spirit that confronts and conquers racism and oppression, strengthening the spirit. The ability not just to survive but to thrive in today's dominant culture. (Kickett, 2011, p. ii)

Marion Kickett (2011) used her own life experience as a Noongar woman to demonstrate how culture can be a strength and promote resilience for First Nations peoples when exposed to adversity (see text box). So, are current practices culturally safe?

> *I am so fortunate to have been taught by my father and other members of his family about my country. This knowledge has enhanced my strong connection to country making me feel a part of it and it a part of me. Such is the case with so many other Aboriginal people throughout Australia. (Kickett, 2011, p. 4).*

Many of the same criminogenic risk and protective factors apply to all people, regardless of cultural background, such as pro-social supports, a sense of belonging, and pro-social attitudes. For First Nations peoples, additional protective factors include building resilience and a "sense of pride in cultural identity, cultural attachment, participation in traditional activities, and connections to land and language" (Usher et al., 2021, p. 11). Culturally appropriate criminal justice responses (by courts and corrections) should embed these elements into sanctions, programs, and ways of working to enhance individuals' resilience through connection to community, land, and spirituality, including cultural activities and promoting cultural pride (Usher et al., 2021).

Ideally, culturally appropriate TICC would be achieved through community-based sanctions (ALRC, 2017; The Healing Foundation, 2021; LCA, 2018). However, work has also been done to embed culturally appropriate TICC in prisons. *The Model of Care for Aboriginal Prisoner Health and Wellbeing for South Australia* highlighted the need for culturally appropriate TICC to focus on Aboriginal prisoners' "social, spiritual and mental health needs" and culturally specific support (Sivak et al., 2017, p. 21). Similarly, a recent study has identified the need for corrective services intervention programs to acknowledge the importance of culture in terms of both historical factors (i.e., the impacts of colonisation) as well as future issues (i.e., literacy and access to housing, employment, pro-social supports; Trudgett et al., 2024). Such models do not currently exist (see Heffernan et al., 2014).

10.5 4R: Future Resistance of Re-traumatisation

Culturally safe sentencing requires the promotion of self-determination, such that First Nations peoples participate in the sentencing process. Most commonly, when the criminal justice system responds to First Nations peoples, mainstream processes or programs are adapted for First Nations peoples and communities rather than co-developing a holistic, culturally safe approach. Obviously, the justice system has fixed parameters, such as sentencing legislation, which restricts the practices and options of judges regarding sanctions. However, sentencing is a tertiary crime prevention strategy (i.e., reactive after the crime has occurred). Sentencing—and indeed the criminal justice system—cannot resolve the traumatic impact of the adversity that First Nations people have experienced and continue to experience. However, as noted in *Gladue*, judges may still play a key role in resisting re-traumatisation. McLachlin CJ and Binnie, LeBel, Deschamps, Fish, and Abella JJ stated:

> Sentencing judges are among those decision-makers who have the power to influence the treatment of aboriginal (sic) offenders in the justice system. They determine most directly whether an aboriginal offender

> will go to jail, or whether other sentencing options may be employed which will play perhaps a stronger role in restoring a sense of balance to the offender, victim, and community, and in preventing future crime. (p. 723)

Culturally safe justice responses require a systemic approach that includes primary and secondary crime prevention to prevent crimes and divert people from the justice system.

10.6 Conclusion

Individualised sentencing is a fundamental precept in Australia, the US, the UK, Canada, and Aotearoa New Zealand. Substantive equality allows for direct and intergenerational trauma to be a factor in the sentencing calculus when sentencing First Nations defendants. If sentencing (and the justice system more broadly) aims to promote community safety, surely the community affected should be consulted to determine what "community safety" means. For First Nations communities, culturally safe responses by the government are a fundamental necessity. Key elements of culturally safe practices directly reflect the trauma-informed principles of practice: consideration of history, gender and culture, safety, trust, empowerment, and choice (in the form of self-determination) and collaboration. This chapter highlights the importance of acknowledging the association between colonisation and the over-representation of First Nations peoples in the criminal justice system.

Key Points

- Developmental and intergenerational trauma are common for First Nations peoples.
- To help address chronic and compounded trauma in Indigenous communities requires culturally safe responses.
- Culture, or Aboriginality, of itself is not a sentencing factor. However, the impact of disadvantages suffered by First Nations peoples and culturally safe sanctions are relevant and should be considered by sentencing judges.

- Substantive equality requires that people are treated differently according to their specific circumstances to reduce disadvantage. First Nations peoples require substantive equality in sentencing.
- Community leaders and Elders should play a key role in helping to inform sanctions that will best achieve the criminal justice system's purpose of keeping the community safe.
- Culturally safe justice responses require a systemic approach, including primary, secondary, and tertiary crime prevention.

References

Anthony, T. (2013). *Indigenous People, Crime and Punishment*. Routledge.

Atkinson, J., Nelson, J., Brooks, R., Atkinson, C., & Ryan, K. (2014). Addressing Individual and Community Transgenerational Trauma. In P. Dudgeon, H. Milroy, & R. Walker (Eds.), *Working Together: Aboriginal and Torres Strait Islander Mental Health and Wellbeing Principles and Practice* (2nd ed., pp. 289–305). Commonwealth of Australia.

Australian Bureau of Statistics (ABS). (2023). *Prisoners in Australia*. ABS.

Australian Health Practitioner Regulation Agency (AHPRA). (2020). *The National Scheme's Aboriginal and Torres Strait Islander Health and Cultural Safety Strategy 2020–2025*. AHPRA and National Boards.

Australian Institute of Health and Welfare (AIHW). (2024). *Aboriginal and Torres Strait Islander Health Performance Framework*. AIHW.

Australian Institute of Health and Welfare (AIHW). (2020). *Child Protection*. AIHW.

Australian Law Reform Commission (ALRC). (1988). *Sentencing* (Report 44). Commonwealth of Australia.

Australian Law Reform Commission (ALRC). (2017). *Pathways to Justice—An Inquiry into the Incarceration Rate of Aboriginal and Torres Strait Islander Peoples: Final Report* (Report 133). Commonwealth of Australia.

Ashworth, A., & Kelly, R. (2021). *Sentencing and Criminal Justice* (7th ed.). Hart.

Barkaskas, P., Chin, V., Dandurand, Y., & Tooshkenig, D. (2019). *Production and Delivery of Gladue Pre-sentence Reports: A Review of Selected Canadian*

Programs. International Centre for Criminal Law Reform and Criminal Justice Policy.

Bennett, P. (2016). *Specialist Courts for Sentencing Aboriginal Offenders: Aboriginal Courts in Australia*. Federation Press.

Bond, C. E. W., & Jeffries, S. (2012). Harsher Sentences? Indigeneity and Prison Sentence Length in Western Australia's Higher Courts. *Journal of Sociology, 48*(3), 266. https://doi.org/10.1177/1440783311413486

Carlson, B., Day, M., & Farrelly, T. (2021). *What Works? Exploring the Literature on Aboriginal and Torres Strait Islander Healing Programs That Respond to Family Violence*. ANROWS.

Clark, T. (2014). Ko Ngā Take Ture Māori: Sentencing Indigenous Offenders. *Auckland University Law Review, 20*, 245–268.

Clark, Y. (2017). *Lateral Violence within the Aboriginal Community in Adelaide, South Australia: From Dilemmas to Strategies*. PhD Thesis, University of Adelaide.

Clark, Y., Augoustinos, M., & Malin, M. (2016). Lateral Violence within the Aboriginal Community in Adelaide: It Affects our Identity and Wellbeing. *Journal of Indigenous Wellbeing, 1*(1), 43–52.

Cooper, A. (2020, December 17). *Indigenous disadvantage a focus in sentence appeal for Aiia's killer*. The Age.

Coulter, D., Forkan, A. R. M., Kang, Y.-B., Trounson, J., Anthony, T., Marchetti, E., & Shepherd, S. (2022). Pre-sentence Reports for Aboriginal and Torres Strait Islander People: An Analysis of Language and Sentiment. *Trends & Issues in Crime and Criminal Justice, 659*, 1–11.

Courts Administration Authority (CAA). (2023). *2022–23 Annual Report*. CAA.

Dickson, J., & Smith, K. (2021). Exploring the Canadian Judiciary's Experiences with and Perceptions of *Gladue*. *Canadian Journal of Criminology and Criminal Justice, 63*(3–4), 23–46. https://doi.org/10.3138/cjccj.2021-0031

Department of Corrections (DOC). (2023). *Annual Report 1 July 2022—30 June 2023*. New Zealand Government.

Edwige, V., & Gray, P. (2021). *Significance of Culture to Wellbeing, Healing, and Rehabilitation*. Public Defenders Chambers.

Ford, J. D., & Courtois, C. A. (2014). Defining and Understanding Complex Trauma and Complex Traumatic Stress Disorders. In C. A. Courtois & J. D. Ford (Eds.), *Treating Complex Traumatic Stress Disorders: Scientific Foundations and Therapeutic Models* (pp. 13–30). Guilford.

Gilmour, S. (2024, February 12). *Beyond the Bars: Neurodisability, Trauma, and the Criminal Justice System* [Conference Presentation]. 2024 Trauma Informed Policing and Law Enforcement Conference, Melbourne.

Gooda, M. (2011). *Social Justice Report 2011: Aboriginal and Torres Strait Islander Social Justice Commissioner.* Australian Human Rights Commission.

The Healing Foundation. (2021). *Make Healing Happen: It's Time to Act*. The Healing Foundation.

Heffernan, E., Andersen, K., McEntyre, E. & Kinner, S. (2014). Mental Disorder and Cognitive Disability in the Criminal Justice System. In P. Dudgeon, H. Milroy, & R. Walker (Eds.). *Working Together: Aboriginal and Torres Strait Islander Mental Health and Wellbeing Principles and Practice* (2nd ed, pp. 165–178). Commonwealth of Australia.

Jeffries, S., & Bond, C. (2009). Does Indigeneity Matter? Sentencing Indigenous Offenders in South Australia's Higher Courts. *Australian and New Zealand Journal of Criminology, 42*(1), 47–71.

Kickett, M. (2011). *Examination of How a Culturally-Appropriate Definition of Resilience Affects the Physical and Mental Health of Aboriginal People*. PhD, University of Western Australia.

Krasnostein, S. (2014). Too Much Individualisation, Not Enough Justice: Bugmy v The Queen. *Alternative Law Journal, 39*(1), 12–14.

Law Council of Australia (LCA). (2018). *Aboriginal and Torres Strait Islander People: The Justice Project Final Report - Part 1*. LCA.

Lewis, P. & Frankland, R. (2019). *Lateral Violence: An Evidence Check Rapid Review Brokered by the Sax Institute for the NSW Ministry of Health, April 2019.* NSW Government.

Legal Services Society (LSS). (2022) *Gladue Report Guide: How to Prepare and Write a Gladue Report* (2nd ed.). Legal Aid BC.

The Magnolia Project and Aboriginal Legal Rights Movement (ALRM). (2023). *Practice Guide for Preparing Mental Health Pre-Sentence Reports with Aboriginal People in the Criminal Justice System in South Australia.*

McLachlan, K.J. (2022). Using a Trauma-Informed Practice Framework to Examine How South Australian Judges Respond to Trauma in the Lives of Aboriginal Defendants. *Journal of Qualitative Criminal Justice & Criminology, 11*(2), 181–210. https://doi.org/10.21428/88de04a1.04778d50

Newton, D., Day, A., Gillies, C., & Fernandez, E. (2015). A review of Evidence-Based Evaluation of Measures for Assessing Social and Emotional Well-Being in Indigenous Australians. *Australian Psychologist, 50*, 40–50. https://doi.org/10.1111/ap.12064

Public Defenders, The (2023). *The Bugmy Bar Book.* NSW Government.

Royal Commission into Aboriginal Deaths in Custody (RCIADIC). (1991). *National Report —Volume Two.* Australian Government.

Robinson, P., Small, T., Chen, A., & Irving, M. (2023). *Over-representation of Indigenous Persons in Adult Provincial Custody, 2019/2020 and 2020/2021.* Statistics Canada.

Sivak, L., Cantley, L., Kelly, J., Reilly, R., Hawke, K., Miott, K., Stewart, H., Mckivett, A., Rankine, S., Coulthard, A., Miller, W., & Brown, A. (2017). *Model of Care for Aboriginal Prisoner Health and Wellbeing for South Australia – Final Report.* Wardliparingga Aboriginal Health Research Unit: SAHMRI. https://www.sahmriresearch.org/Aboriginal-Prisoner-Health-Report

Steering Committee for the Review of Government Service Provision (SCRGSP). (2016). *Overcoming Indigenous Disadvantage: Key Indicators.* Productivity Commission.

Substance Abuse and Mental Health Services Administration. (SAMHSA). (2014). *SAMHSA's Concept of Trauma and Guidance for a Trauma-Informed Approach.* US Department of Health and Human Services.

Trudgett, M., McGrath, A., & Spaccavento, B. (2024). Engaging First Nations Australians in Correctional Treatment: The Perspectives of Program Recipients and Facilitators. *Criminal Justice and Behavior, 51*(1), 24–42. https://doi.org/10.1177/00938548231207059

Usher, K., Jackson, D., Robinson, M., Marriott, R., Walker, R., Sampson, N., Adams, I., & Porter, C. (2021). Indigenous Resilience in Australia: A Scoping Review Using a Reflective Decolonizing Collective Dialogue. *Frontiers in Public Health, 9*(630601), 1–17. https://doi.org/10.3389/fpubh.2021.630601

Victorian Aboriginal Legal Service. (VALS). (2021). *Aboriginal Community Justice Reports.* VALS.

Warner, K. (2011). Equality Before the Law: Racial and Social Background Factors as Sources of Mitigation at Sentencing. In A. v. Hirsch, A. Ashworth, & J. Roberts (Eds.), *Principled Sentencing: Readings on Theory and Policy* (3rd ed., pp. 124–145). Cambridge University Press. https://doi.org/10.1017/CBO9780511979170.008

Williams, R. (2012). *Cultural Safety—What Does It Mean for our Work Practice?* University of Tasmania.

Wilson, M., Jones, J., Butler, T., Simpson, P., Gilles, M., Baldry, E., Levy, M., & Elizabeth, S. (2017). Violence in the Lives of Incarcerated Aboriginal Mothers in Western Australia. *SAGE Open* (Jan-Mar), 1–16. https://doi.org/10.1177/2158244016686814

Workman, A, Kaddour, R., & Griffin, P. M. (2023). Introduction to Culture, Diversity, and Criminal Justice. In A. Workman, R. Kaddour, & P. M. Griffin (Eds), *Culture, Diversity, and Criminal Justice: Towards Culturally Safe Criminal Justice Systems* (pp. 3–16). Routledge. https://doi.org/10.4324/9781003258032-2

Yeong, S., & Moore, E. (2020). Circle Sentencing, Incarceration and Recidivism. *Crime and Justice Bulletin, 226*, 1–22.

Zubrick, S. R., Shepherd, C. C. J., Dudgeon, P., Gee, G., Paradies, Y., Scrine, C., & Walker, R. (2014). Social Determinants of Social and Emotional Wellbeing. In P. Dudgeon, H. Milroy, & R. Walker (Eds.), *Working Together: Aboriginal and Torres Strait Islander Mental Health and Wellbeing Principles and Practice* (pp. 93–112). Commonwealth of Australia.

Case Law

DPP v Herrmann (2019) VSC 694
Munda v WA (2013) 302 ALR 207
Neal v The Queen (1982) 149 CLR 305
R v Bugmy (2012) NSWCCA 223
R v Gladue (1999) 1 SCR 688
R v Grose (2014) SASCFC 42
R v Ipeelee (2012) 1 SCR 433
R v Nelson (2017) SASCFC 40

Legislation

Crimes (Sentencing) Act 2005 (ACT)
Penalties and Sentences Act 1992 (Qld)
Sentencing Act 2017 (SA)
Sentencing Act 2002 (NZ)
Sentencing Act 1995 (NT)

Sentencing Remarks

R v ABT (Supreme Court of SA, #1 J, 25 September 2019)
R v CLS (District Court of SA, Judge #14, 13 June 2019)

R v DG (District Court of SA, Judge #18, 26 September 2019)
R v DLH (District Court of SA, Judge #5, 6 September 2019)
R v KK (District Court of SA, Judge #3, 7 May 2019)

11
Conclusion

11.1 Introduction

Trauma does not cause crime. Many people with a history of trauma do not offend. However, trauma and crime are closely associated.

- Crime may result in trauma for people who are victims.
- Many people who offend have experienced trauma.
- Trauma symptoms and manifestations may be criminogenic risk factors.
- The criminal justice system is traumatic (for victims, people who offend, and workers).

For these reasons, a trauma-informed criminal justice system may improve the experiences of people within it by reducing the risk of additional or future traumatisation and promoting more effective strategies for community safety.

This book used a framework developed by the Substance Abuse and Mental Health Services Administration (SAMHSA, 2014) to explore the degree to which criminal justice agencies are trauma-informed. This book is the first to examine how victim and defendant trauma is realised,

K. J. McLachlan, *Trauma-informed Criminal Justice*,
https://doi.org/10.1007/978-3-031-59290-4_11

recognised, and responded to by justice agencies and sentencing judges and how re-traumatisation can be resisted. Certainly, trauma-informed policing, correctional care, and sentencing are emerging in Australia, Aotearoa New Zealand, the US, the UK, and Canada. However, current practices are in their infancy and tend to focus on community subgroups, such as victims of sexual violence and women and children who have offended.

11.2 A Call for Compassionate Justice

This book has argued that there are many reasons to promote compassionate justice and few reasons to maintain the status quo. The churn of people who re-offend demonstrates that the criminal justice system is not efficiently achieving its aim, to "contribute to a safe and secure community and promote a law abiding way of life" (SCRGSP, 2023, p. 1). While most people convicted of criminal offences are not incarcerated, and crime rates are reducing in Australia (Leigh, 2020) the number of people incarcerated continues to grow. Thus, the current ways of working are not reducing the number of people who are incarcerated or the over-representation of First Nations peoples caught in the justice system. Prison is expensive, it is both criminogenic and traumatic (SACV, 2016), and it is not designed to address the underlying causes of crime (Cullen et al., 2011; Levenson & Willis, 2019). Nevertheless, the criminal justice system continues to rely on prisons ostensibly to protect community safety through an expected (but rarely realised) reduction in future offending. It follows that given their discretionary powers, judges would benefit from a broader range of "smarter" sanctions to be used depending on the individuals involved and their offending trajectory and behaviour.

11.3 A Focus on Resisting Re-traumatisation

In writing this book, I realised that criminal justice agencies and workers should simply focus on resisting re-traumatisation. In implementing a trauma-informed criminal justice system, this is the most important of the SAMHSA (2014) framework. Realising what trauma is and recognising how it impacts the wellbeing and functioning of people are both mechanisms to assist in resisting the re-traumatisation of the self and others. A trauma-informed response (characterised by safety, trust, collaboration, peer support, choice, empowerment, and recognition of culture, history, and gender) also helps to resist re-traumatisation. When professionals, victims of crime, people who offend and others encounter the criminal justice system and feel safer (and not traumatised) as a result, then the criminal justice system is keeping the community safe. As highlighted by Phil Willmot and Lawrence Jones in their book about trauma-informed forensic practice, "a trauma-informed approach will provide a framework that reintroduces, or perhaps introduces for the first time, a more compassionate approach… that sees service users and colleagues as vulnerable, hurt, resilient, but above all, human" (2022, p. 9). Humanising people in the criminal justice system is imperative if we are to achieve the criminal justice system's goal of community safety.

11.4 Conclusion

Kindness and compassion are often confused with weakness. A trauma-informed approach may be perceived as the soft option, not the smart option. It is easy to assume that someone who seeks to be kind is naïve or ill-informed. However, after almost a decade working on the Parole Board, I believe that a compassionate approach takes more effort; to see each person despite their offending behaviours. To feel compassion for both the victims of specific offending and the perpetrator of that offending is effortful. It requires recognition that the cognitive dissonance that results is normal and should not be resolved through thoughtless dichotomies. Faith can be helpful, as demonstrated by the US models of compassionate justice and victim advocate and Police

Commissioner Ray Whitrod (2001), who supported both victims of crime and people who had offended. I do not have a Christian faith, but I do believe in the evidence that shows that repeated punishment and incarceration will not achieve community safety. The criminal justice system cannot use fear and control to reduce crime. Crime can only be addressed through connections between people and the community within which we all live.

References

Cullen, F. T., Jonson, C. L., & Nagin, D. S. (2011). Prisons Do Not Reduce Recidivism: The High Cost of Ignoring Science. *The Prison Journal*, *91*(3_suppl), 48S-65S. https://doi.org/10.1177/0032885511415224

Leigh, A. (2020). *The Second Convict Age: Explaining the Return of Mass Imprisonment in Australia* (Vol. IZA DP No. 13025). IZA—Institute of Labor Economics.

Levenson, J. S., & Willis, G. M. (2019). Implementing Trauma-Informed Care in Correctional Treatment and Supervision. *Journal of Aggression, Maltreatment & Trauma, 28*(4), 481–501. https://doi.org/10.1080/10926771.2018.1531959

Steering Committee for the Review of Government Service Provision (SCRGSP). (2023). *Report on Government Services 2023. Part C: Justice.* Productivity Commission.

Substance Abuse and Mental Health Services Administration. (SAMHSA). (2014). *SAMHSA's Concept of Trauma and Guidance for a Trauma-Informed Approach.* US Department of Health and Human Services.

Sentencing Advisory Council of Victoria (SACV). (2016). *Sentencing Guidance in Victoria Report*. Victoria State Government.

Whitrod, R. (2001). *Before I Sleep: Memoirs of a Modern Police Commissioner.* University of Queensland Press.

Willmot, P., & Jones, L. (2022). Introduction. In P. Willmot & L. Jones (Eds.), *Trauma-informed Forensic Practice* (pp. 1–11). Routledge. https://doi.org/10.4324/9781003120766-1

Index

K. J. McLachlan, *Trauma-informed Criminal Justice*,
https://doi.org/10.1007/978-3-031-59290-4

The manufacturer's authorised representative in the EU is Springer Nature Customer Service Centre GmbH, Europaplatz 3, 69115 Heidelberg, Germany. If you have any concerns regarding our products, please contact ProductSafety@springernature.com

Printed and bound by CPI Group (UK) Ltd, Croydon, CR0 4YY
01/10/2026
02225894-0007